# Sustainable Tourism in Island Destinations

**Tourism, Environment and Development Series**

*Series Editor:* Richard Sharpley
School of Sport, Tourism & The Outdoors, University of
Central Lancashire, UK

*Editorial Board:* Chris Cooper, Oxford Brookes University, UK;
Andrew Holden, University of Bedfordshire, UK; Bob McKercher,
Hong Kong Polytechnic University; Chris Ryan, University of Waikato,
New Zealand; David Telfer, Brock University, Canada

**Sustainable Tourism in Island Destinations**
Sonya Graci and Rachel Dodds

**Slow Travel and Tourism**
Janet Dickinson and Les Lumsdon

**Tourism and Poverty Reduction**
*Pathways to Prosperity*
Jonathan Mitchell and Caroline Ashley

**Tourism Development and the Environment: Beyond Sustainability?**
Richard Sharpley

Please contact the Series Editor to discuss new proposals at
rajsharpley@uclan.ac.uk

# Sustainable Tourism in Island Destinations

Sonya Graci and Rachel Dodds

publishing for a sustainable future

London • Washington, DC

First published in 2010 by Earthscan

Earthscan Ltd, Dunstan House, 14a St Cross Street, London EC1N 8XA, UK
Earthscan LLC, 1616 P Street, NW, Washington, DC 20036, USA
Earthscan publishes in association with the International Institute for Environment and Development

For more information on Earthscan publications, see www.earthscan.co.uk or write to earthinfo@earthscan.co.uk

ISBN: 978-1-84407-779-3 hardback
ISBN: 978-1-84407-780-9 paperback

Typeset by 4word Ltd, Bristol
Cover design by Yvonne Booth


A catalogue record for this book is available from the British Library

Library of Congress Cataloging-in-Publication Data

Graci, Sonya.
  Sustainable tourism in island destinations / Sonya Graci and Rachel Dodds.
    p. cm.
  Includes bibliographical references and index.
  ISBN 978-1-84407-779-3 (hardback) -- ISBN 978-1-84407-780-9 (pbk.)  1.  Sustainable tourism.  2.  Islands.  I.  Dodds, Rachel. II. Title.
  G156.5.S87G73 2010
  338.4'79109142--dc22

                                        2010013416

FSC
**Mixed Sources**
Product group from well-managed
forests and other controlled sources

Cert no. SGS-COC-2482
www.fsc.org
© 1996 Forest Stewardship Council

Printed and bound in the UK by TJ International.
The paper used is FSC certified and the inks
are vegetable based.

# Contents

# List of Figures and Tables

## Figures

## Tables

# Special Preamble
# by Richard W. Butler

*Emeritus Professor, Strathclyde Business School,*
*University of Strathclyde, Glasgow, UK*

Living on a relatively small island (Great Britain) with a large population (over 50 million), one becomes very aware of the unique attractions that islands possess and also their great vulnerability to pressure from development and other human activities, including tourism. The importance of maintaining at least some of an island's characteristics despite intensive development and great population demands is never more clearly revealed than when one visits islands which have failed in that important obligation. Beginning writing this preamble in Hong Kong, part of which is on one of the most densely populated islands in the world, makes one appreciate the continued existence of the island nature of Hong Kong. The sea is never far from one's vision, and the 'concrete jungle' that is Hong Kong is alleviated by the opportunity to at least catch a glimpse of water and the inevitable masses of boats that are a permanent feature of waterways there. Hong Kong, like Singapore, has worked hard to secure some of its natural environment and safeguard areas from the almost relentless march of high-rise developments, and despite heavy visitation, the country parks of Hong Kong, just as parts of Sentosa Island in Singapore, are still able to provide quiet areas of nature or semi-natural settings only a kilometre or less from their respective city centres.

It is perhaps the sight of water almost constantly on an island that gives them their feeling of uniqueness, a sense that they are places apart, separated by water from one another and a mainland. This physical separation requires humans to traverse that space in a different mode of transport to those with which the majority of us are most familiar. When we land on an island, we do that literally, either from water or air, but we are in either case returning to our natural land habitat, but in the case of islands, a land physically separate from elsewhere. The size of an island may be unimportant; it is the separateness that distinguishes it from other places. If an island is very small (and perhaps exclusive, as are many islands that have been developed as upscale tourism resorts) we can let our imagination loose and become Robinson Crusoe, sole master or mistress of all we survey (at least until Man

Friday brings the pre-dinner cocktails). On an island we gain a sense of privacy, exclusiveness, control perhaps, that is much harder to gain in a mainland destination. Here is a place that is 'ours', cut off from others by choice (and perhaps price), allowing us to enjoy our fantasy world.

The long defunct television show 'Fantasy Island' is of course imitated by many island resorts, encouraging us to believe that we are somehow 'special' by indulging at least some of our more reasonable fantasies. As an equally defunct ornithologist, I spent many holidays on small islands (mostly cold-water ones in northern latitudes) pursuing and hoping to observe migratory birds, certainly selfishly enjoying the fact that if I saw a rarity, few others would be able to see it because of the logistics of getting to an island location before the bird moved on or expired. In this day and age of blogs, websites, automated rarity alerting systems, greater affluence and the availability of chartered transport, a real rarity has its privacy invaded by ever increasing numbers of bird watchers prepared to fly several hundred miles at short notice to add it to their life list. To many such 'twitchers', the island involved has become simply the setting for seeing the exclusive rarity, rather than the attraction in its own right. In the same way, the ubiquitous nature of many 'exclusive' luxury resorts means that the island setting sometimes offers little more than the setting for a resort which could equally well have been located on a mainland site. At most in some cases, the island nature of the resort offers an added layer of exclusivity and remoteness but little that is uniquely 'island', despite the inevitable intensive advertising of the island location.

To many islanders of course, the improvements in transportation that enable bird watchers to reach their destination in a very few hours, and which tourism development in particular has brought, are greatly welcomed, as they represent improved communications, increased safety, more frequent service, reduced travel times and often lower costs for imported goods. It is often the newly arrived retired permanent resident who objects to the 'modernization' of the island, although at the same time they probably appreciate the satellite television, frequent arrival of mail and newspapers, greater choice of items to purchase and emergency geriatric medical care when they need it. The pejorative term 'white settlers' who wish to 'pull the ladder up after them' is not confined to newly arrived island residents, but such immigrants are often more noticeable on small islands where they may exert disproportional influence on development.

It is the particular vulnerability of island environments, human and non-human, that is generally of most concern. Islands in general are characterized by limited species diversity, often a function of size as well as of location, which means even minor environmental change can be of much greater significance than on a mainland location where replacements can more easily be found. The increased danger from exotic species introduction is a major issue, as shown by the effect of rats having been introduced, often by accident from visiting boats on several small islands, having disastrous effects on ground nesting birds and other species. Culls of rats and hedgehogs in recent years are indicative of corrective steps that have to be taken. The isolated nature of islands in particular is what allows some of them to retain rare endemic species, the most well known example of such a phenomenon being the Galápagos Islands, and the species there, combined with their tameness that results from their not being exposed to humans make them a major attraction for tourists. The continuing increased pressure on the islands and their wildlife that the Galápagos Islands are experiencing is mirrored elsewhere on islands ranging from the Arctic to the Antarctic.

The appeal of islands to visitors is age old; they have been seen as suitable sites for settlement, defence, trade and resource extraction and processing long before they became attractive to tourists. Few islands with permanent populations remain unchanged or purely natural, but that does not mean that their physical environment is unimportant. While tourism may represent only the latest in a series of threats to environmental integrity, it may, if one wishes to be optimistic, be an economic activity which could encourage the maintenance and protection of at least some of the natural environment. Despite the obvious impacts of tourism, now well documented in the tourism literature, there has to be a vested interest by resort developers and governments involved in tourism in ensuring the appeal of their islands remains. While this may be a utilitarian and financial rationale for environmental protection, without such actions island destinations can and do go the way of mainland destinations, through the tourism life cycle and into decline. Although their island location may delay the onset of the full negative effect of tourism, overdevelopment and loss of appeal can be seen in resorts in island locations such as the Balearics, the Greek islands, Cyprus, Malta and the Canaries in Europe, and in the West Indies and South Pacific islands as well. Island destinations in the Indian Ocean are now experiencing heavy development, albeit at the luxury end of the market, but luxury does not automatically mean reduced or mitigated impacts, the development of facilities felt needed for the high-end of the market may have greater impacts than development associated with the much maligned mass tourism market.

To date, most researchers have been concerned with site-specific environmental impacts resulting from tourism development. We are at the point now that we also have to consider global impacts on island tourism destination environments stemming indirectly from tourist (and other) activities, such as changing climatic conditions and rising sea levels. If we want to maintain the islandness of islands (however we may define that element), along with their often unique environments, action is needed in many areas. Tourism may only be one part of the overall problem of island development and change, but it is a part which should be capable of sensitivity and appropriateness in its development and use of island resources. The theme of this volume is the relationship between tourism, development and the environment of islands and the examples featured succeed in capturing the flavour and urgency of the situation in island locations. They should help to teach all who care about islands and their character some of the steps that we need to take to ensure that character remains in the future.

# Foreword by Ilan Kelman

*Center for International Climate and Environmental Research, Oslo, Norway*

Islands are mysterious, romantic, tranquil, dazzling, inspiring, and exquisite – or so island myths and novels tell us. Even where reality mirrors this idyllic image, islands face immense challenges while providing important opportunities for better understanding how to resolve the challenges. Island communities – whether tropical or at higher latitudes, coastal or inland, salt water or fresh water – display rich and diverse cultures, languages, societies, histories, governance forms and livelihoods.

Yet inherent island characteristics such as isolation, restricted land area, small populations and limited domestic land-based resources frequently bring about significant environmental and social challenges. Meanwhile, island languages, cultures and knowledges are being lost as youth migrate to mainland cities and as local island knowledge is devalued by the onslaught of cultural homogeneity.

The same island characteristics breeding these challenges can also yield opportunities for tackling them. Small, isolated populations form tight kinship networks, a strong sense of identity and unique cultural heritage. Community opportunities are often bolstered by remittances from islanders overseas. Millennia of experience of dealing with environmental and social changes in isolation provide islanders with the flexibility to adjust, at least to some degree, to contemporary changes such as human-caused climate change, improving Internet connectivity, and swifter although fossil-fuel-based transportation modes. Despite the hurdles, islands present impressive advantages for building and maintaining healthy and prosperous communities.

One example is island tourism livelihoods – bringing challenges and opportunities, those of tourism livelihoods more generally in addition to those specific to island tourism contexts. In fact, island destinations frequently use island branding in their marketing. The Canary Islands and Madeira are advertised to northern Europeans as winter island getaways. Hawaii frequently uses its natural and cultural island heritage as part of the bid to attract tourists, especially beyond those seeking beaches. The Galápagos Islands and Rapa Nui make extensive use of the locations' islandness and isolation as promoting the unique natural heritage and cultural heritage respectively.

Is island tourism, really that unique compared to non-island tourism? That is an especially important question since fixed definitions for the terms 'island', 'islandness', and 'isolated' do not exist. Yet the importance of islands and islandness emerges at many levels.

More than 10 per cent of the world's population are islanders. That is far from the majority, but is far from insubstantial. More than 20 per cent of sovereign states are islands or archipelagos along with over 90 per cent of non-sovereign territories, with a variety of governance forms ranging from Prince Edward Island to Niue to Aruba. Island knowledge and experience do not apply just to themselves. Analogies and parallels appear with non-islands. Mountain villages can be as isolated while cities comprising islands such as Stockholm and New York are themselves worthy of island-related study. Deltas and Arctic communities display multiple island characteristics as well.

The tourism livelihoods that emerge from, and create the appeal of, islands find numerous overlaps and parallels with these other locations. Consequent challenges that emerge range from culture or nature being commodified or created for tourists to islanders being overwhelmed by outsiders treating the island as nothing more than a holiday home. How can these island livelihood vulnerabilities be better understood and tackled?

*This book provides some answers.* It grasps the challenge of sustainability within tourism livelihoods to explore the vulnerabilities that tourism livelihoods create and redress. The island context becomes poignant given the diversity of the case studies, yet the familiarity of many of the topics is often enhanced by the island context. The smallness of the case study of Honduran islands amplifies the disparity in views among different people involved in the tourism sector. The isolation of a Chinese island seems to reduce the awareness of environmental and sustainability subjects among those with tourism livelihoods.

Of particular importance is the focus on non-sovereign islands (subnational island jurisdictions) rather than considering only islands that are countries. Consequently, one of the struggles experienced within tourism livelihoods is the country's desires compared to the islander's desires and the vulnerabilities that can be created by tourism livelihoods being influenced or dominated by mainlanders who seek cash rather than island life. A Thai island devastated by the 26 December 2004 tsunamis lacks planning and development oversight, which could potentially be driven by national interests promoting Thailand as a tourist destination.

Yet highlighting the 'vulnerability' part of such situations can be criticized as being too technocratic, too negative or too disempowering. Avoiding overemphasis on such connotations is important, but so is recognizing the reality of the many vulnerabilities faced by islands, islanders and island livelihoods. The reality is that vulnerability exists and that it can and should be addressed. Tourism both supports and hinders that. Island strengths and island advantages can and should be used to support vulnerability reduction, including the appropriate use of tourism livelihoods.

Smallness, such as in diseconomies of scale or economies of smaller scales, provides elegance and avoids the cumbersome expanse of larger scales. Isolation breeds a culture of self-help and self-sufficiency, which is a fundamental tenet for vulnerability reduction. Bornholm, Denmark, for example, has pioneered numerous initiatives regarding local sustainability and local products that make the island a better place to live and work while providing a selling point for tourists.

These island traits enhance creativity in generating livelihoods that can be used for long-term vulnerability reduction and livelihoods. An example is developing and testing vehicles that run on coconut oil on islands of Vanuatu. That could support on-island tourism without dependency on external fossil fuels, while being cautious not to permit coconut plantations to take over local ecosystems in order to supply the coconut oil needed for the vehicles.

Similarly, tourists frequently demand more water and more electricity, while producing more waste, than locals. Appropriate island tourism should see that as an opportunity to tackle these problems directly, rather than being subservient to the tourist demands.

*This book does so.* In fact, the importance for researchers, policy-makers, and practitioners comes through in the practical approaches and techniques presented for managing island tourism and island tourism livelihoods. Partnerships for participatory processes for sustainable tourism are described for an Indonesian island. A Spanish island displays good practice in developing integrated, workable and working policies for sustainable tourism. Leadership in creating a tourism future desired by the islanders appears on a Tanzanian island. Across three continents.

As such, immense power emerges from this book going beyond problem identification. That, frequently, is the easy part. That, perhaps, is why vulnerability is often emphasized, sometimes in a superficial and unhelpful manner. Looking at the depth within island vulnerability, as shown by some of the case studies here, and the manners in which island vulnerability can be reduced, as shown by the other case studies here, ensures that direction and guidance for moving forward supports those who wish to do better.

The richness and diversity of the examples within this book show that the theory of island vulnerability reduction is neither small scale, nor isolated, nor remote from reality. Instead, tourism can be used as a force supporting some aspects of sustainability, especially where isolation and remoteness are used to create advantages, namely the beauty, poetry, and allure portrayed in the island myths and novels.

Perhaps the challenge of being an islander is not to emulate, nor to become closer to, the mainland. It is certainly not to 'improve' the oft-alleged but rarely proven 'backward' island way. Instead, the challenge is to maintain viable islandness without succumbing to vulnerability, but using islandness to reduce vulnerability. Throughout, the underlying question is always: can tourism ever be fundamentally sustainable?

Island strengths can turn the vulnerability process into vulnerability reduction opportunities to resolve island challenges on the islanders' own terms. That yields further opportunities for exporting island expertise and experience to apply island lessons elsewhere around the world. But care is always needed not to get caught up in the rhetoric, idealism, or greed of tourism and tourism livelihoods. *This book brings an important reality check to that challenge.*

# Authors' Preface

This book is the fourth title in the Earthscan series *Tourism, Environment and Development*. The purpose of this series is to explore, within a variety of contexts, the developmental role of tourism as it relates explicitly to its environmental consequences. Each book reviews critically and challenges 'traditional' perspectives on (sustainable) tourism development, exploring new approaches that reflect contemporary economic, socio-cultural and political contexts.

The purpose of this title, which is focused on sustainable tourism development in islands, is twofold. First, it aims to provide an innovative discussion regarding issues of sustainability, focusing on island tourism destinations. It builds on and consolidates the existing literature on sustainable tourism in island destinations and seeks to add to this by providing innovative discussions and practical examples through the use of the authors' various research in island destinations. We examine sustainability issues in an island context and focus, through an illustrated case study approach, on the challenges that islands face in achieving sustainable tourism. Innovative mechanisms such as multi-stakeholder partnership structures and community capacity-building approaches are then put forward as ways that can move the sustainability agenda forward in destinations that face specific challenges due to their geography and historic development. These case studies provide a foundation that suggests that alternative approaches to tourism development are possible if it retains sustainability as a prerequisite of tourism development. Secondly, the book aims to contribute to the series as a whole. A number of issues that we raise can be considered a detailed analysis of what affects island destinations and can be discussed independently of the other books as a series. To date, although there has been a lot of literature about islands and also about tourism, there have been few texts on practical examples of both successes and challenges of sustainable tourism in islands. Therefore, while this book seeks to investigate the tourism context specifically in islands, it is also complementary to the series as a whole as it contributes to the examination of tourism development in light of sustainability.

Although there are many organizations, articles and books about small island developing states (SIDS) and island states, we have decided to expand this focus. The case studies in this book are sub-jurisdiction islands (islands that are part of larger nations), semi-autonomous islands as well as autonomous islands, because it was felt that although there are almost 40 island countries, there are countless islands which are semi-autonomous, archipelagoes, territories or indeed just part of a larger country. We have chosen eight case studies to be described in detail (see locations on the map below), although numerous other islands are also used as examples. Of the eight detailed case studies, the first four (Chapters 5–8) focus on problems and challenges, while the others (Chapters 9–12) illustrate more successful solutions. As not all island countries' lessons can be extrapolated to smaller islands, it is hoped that this book may illuminate issues and successes in islands which can be applicable to island states as well as sub-jurisdiction islands.

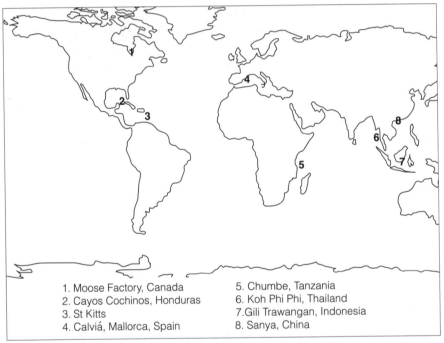

1. Moose Factory, Canada
2. Cayos Cochinos, Honduras
3. St Kitts
4. Calviá, Mallorca, Spain

5. Chumbe, Tanzania
6. Koh Phi Phi, Thailand
7. Gili Trawangan, Indonesia
8. Sanya, China

*World map and chapter case studies*

# List of Acronyms and Abbreviations

| | |
|---|---|
| AOSIS | Alliance of Small Island States |
| CHICOP | Chumbe Island Coral Park Ltd |
| CIA | Central Intelligence Agency |
| CSI | UNESCO Directorate for Environment and Development in Coastal Regions and Small Islands |
| CSR | corporate social responsibility |
| CTO | Caribbean Tourism Organization |
| CURLA | Centro Universitario Regional del Litoral Atlantico |
| DFID | Department of Foreign and International Development |
| DMO | destination marketing organization |
| EA | environmental auditing |
| EIA | environmental impact assessment |
| ENGO | environmental non-governmental organization |
| FIM | floating underwater information modules |
| FIRE | Forum for Island Research and Experience |
| GDP | gross domestic product |
| GLISPA | Global Island Partnership |
| GSEII | Global Sustainable Energy Islands Initiative |
| HCRF | Honduran Coral Reef Foundation |
| IIS | Institute of Island Studies |
| ICLEI | International Council for Local Environmental Initiatives |
| ICRAN | International Coral Reef Action Network |
| ICRI | International Coral Reef Initiative |
| ICZM | Integrated Coastal Zone Management |
| IFAD | International Fund for Agricultural Development |
| IH&RA | International Hotel and Restaurant Association |
| IPCC | Intergovernmental Panel on Climate Change |
| IUCN | International Union for Conservation of Nature |
| LA21 | Local Agenda 21, Earth Summit 1992 |
| LAC | limits of acceptable change |
| LDC | less developed countries |
| MCN | Micronesia Conservation Trust |
| MEAB | Marine Education, Awareness and Biodiversity Program |

| | |
|---|---|
| MNC | multinational corporation |
| MPA | marine protected area |
| MTA | Malta Tourism Authority |
| NAPENTHES | Danish NGO |
| NEAP | National Environmental Action Plan |
| NFWF | US-National Fish and Wildlife Foundation |
| PCS | Palau Conservation Society |
| PPT & CTO | Pro Poor Tourism & Caribbean Tourism Organization |
| RES | renewable energy source |
| SADC–REEP | South African Development Cooperation – Reef Environmental Education Program |
| SEZ | special economic zone |
| SIDS | small island developing state |
| SLA | sustainable livelihoods approach |
| SME | small and medium-sized enterprises |
| SPREP | Pacific Regional Environmental Programme |
| SSTIP | set of sustainable tourism indicators |
| STINAPA | Stichting Nationale Parken Nederlandse Antillean |
| TALC | tourism area life cycle |
| TIAC | Tourism Industry Association of Canada |
| TOI | Tour Operators Initiative |
| TOMM | tourism optimization model |
| TSA | tourism satellite account |
| UN | United Nations |
| UNCED | United Nations Conference on Environment and Development |
| UNCSD | United Nations Conference on Sustainable Development |
| UNCTAD | United Nations Conference on Trade and Development |
| UNEP | United Nations Environment Programme |
| UNESCO | United Nations Educational, Scientific and Cultural Organization |
| UNWTO | United Nations World Tourism Organization |
| USAID | United States Agency for International Development |
| VFRs | Visiting friends and relatives |
| WCED | World Commission on Environment and Development |
| WCMC | UNEP World Conservation Monitoring Centre |
| WESSA | Wildlife and Environment Society of South Africa |
| WTO | World Tourism Organization |
| WTTC | World Travel and Tourism Council |
| WWF | World Wide Fund for Nature |

# PART I

# SUSTAINABILITY IN ISLAND DESTINATIONS

# 1
# Tourism, Growth and the Need for Sustainable Tourism

## Introduction

Tourism is often identified as a promising growth sector in many islands as it offers opportunities for economic diversification and can contribute to growth in many other tourism-related activities such as agriculture, fishing and services such as transportation (UN, 1996). Currently, tourism activities in islands across the world range from over-developed to barely touched and, due to the potential for tourism growth as a contributor to the economy, the sustainability of such an industry should be considered.

Island economies are the focus of this study due to their dependence on tourism, insular geography, fragile ecosystems and complexities of planning, development and management. The characteristic complexities of island destinations give rise to a multitude of issues, especially relating to the potential success of sustainable tourism development.

In order to understand tourism in islands, it is first necessary to understand tourism, its historic growth and its impacts. This chapter will outline the growth and impacts of tourism and provide definitions for sustainable tourism as well as providing a brief history of sustainable tourism development as it relates to sustainable development.

## Growth of tourism

Although some contest whether tourism should be regarded as an industry, tourism is commonly recognized as one of the world's largest employers and providers of services and continues to expand at a rapid rate (UNWTO, 2006; WTTC, 2007). The magnitude of this industry is demonstrated by the World Tourism Organization (WTO) statistics, which indicate that, by the year 2010, international tourist arrivals will almost reach one billion tourists (Bruner et al, 1999). In 2008, worldwide tourism arrivals reached 924 million. In 2006, the World Travel and Tourism Council (WTTC) projected that the direct and indirect impacts of tourism were expected to contribute

**Figure 1.1** *Island tourism*

10.3 per cent of the global gross domestic product and create nearly 10 million new jobs for the world economy for a total of 234.3 million jobs (WTTC, 2006). The United Nations World Tourism Organization (UNWTO) forecast study, 'Vision 2020', predicts a tripling in the volume of the world tourism market between 1995 and 2020 (Frangialli, 1999). According to this report, changes in the demographic structure and social patterns of the developed and newly industrialized countries mean that more people from these areas will have the time, inclination and income to travel (Frangialli, 1999). Despite the recent worldwide recession, and potential for incorrect and inflated measurements, tourism continues to grow, illustrating its global importance.

Tourism has a high multiplier effect and has a significant impact on other industries – a decline of one million US dollars in tourism earnings affects about two to four times that in generated earnings and affects agriculture, food processes, transportation and handicrafts (Edgell, 1999). Tourism dollars, especially for a destination dependent on tourism, will result in both the positive and negative export of services, economic development (infrastructure, transportation, agriculture) and impacts on the local economy.

In many cases, tourism development has been a profitable economic tool, making it an alluring industry and form of development for many countries and regions around the world. The benefits, however, are also often accompanied by many negative effects that result in impacts of both an

**Figure 1.2** *Is this island paradise?*

environmental and a social nature (Bohdanowicz, 2005; Dodds, 2008; Lansing and DeVries, 2006; Manaktola and Jauhari, 2008; Perez-Salom, 2001; Theobald, 1998). These impacts can be severe and may consist of air, water and ground pollution, erosion, damage to coral reefs and marine life, leakage, destruction of greenfield sites, acculturation, increased crime rates and reduced access to common areas.

The development and long-term success of the tourism industry depends on a constant availability of natural and cultural resources. The appeal of a destination is based on pristine resources, yet it is these resources that are also affected most by overexploitation and degradation (Bohdanowicz, 2005; Butler, 1993; Butler, 1998; Coccossis, 1996; Dodds, 2007a,b; Murphy, 1994). As tourism is a resource-intensive industry using a constant amount of energy and water and producing wastes, this has resulted in a significant environmental footprint (Bohdanowicz, 2005). Given tourism's significance to global and local economies and its impact on the natural and social environment, the need to implement sustainable practices has come to the forefront of global issues (Bramwell and Lane, 1993; Butler, 1993; Dodds, 2007a,b, 2008, 2009; Graci, 2010; Hunter Jones et al, 1997; Ioannides, 1996; Kripendorf, 1982; Lansing and DeVries, 2006; Manaktola and Jauhauri, 2007; Mastny, 2002; McElroy and Albuquerque, 1998; Murphy, 1994; Pryce, 2001; Sharpley, 2000; Stipanuk, 1996; Theobald, 1998; WTTC, 2002).

Figure 1.3 *Need for sustainable tourism: sharks as tourist food?*

## Need for sustainable tourism

Probably the main motivations for developing a tourism industry derive from its assumed potential to generate employment and economic development (Edgell, 1995; Fayos-Sola, 1996; McElroy and Dodds, 2007; Puppim de Oliviera, 2003; Wilkinson, 1997). Tourism generally produces beneficial economic results but mixed social and environmental impacts. Tourism needs to be viewed as more than just economic activity as it influences the socio-cultural and environmental aspects of most countries, let alone islands in the world. It is for this reason that sustainable tourism started to be discussed. Over 20 years ago Kripendorf (1987) wrote about tourism's role as a potential burden on cultures, economies and the environment and that more sustainable forms of tourism need to be considered. Living standards and quality of life can be raised by income, local communities can be transformed, new employment and educational opportunities can be gained and improved international understanding can all be a result of tourism initiatives (Bramwell and Lane, 1993; Clifton and Benson, 2006; Eber, 1992; Elliot, 1997; Green and Hunter, 1992; Hall and Jenkins, 1995). The issues that call for more sustainable forms of tourism and tourism development arise from the same concerns over general sustainable development. Some of the issues and impacts affecting destinations include:

- dependency of a host community's economy on tourism;
- competition;
- leakage;
- government debt to finance development;
- loss of habitat areas and resources due to development and pollution;

- decline in biodiversity of species and ecosystems;
- erosion;
- loss of natural and architectural heritage in the face of rapid expansion;
- decline in quantity and quality of water resources;
- sea, land, noise and air pollution;
- increased congestion and strains of infrastructure;
- rapid decline of traditional pursuits by locals because of a change in habits due to tourism;
- excessive use of natural areas;
- encroachment of buildings, facilities and roads close to coastline;
- crowding and pressure on services;
- displacement of local population;
- inflation;
- foreign customs and expectations creating conflicts.

(Agarwal, 2002; Dodds, 2008a; Filho, 1996; Graci, 2010; Harrison, 2003; May, 1991; Mbaiwa, 2005; McElroy, 2002; Milne 1993; Mycoo, 2006; Stabler and Goodall 1996; Swarbrooke 1999; UNEP 1996; United Nations Commission on Sustainable Development (UNCSD) 1999; Wheeler 1993; Wilkinson 1989).

Tourism can also magnify issues surrounding or affecting itself such as prostitution, commercialization, inflation, begging and leakage (Butler, 1999; Cooper et al, 1998; Kirstges, 2002). Leakage can be understood as revenue generated by tourism in one country that is lost to another country's economy. As with many developing economies, a high percentage of foreign exchange income is generated by tourist leakage out of the economy. This leakage can be in the form of repatriation of benefits to multinational corporations, fees to hotel management companies, remuneration of foreign staff and imports of goods and services (Hashimoto, 2004; Swarbrooke, 1999). The less diversified the economic structure of a destination, the higher the level of imports and leakages.

According to the UN (2003) over 40 per cent of Mediterranean coastal beaches in Europe are affected by erosion and one million hectares of wetlands in the past 50 years have been lost. Singh and Singh (1999) note that 75 per cent of total pollution that enters oceans comes from human activity on land. At peak times a ratio of 'up to 130 tourists per inhabitant has been calculated in the most populated coastal regions' (UNCSD, 1999: 13). The tendency historically to develop mass tourism has often been associated with serious impacts (Malvarez et al, 2003; Vera Rebollo and Ivars Baidal, 2003). This mainstream 'sun, sea and sand' tourism generally leads to low yield tourism with excessive use of natural resources and little benefit for the local community. Several tourism island destinations have suffered from their lack of planning or concern for the environment, which has resulted in mass tourism or unchecked development. Many islands are facing a decline in tourism due to this overdevelopment that has led to the degradation of the resources that it is ultimately trying to sell. Therefore, it is pertinent for island destinations to understand the impact that tourism can have on the environment and plan and manage tourism accordingly for a viable and sustainable future.

Figure 1.4 *Sustainable tourism development in the Caribbean?*

## Defining sustainable tourism

Over 200 different definitions of sustainable development and sustainable tourism have been identified and many critiques note that it is an ambiguous and idealistic concept with no widely internationally accepted definition (Clarke, 1997; Collins, 1999; Johnston and Tyrell, 2005; Miller, 2002). 'Sustainability, sustainable tourism and sustainable development are all well-established terms that have been used loosely and often interchangeably' (Liu, 2003: 461). These definitions range from tourist-centric, economically focused points of view that pay little attention to natural resource demands to a more eco-centric, multi-sectoral approach that focuses on resource management as the primary factor (Hunter, 2002). These variants do not commonly identify socio-cultural aspects that are imperative to incorporate into a definition of sustainable tourism. Therefore, a definition that incorporates all aspects of sustainable development, including economic, environmental and socio-cultural aspects, in the context of tourism, is necessary. Butler's (1993) definition of sustainable development in tourism is one definition that incorporates all three facets. Butler defines sustainable development in relation to tourism as:

> *Tourism which is developed and maintained in an area (community, environment) in such a manner and such a scale that it remains viable over an indefinite period and does not degrade or*

*alter the environment (human and physical) in which it exists to such a degree that it prohibits successful development and well-being of other activities and programmes. (Butler, 1993: 29)*

This definition of sustainable tourism can be applied to all tourist destinations, mass or alternative, built or in the planning stages, and to all types of tourism products. It enables a practical approach to incorporating sustainability in tourism planning and development rather than a very theoretical definition that does not incorporate all tourism activities. It is through this definition that the premise of acquiring a sustainable tourism industry for the well-being of the global environment can be understood. The most recent, most comprehensive definition of sustainable tourism has been put forth by the WTO in 2005:

*Sustainable tourism development guidelines and management practices are applicable to all forms of tourism in all types of destinations, including mass tourism and the various niche tourism segments. Sustainability principles refer to the environmental, economic and socio-cultural aspects of tourism development, and a suitable balance must be established between these three dimensions to guarantee its long-term sustainability... Sustainable tourism development requires the informed participation of all relevant stakeholders, as well as strong political leadership to ensure wide participation and consensus building. Achieving sustainable tourism is a continuous process and it requires constant monitoring of impacts, introducing the necessary preventive and/or corrective measures whenever necessary. Sustainable tourism should also maintain a high level of tourist satisfaction and ensure a meaningful experience to the tourists, raising their awareness about sustainability issues and promoting sustainable tourism practices amongst them. (www.world-tourism.org)*

This definition is perhaps the most comprehensive definition of sustainable tourism as it incorporates not only the idea that sustainable tourism can be applied to all aspects of tourism, but that in order for it to be successful it must include the participation of all stakeholders and political leadership. It also indicates that it is a continuous process and that measurement is necessary to ensure success. Finally, it identifies that it should also bring about a high level of tourist satisfaction and engage the market in sustainable tourism practices. The premise of this book is based on this definition, as it not only focuses on the impacts of tourism but examines the issue further by identifying how to manage these impacts and control tourism development accordingly.

## History of sustainable tourism

The environmental and social impacts of the tourism industry since the Rio Earth Summit in 1992 have come to the forefront of global issues. Tourism, as an economic sector that needs to be managed sustainably, has been discussed at length through global conventions, policies within the United Nations and at the individual country, regional, destination and organizational level (Bohdanowicz, 2005; Bramwell and Lane, 1993; Butler, 1993; Dodds, 2008; Hunter Jones et al, 1997; Ioannides, 1996; Kripendorf, 1982; McElroy and Albuquerque, 1998; Sharpley, 2000). Yet sustainability considerations have been mainly conceptual to date and have not yet been translated into industry-wide practice.

At the time of writing, almost 25 years have passed since the 1987 World Commission on Environment and Development (WCED), where sustainable development had initially become a major global concern. At this event, the deteriorating condition of the world's natural resources inspired an agreement among world leaders that sustainable development should be the central principle of governments, private institutions and organizations (WCED, 1987). This event brought attention to the fact that the destruction of the natural environment is clearly associated with the effects of human economic activities and developments (Middleton, 1998). The concept of sustainable development, defined as 'development that meets the needs of the present without compromising the ability of future generations to meet their own needs', provided an alternative to past development schemes that were less practical as they were based largely on economics without sufficient thought to the long-term viability of the development and its externalities (WCED, 1987). Unlike these previous theories of development, sustainable development incorporated ecological, social and economic aspects and became the new global agenda for change (Becherel and Vellas, 1999; Sharpley and Telfer, 2002; WCED, 1987).

Subsequent to the WCED (for tourism is not mentioned in their documentation), the United Nations has viewed tourism as a key sustainable development issue in light of the industry's both beneficial and destructive nature. Tourism is a service delivered by people that provides experiences and involves the transportation of participants, their accommodation and entertainment, giving rise to potentially disruptive side-effects. The capacity of tourism to impact destination economies, societies, cultures and environment, both positively and negatively, is well documented and its adverse repercussions have exposed the industry to strong criticism (Anguera, Ayuso et al, 2000; Bramwell and Lane, 1993; Butler, 1993; Dodds, 2003; Henderson, 2007; Hunter Jones et al, 1997; Ioannides, 1996; Kripendorf, 1982; McElroy and Albuquerque, 1992; Sharpley, 2000). The other side to this argument, however, is that tourism can supply much needed infrastructure, income and employment which will boost destination economies and raise standards of living. In addition, if planned properly, tourism can also protect resources and help finance conservation (Dodds, 2003, 2007a; Henderson, 2007; McElroy, 2002a; Swarbrooke, 1999). Given this dichotomy, tourism was identified as one of the five main industries in need of achieving sustainable development at the United Nations conference in Rio de Janeiro in 1992 (Budeanu, 1999; Pryce, 2001; Theobald, 1998).

The key points recommended by the WCED (1987) and accepted by the UNCED in 1992 to be incorporated by all industries focused on the following:

- maintaining ecological diversity;
- increasing social equity;
- enabling more productivity in developing areas;
- increased community/local control;
- increased regional self reliance;
- intervention by government;
- partnerships (business/government);
- economic viability (Howie, 2002: 5).

In 1993, *Sustainable Tourism Development: A Guide for Local Planners* (WTO, 1993) was published, followed by *Agenda 21 for the Travel and Tourism Industry* produced in 1995 by the World Tourism Organization (WTO), the World Travel and Tourism Council (WTTC) and the Earth Council. This document's aim was to establish systems and procedures to incorporate sustainable development considerations into the decision-making processes of tourism activities. It emphasized the importance of partnerships between government and industry, and demonstrated the benefits of making the whole industry sustainable and not just the niche eco-tourism sector (Pryce, 2001). Subsequently, sustainable development has become the foundation and framework for tourism planning in many contexts (Dredge, 2006).

Despite this movement in the early 1990s to develop a framework or blueprint for sustainable development for the tourism industry, little has been accomplished to move the agenda forward. This is perhaps because some 'bottom-up' approaches are only applicable to particular areas or that there is still little widespread adoption of sustainable tourism practices.

## Need for practical application of sustainable tourism

Perhaps due to several definitions and interpretations of sustainable tourism, there is often confusion in the industry and slow implementation of the concept (Godfrey, 1998). There is also a problem with the practical implementation of sustainable tourism practices. According to Liu (2003), there is an urgent need to develop policies and measures that are not only theoretically sound but also practically feasible. 'Without the development of an effective means of translating ideals into action, sustainable tourism runs the risk of remaining irrelevant and inert as a feasible policy option for the real world of tourism development. In particular, ways of applying the principles of sustainable development to mainstream, conventional mass tourism should be studied' (Liu, 2003: 472). In order to implement the principles of sustainability in a practical and feasible fashion, what must be understood are the reasons for this gap between attitude and action. Despite the numerous reports, studies and discussions on sustainable tourism, what is impeding its successful implementation and how these impediments can be overcome must be identified. In addition, innovative management strategies need to be identified so that island destinations can learn from best practices and adapt them to their own situations.

## Tourism in islands

Tourism in islands can be similar to tourism in other areas of the world. Similar to much tourism development around the world, tourism in islands provides economic welfare, increased foreign exchange and employment. International policy and practice also often highlight the special interests and uniqueness of islands in terms of sustainable development and livelihoods. The following are three examples:

- The *Johannesburg Plan of Implementation* from the World Summit on Sustainable Development held in August and September 2002 in South Africa (see Chapter VII).
- *The Hyogo Framework for Action* agreed at the World Conference on Disaster Reduction in January 2005 in Japan (e.g. paragraphs 13g and 25).
- The *Gozo Statement on Vulnerable Small States* from the Commonwealth Heads of Government Meeting in November 2005 in Malta.

Just like tourism in many other parts of the world, tourism in islands can also have numerous negative consequences such as inflation, increased fragility of geological, marine, cultural and historical attractions, loss of local control and leakage. The very elements that attract tourists often make them more vulnerable to the pressures of tourism. In islands, much of the focus on tourism development to date has been on economic aspects rather than social, environmental and human, which has resulted in overdevelopment and the proliferation of mass tourism and its consequences (Conlin and Baum, 1994; Lim and Cooper, 2009; Royle, 2001).

## Overview of this book

It is hoped that this book offers practical examples where the reader will benefit from descriptive case studies rather than theoretical or prescriptive discussion. The book is divided into four sections. Part I outlines the historical growth of tourism, the need for sustainable tourism, sustainable tourism definitions as well as a brief description of overall impacts. The second chapter sets the stage for the book by examining pertinent theories to sustainable tourism development. Stakeholder theory, sustainable livelihoods and the tourism area life cycle are outlined. The life cycle model is a useful tool to evaluate the life cycle stage of destinations and will be further contextualized at the beginning of each case study. The general introductory context of islands, their insularity and overall issues they face will then be presented.

Part II outlines the challenges to developing sustainable tourism island destinations. A detailed description of challenges followed by three case studies that illustrate real-life examples of the negative impacts of tourism development in islands are provided. The first case study, Sanya in Hainan Island, China, illustrates that despite being designated as an 'eco-province' and attempting to claim that it is an island that manages its environment, this does not necessarily translate into practice. The island of Hainan has impediments to sustainable tourism development due to the lack of environmental awareness among key stakeholders. The second case study showcases the Cayos Cochinos Islands in Honduras. This case study illustrates the differing ideals of development that varying stakeholders have in developing sustainable tourism. It also discusses the challenges that the community faces in building community capacity and being empowered in the decision-making process. The third case study, of Koh Phi Phi, Thailand, showcases what can happen without adequate planning and overdevelopment and when the focus is on economic returns rather than social and environmental well-being. The fourth case study illustrates St Kitts, an island economy which has not planned for long-term sustainability; instead it has copied other destinations, which has led to an uncompetitive and potentially failing economy.

Part III discusses successes to sustainable tourism development in islands and identifies innovative, practical initiatives to move the agenda forward. Although islands are often seen as vulnerable and isolated, it is usually the very characteristics of islands that showcase strengths. This chapter on successes in island tourism outlines a number of island examples worldwide, which have demonstrated good practice. Then three case studies showcasing innovative initiatives are presented. The first case study, of Gili Trawangan, Indonesia, provides an example of a collaborative multi-stakeholder partnership while Calviá, Mallorca, Spain showcases a policy approach which is inclusive, integrated and applied. Chumbe in Tanzania provides an example of leadership and long-term vision for conservation through tourism. Finally, Moose Factory Island in Canada illustrates that a sustainable livelihoods approach is what is needed to build community capacity. The final section of this book outlines innovative initiatives that islands can use to help overcome challenges of sustainability. Collaborative partnerships, leadership, building community capacity, implementing a cohesive policy strategy and continuous improvement are discussed.

Part IV discusses the way forward. Eight key elements for achieving sustainable tourism development are provided and discussed, relating back to the case studies in this book. The book concludes with ideas for further study and research and then offers a section of resources that may be useful for managers, students and planners in islands.

This book is unique in that the case studies outlined are not only island states or countries but islands that are part of larger nations. Often, it seems that the discussions of islands focus only on small island developing states (SIDS) or individual countries to illustrate island vulnerabilities and challenges (such as the islands of the Caribbean and South Pacific). This book discusses islands that are located around the world and can share characteristics of SIDS or other independent nations, as well as those representing developed and developing nations, and we hope to offer insight into a wide range of situations that islands may face. Although this book does not offer case studies of cold-water islands, it does discuss some examples in both the challenges and successes sections and the authors believe that as tourism development on islands happens in both warm and cold-water islands, challenges faced and initiatives succeeded also offer comparison.

# 2
# Setting the Stage

In order to understand tourism and islands it is necessary to first understand the many stakeholders involved as well as the life cycle of destinations of islands and livelihoods that are affected.

Islands are seen as useful locations to explore concepts of sustainability (Dodds, 2007b; Douglas, 2006; Giannoni and Maurpertuis, 2007; Kelman, 2007b, 2009; McElroy and Albuquerque, 1992; Nowak and Selhi, 2007) and can be used to better understand the 'sustainable livelihoods approach'. This approach has been adopted and increasingly applied to sustainability and development activities. Chambers and Conway's (1992: 6) definition of a sustainable livelihood is as follows:

> *A livelihood comprises the capabilities, assets (stores, resources, claims and access) and activities required for a means of living: a livelihood is sustainable which can cope with and recover from stress and shocks, maintain or enhance its capabilities and assets, and provide sustainable livelihood opportunities for the next generation; and which contributes net benefits to other livelihoods at the local and global levels and in the short and long term.*

The definition is useful operationally despite the absence of explicit social elements and some instance of circularity. In simple terms, it can be seen to illustrate the preservation of community and individual relationships that are beneficial, healthy and ensure well-being.

The Sustainable Livelihoods Approach (SLA) is an approach centred on people and their livelihoods. As outlined by Carney (n.d.), this approach is a difficult balancing act as different power and relationships are evident and livelihoods are usually in the private sector albeit heavily influenced by public policy and government. According to the Department of Foreign and International Development (Ashley and Carney, 1999: 7), sustainable livelihood principles should be:

- people centred;
- responsive and participatory;

- multi-level;
- conducted in partnership;
- sustainable;
- dynamic.

The SLA approach places people, particularly rural poor people (or in this case islanders), at the centre to determine how interrelated influences affect how people create a livelihood for themselves. To understand sustainable livelihoods is to gain an understanding of the *assets* that these people use and have and to what extent these assets are *vulnerable* (IFAD, n.d.). Assets can include natural resources, technology, access to education and health facilities, sources of income and credit and networks of social support. The context of vulnerability must take into consideration trends (political, technological, social, environmental and political), shocks (e.g. natural disasters, epidemics, civil strife) and seasonality (prices, employment opportunities, production capabilities). The livelihood strategies are then assessed in relation to prevailing social, political and institutional environments which affect the ways in which people use their assets to achieve their goals. The SLA can inform innovative approaches to sustainable island tourism as the approach focuses on people rather than resources they use and their constraints are expressed by the people themselves. 'Sustainable livelihoods has a core focus on the community, though this approach is to stress an understanding on understanding and facilitating the link through from the micro to the macro, rather than working only at the community level' (Ashley and Carney, 1999: 4). Similar to a multi-stakeholder approach, SLA emphasizes that the local people have a voice and their interests and needs are considered for more sustainable development to occur. It is also adaptive as it depends on the situation and context at hand. As tourism continues to grow and its sustainability can be affected by growth (increasing competition, globalization, environmental disasters and social strife), the livelihoods of islanders are also affected. Using SLA questions the effectiveness of development activity as historically it has been focused on resources and facilities (water, land, infrastructure, services) rather than on people themselves (Ashley and Carney, 1999).

SLA is a process of which a facilitating and supporting approach to people is key. The following steps lay out such a process and individuals or organizations may play a part in one or many of these steps.

### Step 1: Analyse how people thrive and survive and identify key opportunities

Key questions which can be used for community group discussions can include:

- What are the comings and goings in the community?
- What is the most difficult time of year for you and why?
- How do you manage during those months?
- What are things that people are talking about in your community at the moment?

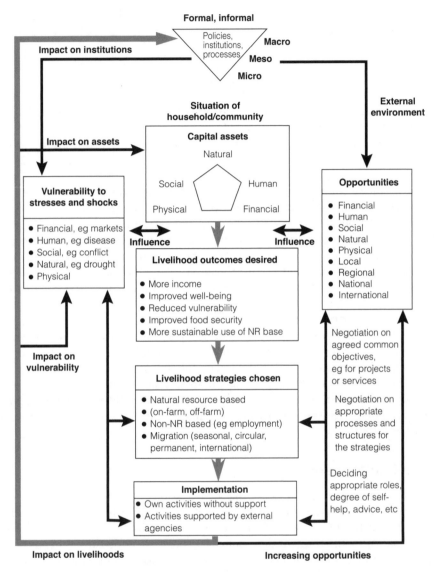

*Source:* Carney (n.d.)

**Figure 2.1** *Khanya's sustainable livelihoods framework
(redrawn from original)*

- Where do the young people hang out? What do they do/talk about?
- What are relationships with outsiders and outside institutions currently like?
- Who are the most helpful groups or people who come into this community?
- How is tourism going these days?

- Who is getting richer? Can you think of a household that is better (or worse) off now than a few days before? Why are they richer (or poorer) now – what happened?
- Who is the richest person in this village – what makes them rich?
- Is there anything else we should know about?

*Step 2: Attain agreement among key stakeholders on the desired outcome – the development 'prize'*

This 'prize' may be reduced risk of disease, improved access to information, etc.

*Step 3: Clarify the operational context and development factors that determine what is feasible (the scope, scale, size and risk of intervention) and help identify the best entry points*

Such processes might include a commitment to poverty eradication, sound decentralized policy, a move towards cross-sectoral working groups, strong economic growth, environmental protection of the reef, etc.) This step often requires a good deal of iteration with Step 2 (defining the desired outcome).

*Step 4: Decide on the nature of the 'intervention'*

Action to reduce transactional costs can take place at all levels. This may range from sectoral policy reform to community capacity, building projects or even food aid. There is no typical sustainable livelihoods programme or project that arises from the use of this approach. (Adapted from Carney, n.d.: 17)

Key issues for this process include engaging stakeholders, building capacity, developing a vision and focusing on empowering ways to deliver outcomes and objectives.

## Stakeholder theory

As the sustainable livelihoods approach focuses on engaging stakeholders, it is also necessary to understand who the stakeholders are in an island destination. Throughout this book there are numerous discussions on integrating stakeholders in the tourism development process. It is pertinent therefore to identify who the stakeholders are in the island tourism context and provide a brief description of their pertinence. Stakeholder theory will also be discussed and how it has been used in other tourism studies.

As the sustainability of many destinations economies, especially islands, is now dependent on tourism, planning and management of the destination is needed. Bramwell and Lane (1993) and Ioannides (2001) believe that sustainable tourism is the responsibility of all stakeholders, and because of this, there is a need to understand stakeholder roles and their role in sustainable tourism practices. Stakeholder theory has evolved over the years to explain the stakeholder–organization relationship. This theory, however, has traditionally focused on the responsibilities of the organization towards its stakeholders. In recent years, attention has turned towards stakeholder identification, responsibilities and power in order to understand the influence of stakeholders

(Donaldson and Preston, 1995; Mitchell, Agle et al, 1997). The organizational setting of a company can be similar to that of an island as islands are also groups of resources just like companies (Ryan, 2002). For the long-term viable management of an island destination, it is important to understand the views of stakeholders as they can motivate or impede sustainability in organizations (competitive advantage, regulatory compliance, economic considerations, etc.) (Bansal and Roth, 2000; Carroll, 2000; Lantos, 2001).

The idea that organizations have stakeholders has now become common-place in management literature and has been used by numerous authors to explain decision-making in both an organizational and a government/destination context. A stakeholder is defined as:

> *any group or individual who can affect or is affected by the achievement of an organization's objectives. Thus a group or individual qualifies as a stakeholder if it has a legitimate interest in aspects of the firm's activities and has either the power to affect the firm's performance or has a stake in the firm's per-formance. (Freeman, 1984: 55)*

This is a broad definition as it leaves the notion of stake and the field of pos-sible stakeholders open to include virtually anyone. It does not discuss the implication or necessity of reciprocal impacts that occur in most situations involving relationships, transactions or contracts. Only those who cannot affect the firm (have no power) and are not affected by it (have no claim or relationship) are excluded. In order to understand the impacts of stakeholders on an organization or, in this context, an island destination, it is important to adopt a broad definition in order to encompass all possible relationships and associated claims and interests. However, a broad definition makes it difficult for many organizations/destinations to identify and manage their stakeholders as this implies that the number of stakeholders is vast and many organizations do not believe that all affected parties should be considered stakeholders (Mitchell, Agle et al, 1997).

Defining stakeholders is a way to broaden management's vision of its roles and responsibilities beyond the profit maximization function to include all interests and claims of non-stockholding groups. Stakeholder theory does not simply describe existing situations or predict cause–effect relationships, it also recommends attitudes, structures and practices which, collectively, constitute stakeholder management (Cheyne and Barnett, 2001; Donaldson and Preston, 1995).

## Defining stakeholder influence

In order to identify which stakeholders are the most influential and receive the bulk of the attention in regard to decision-making and influence, it must be understood that there are complex stakeholder dynamics. All stakeholder interests must be recognized for the good of the organization, or in this case the island destination. Nevertheless, stakeholders' interests do not play an equal role in the decision-making process. Stakeholder relationships, both actual and potential, need to be evaluated to better understand who and what really counts. Mitchell, Agle et al (1997) developed a theory of stakeholder salience within the general context of stakeholder theory, to identify an organization's stakeholders and their associated influences. This theory attempts to define how stakeholders affect the decision-making process of an organization. This theoretical concept can be applied to a destination, as it is, in many ways, similar to the organization in structure and context.

## Theory of stakeholder salience

The theory of stakeholder salience is based on three attributes: power, legitimacy and urgency (Mitchell, Agle et al, 1997). Salience is defined as the degree to which managers give priority to competing stakeholder demands (Mitchell, Agle et al, 1997). Most theories of a firm (or destination) only account for legitimacy and power but this theory includes urgency, which is the degree to which stakeholder claims call for immediate attention. This adds a catalytic component to the theory of stakeholder identification, because urgency demands attention (Mitchell, Agle et al, 1997). Table 2.1 defines the three attributes in the context of this theory.

This theory also identifies the importance of managers or decision-makers. These are the only group of stakeholders who enter into a relationship with all other stakeholders and have direct control over the decision-making process of the firm. It is the firm's manager (or destination's decision-maker) who determines which stakeholders are salient and therefore receive attention. This theory posits that managers who want to achieve certain results pay particular attention to various classes of stakeholders, that managers' perceptions dictate stakeholder salience, and that the various classes of stakeholders may be identified based upon the possession, or attributed possession, of one, two or all three of the attributes (Flagestad, 2001; Mitchell, Agle et al, 1997). Table 2.2 classifies each type of stakeholder and the attributes they possess. This classification justifies the identification of entities that should be

**Table 2.1** *Definitions of stakeholder attributes*

| Attribute | Definition |
| --- | --- |
| Power | A relationship among social actions in which one social actor, A, can get another social actor, B, to do something that B would not have otherwise done. This is the ability of those who possess power to bring about the outcomes they desire. |
| Legitimacy | A generalized perception or assumption that the actions of an entity are desirable, proper, or appropriate within some socially constructed system of norms, values, beliefs and definitions. |
| Urgency | The degree to which stakeholder claims call for immediate attention. Based on time sensitivity which is the degree to which managerial delay in attending to the claim or relationship is unacceptable to the stakeholder and criticality which is the importance of the claim or the relationship to the stakeholder. |

*Source:* Mitchell et al (1997): 869

**Table 2.2** *Explanation of stakeholder typology*

| Number | Type | Attributes | | | Description |
|---|---|---|---|---|---|
| | | Power | Legitimacy | Urgency | |
| 1 | Dormant | X | | | • Without a legitimate relationship or urgent claim, their power remains unused.<br>• Little or no interaction with firm but has potential to acquire a second attribute.<br>• Example is a stakeholder that can command attention in the news media. |
| 2 | Discretionary | X | | | • Do not have power or urgent claims to influence the firm.<br>• No pressure on managers to engage in an active relationship.<br>• Example is a non-profit organization that accepts donations. |
| 3 | Demanding | | | X | • Mosquitoes buzzing in the ears of managers.<br>• Example is a lone picketer who may gain the attention of a manager but without power or legitimacy their claims will not be considered. |
| 4 | Dominant | X | X | | • Form the dominant coalition.<br>• Have a formal mechanism in place that acknowledges the importance of their relationship with the firm.<br>• Examples are employees and customers. |
| 5 | Dependent | | X | X | • Depend on other stakeholders for the power necessary to carry out their will.<br>• An example would be local residents affected by an organization and requiring the aid of another group to have their claims heard. |
| 6 | Dangerous | X | | X | • Coercive and possibly violent.<br>• Examples are wildcat strikes, employee sabotage and terrorism. |
| 7 | Definitive | X | X | X | • Clear and immediate mandate to attend to and give priority to definitive stakeholders' claims.<br>• Hold the most influence in an organization.<br>• Examples are shareholders and the corporate decision makers. |
| 8 | Non-stakeholder | | | | • No power, legitimacy or urgency in relation to the firm and thus holds no salience. |

*Source:* Mitchell et al, 1997; Flagestad, 2001

considered stakeholders of the firm. It also constitutes the set from which managers select those entities they perceive as salient.

Stakeholders can move from one category to another by acquiring one of the missing attributes. This is important because, depending on the issue, stakeholders can change in salience, requiring different degrees and types of attention (Flagestad, 2001; Graci, 2009; Mitchell, Agle et al, 1997).

Mitchell, Agle et al's (1997) theory demonstrates that the importance of a stakeholder increases according to the number of attributes they possess. This is helpful in prioritizing stakeholders. It is unclear, however, which attribute should be emphasized over others for continued systematic sorting of stakeholders into priority groups. Prioritizing stakeholders will therefore depend on the manager's judgement and thus will be different with each issue facing an organization. There is also a question regarding the extent to which the three dimensions are independent of each other. In many instances, power and legitimacy may be difficult to separate (Flagestad, 2001; Graci, 2009; Harvey and Schaefer, 2001; Mitchell, Agle et al, 1997).

## Stakeholder theory and its application to sustainability in the tourism industry

Several empirical studies have been conducted to explore the relationship between stakeholder influence and sustainability in an organization (Alvarez Gil et al, 2001; Bansal and Roth, 2000; Berman et al, 1999; Cheyne and Barnett, 2001; Clarkson, 1995; Flagestad, 2001; Harvey and Schaefer, 2001; Henriques and Sadorsky, 1999). According to stakeholder theory, organizations carry out activities to appease their main stakeholders. By satisfying these stakeholders, support and resources are acquired which ensures the long-term success of the organization (Alvarez Gil et al, 2001). This theory identifies that organizations/destinations will adopt sustainability if stakeholders demand it.

Sautter and Leisen (1999) use stakeholder theory as part of a tourism-planning model. These authors developed a tourism stakeholder map adapted from Freeman's (1984) model to include the salient stakeholders in the tourism industry. Depending on the specifics of the organization (sector,

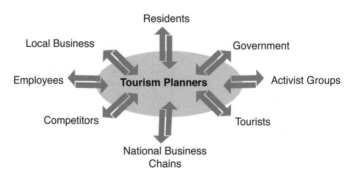

*Source:* Sautter and Leisen (1999): 315

**Figure 2.2** *Tourism stakeholder map*

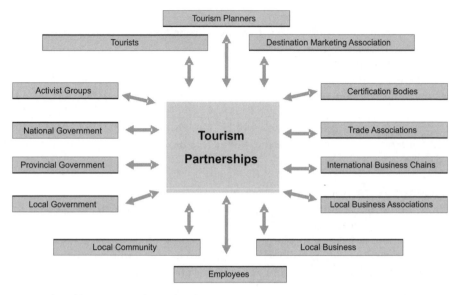

*Source:* Adapted from Sautter and Leisen (1999)

**Figure 2.3** *Stakeholder map of island tourism destinations*

location and type of facility), stakeholders may be added or deleted (Sautter and Leisen, 1999). This comprehensive map provides an excellent starting point for the development of a stakeholder map for any island tourism destination. Stakeholders could be added or deleted depending on the situation on the island and is affected by or can affect tourism development.

For the purpose of identifying stakeholders in island destinations, the authors chose to adapt and expand on Sautter and Leisen's (1999) stakeholder map. Figure 2.3 identifies a modified version of the map with identified key stakeholders. Each stakeholder will be discussed in further detail.

### The public sector

The public sector influences tourism in a number of ways and can play a role in the development of sustainable tourism. The public sector, which comprises a number of agencies at the local, state and national levels and internationally, usually has the mandate to represent the whole population and not just particular interest groups or stakeholders. The public sector should not be constrained by short-term financial objectives, as its mandate should be the longer-term view that incorporates the best for the destination. The public sector has responsibilities for:

- legislation and regulation;
- funding and fiscal incentives;
- land use planning;
- development and building control including the role of environmental impact assessments;

- provision of infrastructure;
- the example the public sector can set through its role as an active player in the tourism industry;
- official standards;
- the designation of particular areas for special protection;
- government control over tourist numbers (Swarbrooke, 1999: 88).

To be successful, public sector policy has to be coordinated effectively, and different departments in the public sector at all levels need to work together.

## Local government

In an island destination, the local government can consist of one person or can be a number of agencies that work together on various aspects of the destination. They can also be elected by the community or, in many cases in the developing world, appointed through custom and tradition. Nevertheless, the role of the local government is to ensure good governance of its community and in the island context this can be a very powerful position. Even though the tourism industry is loosely regulated, there is still the threat of regulation and the local government can institute legislation that all stakeholders will have to follow. Consequently, the local government also has the power to not enforce regulation and, as is seen in the various examples throughout this book, has the potential to become corrupted or not have the financial wherewithal to enforce regulations that can lead to the failure of the government to protect the community's resources. The local government, however, is very powerful in terms of hindering or moving the agenda in all island destinations.

## State and national government

In some islands that are not states or countries on their own, they are part of a larger governance system of a larger country. In this case, state and national governments have varying degrees of power in island destinations. As islands are usually far removed from mainland destinations, they are insular in dealing with their affairs. State and national governments may collect taxes from island destination; they may also provide money for infrastructure; and most importantly, as in the case of several islands, they may institute policies such as marine park designations. However, due to the distance of islands from the mainland, islands usually seem to govern their own affairs. The state and national governments are not as influential as the local governments, since policy is only effective if it is enforced. Support is usually required from the local governments.

If the island is a state or country unto itself, it may also have state and national government. In some islands all three levels of government are present and must work together to ensure good governance. Often different levels of government are accountable or responsible for different elements of planning, education and the like, and coordination and collaboration can be challenging as each have their own priorities or agendas.

## The tourism industry

The tourism industry is normally seen as being responsible for degradation in many island destinations. Multinational and foreign corporations who own hotels on islands are seen to be detached from the well-being of the state of the environment and community. Tourism businesses are often portrayed as being concerned solely with profit and having a short-term perspective towards development. Despite the fact that industry potentially can be the cause of many negative impacts in a destination, it also has the power to move the sustainability agenda forward. The tourism industry comprises numerous variations of businesses: locally owned, one-person enterprises; locally owned small and medium enterprises; nationally owned chains which operate across a domestic market; nationally owned chains which also operate in other countries: foreign owned small and medium enterprises; foreign owned one-person enterprises; multinational corporations; and a mix of everything in between (Swarbrooke, 1999). Industry is often criticized for its short-term focus and exploiting the environment and local populations rather than conserving them; however, many tourism organizations are also the leaders in pushing sustainable tourism in island destinations as they are often the most organized, goal-oriented and forward thinking. Industry can be the innovators in terms of stakeholder engagement, implementing new technologies and efficiencies and partnerships with government to ensure voluntary action through codes of conduct, and international initiatives such as the International Hotel Environmental Initiative (now called the International Tourism Partnership) or The Tour Operators Initiative (TOI).

## Multinational corporations

Multinational corporations (MNCs) can also play an influential role in the sustainability of island destinations. Although the tourism industry is made up mainly of small and medium-sized enterprises (SMEs), large MNCs own or influence a large portion of accommodation facilities (hotels, motels, cruise ships), transportation (airlines, cruises, motor coach companies) and mainstream travel distribution (tour operators, travel agents) and therefore should not be ignored in the quest for sustainable tourism. Business travel and, additionally, mass tourism, is still mainly operated by businesses owned by MNCs (e.g. TUI, Sol Melia, Accor, Intercontinental, etc.). As MNCs are scrutinized by international media, they usually follow the laws and regulations as designated in developed countries. Some MNCs have a sustainability strategy and clearly report on corporate social responsibility (CSR) practices. They have the power to create change in an island and many MNCs have policies that lead to the development of partnerships with the local community (i.e. the Holiday Inn Brand works with suppliers in local communities such as bakeries and dry cleaners). Intercontinental hotels group 'greened' their purchasing policy that trickled down their supply chain affecting millions of US dollars purchased in local economies. MNCs, however, are usually the accommodation or other facility on the island that is the biggest and most expensive to stay in. Due to their size, they also are usually responsible for using a lot of land and resources. They can, however, play an influential role in moving the agenda forward in an island as they are powerful stakeholders. If they threaten to pull out of an island, the fear is that revenue will be lost.

## Local businesses

Locally owned businesses consist mostly of small and medium-sized operations that represent the grass roots of the tourism industry in any destination but especially an island. Local businesses ensure that the multiplier effect is increased in the island tourism destination as the income generated by these ventures is often multiplied and shared across the destination. Local businesses often also lead to capacity being developed in the community through entrepreneurship and the hiring and training of local people as staff. Local businesses are important stakeholders as they have a vested interest in the destination and collectively can make an impact on the environmental and social status of a destination. They can also, however, be interested only in short-term profits and have little understanding or interest in promoting or moving towards sustainable tourism.

## Foreign-owned businesses

Foreign-owned businesses can also be small and medium-sized operations or of a larger status. The difference is that they are foreign-owned. In many islands, Westerners settle to enjoy island life and open a tourist business (accommodation, tour operator, specialty service such as a dive shop or adventure tourism outfitter, restaurant). These foreigners usually consider themselves as living in the community and have a relationship to the destination. Like local businesses, they can play a large role in sustainable tourism and in many cases have been the influence to move the sustainability agenda forward in a tourism destination. They can have a vested interest in protecting the destinations' livelihood, as it is not only their source of income but also their community.

## Industry associations

Industry associations can act as a motivating factor to promote and institute environmental initiatives in the accommodation industry. Industry associations, such as the International Air Transport Association or Tour Operator Associations, may provide support, guidance, lobbying, marketing, financial assistance, technical assistance, advertising and certification programmes to its members. The purpose of this guidance is to promote the industry's social and environmental concerns in order to create a positive reputation, avoid increased scrutiny from stakeholders and decrease the potential for new regulations (Berry and Rondinelli, 1998; Henriques and Sadorsky, 1999; Kelley, 1991; Post, Lawrence et al, 1999; Pryce, 2001; Rivera, 2002b; Stabler and Goodall, 1996; Thompson, 1997).

## Destination marketing associations

Destination marketing organizations (DMOs) are tasked with the role of marketing their region to travel consumers and travel trade intermediaries (Choi, Lehto and Oleary, 2007). Not all island tourism destinations have destination marketing associations. These associations may be at the international level such as the Pacific Asia Travel Association; national level such as the Canadian Tourism Commission; or may be specific to the destination. The role of the destination marketing organization has been strengthened as destinations have attempted to play a more proactive role in fostering and managing the benefits of tourism development. At the international level, these organizations seek to advance tourism development across cooperating nations. National destinations have established national tourist offices. This has also been created at the provincial and state level. Many cities also have their own convention and visitor bureaus and smaller municipalities and regions can also set up regional tourism offices. The DMO as the main avenue for marketing a destination may play a strong role in ensuring that sustainable tourism occurs in the destination and that the image it is trying to market is upheld in the destination. Traditionally, services provided by DMOs include promotional and advertising campaigns, publishing and distributing visitors' guides, and online marketing, training, research and product development (Dodds, n.d.).

## Suppliers

A growing number of organizations are recognizing the need to extend their level of sustainability to their suppliers. A supplier in the tourism industry is a firm or organization that supplies the tourism industry with the basic factor inputs such as labour, materials, equipment and facilities (Ritchie and Crouch, 2005). This is especially pertinent in the tourism industry where success is based on location quality that comes from the support of local businesses. Increasingly, tourism organizations are seeking to improve the level of sustainability throughout their supply chain in order to enhance quality, increase innovation and support the community (Henriques and Sadorsky, 1999; Lippmann, 1999; Post, Lawrence et al, 1999). In the case of an island destination, where all factors are interrelated, suppliers to the tourism industry need to adopt sustainability practices. For example, an island will not be able to reduce its waste if the supplier of water refuses to use refillable containers and ban plastic water bottles. Therefore suppliers must be consulted to determine how the supply chain can embrace sustainability principles and reduce the impact on the environment. This is also the case in terms of social impacts, as a supplier may use inhumane labour practices in its manufacturing, but it is up to the industry it supplies to ensure it is onboard with sustainable social practices.

## Non-governmental organizations

A number of public pressure groups, which operate independently of the tourism industry, are playing a role in the development of more sustainable forms of tourism. The voluntary sector consists of tourism-specific groups whose main focus is sustainable tourism, such as Tourism Concern or The Icarus Foundation; environmental non-governmental organizations (ENGOs) such as the World Wildlife Fund (WWF) that take an interest in tourism; and local development organizations in destinations that have an interest in sustainable forms of tourism development. These organizations act as watchdogs for tourism development in the industry and have a mandate to educate the industry and tourists about sustainable tourism; work in conjunction with governments and industry to ensure sustainable development; and ensure that social and environmental impacts are assessed and mitigated in tourism development. These organizations also have the capability to pressure government for legislation and influence consumer choice. They also can participate in partnership agreements with industry and governments. For example, the Rainforest Alliance and Conservation International have successfully influenced the development of several sustainable tourism programmes in the developing world by participating in voluntary agreements with the tourism industry. ENGOs, however, may not be present in many areas of the world and so while their influence can be quite strong if they exist, their absence is also felt (Post, Lawrence et al, 1999; Swarbrooke, 1999).

## Tourists

Tourists may act as a motivating or impeding force in the quest for sustainable tourism. Tourists respond positively to an organization's or destination's actions by purchasing its product or voicing their discontent by boycotting a product. Island destinations that improve their public image by increasing their level of sustainability have the potential to gain new consumer markets by attracting green consumers and socially conscious investors (Anguera, Ayuso et al, 2000; Post, Lawrence et al, 1999; Robinson, 2000).

As customers are largely responsible for the consumption of resources and the generation of waste, island destinations may seek their customers' commitment to practise environmental and social initiatives (Cespedes Lorente, Burgos Jimenez et al, 2003). The attitudes of consumers are changing and more of them prioritize preservation of the natural environment over economic growth (Gonzalez-Benito and Gonzalez-Benito, 2005).

There is, however, an alternative opinion among customers. There is the perception among clients looking for a high-end, luxury experience that a sustainable destination means one that will affect the level of service. As luxury is usually equated with opulence, customers may perceive a destination that focuses on water conservation as not being able to provide copious amounts of fresh water. This is a challenge, as in many islands fresh water is scarce; thus there is a need to educate consumers that sustainability does not mean a disruption of their experience. Additionally, sustainability does not always mean 'basic', and tourists are often confused by either too much information, not enough information or false claims of sustainability.

## Local community

Members of the local community often have particular concerns about the impact of tourism on their well-being. The local community should be actively involved in tourism planning and should have a say in the development of tourism activities. The community can mobilize public opinion, collaborate with non-governmental organizations and influence government in favour of or against tourism development (Thompson, 1997). The local community can be an influencing factor in the development of sustainability initiatives, or if not consulted, can be a detriment. It is imperative for local communities to be consulted when tourism is being developed. Many of the employees that work in tourism on island destinations are from the local community and this link provides further reason for collaboration (Anguera, Ayuso et al, 2000; Henriques and Sadorsky, 1999).

## Employees

Employees can be a strong motivating or impeding factor for increasing the level of environmental commitment in an accommodation facility. A successful environmental programme depends on the support and involvement of employees. Employees can also be impeding factors in the implementation of environmental commitment initiatives, as they may not be willing to participate or take on extra associated duties. Employee support, however, is imperative as lack of it can lead to the failure of an environmental programme (Berman, Wicks et al, 1999; Ghobadian, Viney et al, 1998; Henriques and Sadorsky, 1999; Johnson, 1998; Johnson, 2002; Pryce, 2001; Welford, 1997).

## General managers

Within an organization, the general manager is seen as a key actor in the onset, development and implementation of sustainable tourism. General managers are the senior management of an organization and have cross-functional responsibilities. They are described as powerful decision-makers that allocate resources and significantly impact on the processes of an organization (Narayanan and Nath, 1993). General managers have a direct influence on organizational practices including the overall development and implementation of sustainability initiatives in the facility. They have a significant influence on practices that are implemented within the island destination and have the power to influence or hinder the development of these initiatives. The tourism industry is an interesting example for examining the extent to which managerial efforts help balance contradictory factors to adopt sustainability initiatives. For example, general managers have to try to reconcile requests from clients for high comfort and high consumption of water, requests from shareholders to cut costs on the water supply as well as demands from the public and employees to implement sustainability initiatives (Cespedes Lorente, Burgos Jimenez et al, 2003).

It is also interesting to note that studies have found that tourism businesses run by managers born in industrialized countries display higher levels of environmental commitment (Rivera and DeLeon, 2005). General managers from industrialized countries may be more likely to adopt proactive sustainability initiatives because of their increased awareness of international environmental requirements and easier access to environmental management information. Facilities with general managers from industrialized countries may also be subjected to increased scrutiny by local environmental groups and government agencies. Hence it can be expected that these general managers would be more likely to endorse and adopt environmental initiatives that improve their facility's reputation (Rivera and DeLeon, 2005).

General managers are either the catalyst or hindrance to a successful implementation of sustainability initiatives. A general manager's knowledge and values in regard to sustainability is imperative for a successful programme to be implemented. An organization's general manager is more receptive to changes in the organizational agenda, products and processes if these fit with their own personal values (Graci, 2009).

## Media

The media can play a significant role in tourism development through shaping tourist behaviour and raising awareness of issues relating to sustainable tourism. The media can influence society's perceptions of a company, especially in respect to environmental crises. The media can also encourage governments to take regulatory action on facilities (Henriques and Sadorsky, 1999; Swarbrooke, 1999). The media, however, can also promote destinations that are not sustainable in its focus, such as ones which have oppressive political regimes or destinations that are degraded beyond repair.

Stakeholders play varying roles in the quest to move towards sustainable tourism. Depending on the political, environmental and social situation on the island, stakeholders at times may be present and may hold differing forms of influence. As will be illustrated in this book, the role of stakeholders may help or hinder the move towards sustainability.

As all stakeholders have a 'stake' or investment into a destination, it is important to consider all different viewpoints in order to understand how they can affect sustainable tourism initiatives.

## The tourism area life cycle (TALC)

Another method used to explain tourism and explain the process by which a destination develops is the tourism area life cycle (Butler, 1980). As more regions and countries (developed and developing) are keen to develop tourism, there is clearly a growing need to consider the sustainability of the tourism resource through an evolutionary model in order to explain the observed growth.

Attempts to model this dynamic element now constitute a major theme of research in the tourism literature. This emphasis is commonly referred to as the *resort cycle concept*. The cycle implies growth, usually excessive, and this illuminates the problems of unstructured tourism growth, while highlighting the need for sustainable tourism. Butler points out that tourism is an activity that, because of its reliance upon the maintenance of natural environment and natural processes, should lend itself toward sustainable development (1993). If a destination continues to develop unchecked and with little planning, eventually the quality of the tourist experience is reduced and a destination's comparative natural/unique/real advantage is lost or reaches a decline (see Figure 2.4).

Butler's (1980) destination life cycle model has been used to describe the tourism development process in many tourism destinations. The life cycle model describes six stages of an evolutionary sequence that a tourist area passes through: exploration, involvement, development, consolidation, stagnation and rejuvenation or decline. Dodds and McElroy (2008) characterize

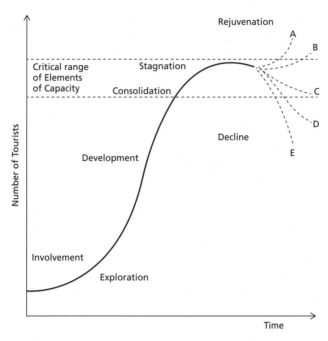

Source: Butler (1980)

**Figure 2.4** *Destination life cycle*

Butler's changes in the nature and extent of facilities provided by stages in the development process:

- *Exploration*: initial discovery of a tourist area. Little visitation by 'explorers'.
- *Involvement*: typified by basic and/or limited provisions, initial publicity and marketing initiations for the tourist product. The product creates/fulfils a need in the marketplace.
- *Development*: expansion of more facilities and tourists. Accessibility is improved and outside investment or competition is attracted to the destination. Companies raise entry barriers through cost and quality to make imitation more difficult. This stage usually marks the beginning of rising antagonism by the local or host community.
- *Consolidation*: the maximum number of tourists has reached capacity levels. Tourist interest is no longer peak and ownership turnover is high although the destination is well known and established. Demand starts to stagnate and competition intensifies.
- *Stagnation*: tourist numbers languish and efforts are made to maximize profits.

Following stagnation, two likely scenarios are suggested by Butler:

- *Rejuvenation*: efforts are made to revitalize levels of interest.
- *Decline*: demonstrates a waning market.

As airports, accommodation and other tourist facilities are provided, awareness grows, but visitors will eventually decline as carrying capacities are reached. Each stage is accompanied by changes in the nature and extent of facilities provided and the local/non-local provision of these. Generally, no local involvement is apparent until the decline stage as employees are able to purchase facilities at significantly lower prices as the market declines (Butler, 1990). Controversy about the exact shape and pattern of the life cycle curve and detailed specification of its parameters has been an ongoing characteristic of the literature and there has been much discussion of the operationalization of the life cycle model in relation to broad evolutionary patterns (Agarwal, 1997). The model, however, is agreed to be a useful way to describe varying elements of development.

There has been much discussion of the operationalization of the life cycle model in relation to broad evolutionary patterns (Agarwal, 1997). Controversy as to the exact shape and pattern of the life cycle curve and detailed specification of its parameters has been an ongoing characteristic of the literature. Choy (1992) disagrees with the efficiency of Butler's cycle, that it is not applicable to all destinations, and can be misleading in the case of Pacific island destinations. Choy argues that it is better to treat each destination individually as a unique entity rather than describe the evolution of the tourist model and is at best a diagnostic tool to be utilized after the fact. Getz (1992) emphasizes that the life cycle model describes stages of tourism development but tourism planners need to be more aware of monitoring. Forecasting a number of important product-, market- and impact-related indicators would reveal the health of the industry from a private sector and public good view. Getz (1992) also discusses the problems associated in differentiating the hypothetical life cycle stages of the model in regard to 'capacity' as a management context and 'rejuvenation' as a planning initiative. Although there are criticisms, the cycle could be applied to a micro level for the specific resort, or to a macro or regional scale, and is therefore put forth as a useful tool to establish at what stage of development an island's tourism may have reached. The case studies in this book illustrate this and also provide a larger perspective on how the life cycle affects the development of sustainable tourism in island destinations.

## Conclusion

The key theories that focus on sustainable livelihoods, stakeholders and the tourism life cycle set the stage for the upcoming discussion and analysis in the book. What will be discussed is how sustainable tourism can be implemented in island states and what is currently challenging this development. Stakeholders play a key role in moving the sustainability agenda forward in an island destination and the tourism life cycle identifies at what stage a destination is at in development and projects where the destination could possibly go. The next chapter is on island destinations and identifies what makes them unique.

# 3
# Island Tourism

## Introduction: Defining islands

The word island creates an image of fantasy and escape from routine and stress; a paradise with an exotic lifestyle (Baum, 1997). Islands are seen to have a slower pace of life and unique culture in comparison to their mainland counterparts.

An agreed-upon definition for the term 'island' does not exist. There are almost as many definitions as there are islands. The most basic definition is 'land surrounded by water on all sides'. However, international organizations do not always use the same criteria. For one it might be the area, for another how far it is from the continent, whether or not it is inhabited and/or the number of inhabitants. For the European Community if there is a capital city on an island it is no longer considered an island. Therefore for the purpose of this book an island is considered simply to be a land mass surrounded by water, which is not a continent.

Increasingly, people travel to obtain the island experience and visit communities that are isolated, display rich and diverse cultures, unique environmental attributes and exotic species (Douglas, 2006; Giannoni and Maupertuis, 2007; Lim and Cooper, 2009; Lopez and Baum, 2004). Island communities have varied languages, histories, societies, governance forms and livelihoods (Baldacchino, 2007; Kelman, 2009).

Recognizing the contribution of tourism as an economic diversification tool, island communities have been trying to introduce tourism as a major economic alternative to traditional livelihoods such as fishing and agriculture (Lockhart, 1997). Tourism on islands has developed not just due to exotic locations and beautiful beaches (as is the case with Mauritius, Seychelles, Bora Bora and the Maldives for example) but also because of their historical significance. Zanzibar in Tanzania was a slave trade port and St Helena off the coast of Angola became famous for the imprisonment of Napoleon Bonaparte – both are now important tourism attractions. Some islands historically gained recognition from their military strategic importance such as Hawaii's Pearl Harbor, the Andaman and Nicobar Islands, Gibraltar, Guam and Malta. Madagascar, Rottnest Island in Australia and the Island of Komodo in

Source: © Nick Palin

**Figure 3.1** *Island paradise*

Indonesia have gained their recognition from conservation that promotes and protects rare animal, bird or mammal species. Whatever the reason for an island's popularity, tourists are attracted to these destinations and their unique way of life.

## Contribution of tourism to islands: Growth and GDP

More than ten per cent of the world's populations are islanders. Although this is not a majority, it is far from insubstantial. More than 20 per cent of sovereign states are islands or archipelagos along with over 90 per cent of non-sovereign territories, with a variety of governance forms (Baldacchino and

Milne, 2009). When examining global tourism growth, the number of islands that are specializing in tourism is increasing. Seven of the 15 fastest-growing countries between 1985 and 1995 were tourism economies and most of them were island tourism economies with more than 30 per cent of gross domestic product (GDP) coming from tourism (Giannoni and Maupertuis, 2007). Annual growth in international arrivals to small island states between 1990 and 2002 was generally much higher than average international arrivals (Nowak and Sahli, 2007). Seven of the ten most prosperous states in the world in 2005 – Iceland, Aruba, Bermuda, Bahrain, French Polynesia, Jersey, Luxembourg – have populations of less than one million people and all except one is an island (Baldachino, 2005). In many instances, tourism is more important in an economic sense to island destinations than it is in many mainland destinations as it is a larger and more significant portion of their economies. As identified in Dodds (2006):

> *International tourism receipts combined with passenger transport currently total more than US$ 800 billion – making tourism the world's number one export earner, ahead of automotive products, chemicals, petroleum and food. In the Caribbean (31 Caribbean Tourism Organization (CTO) member countries), the equivalent figures for 2005 are 22.5 million stay-over arrivals, 19.8 million cruise passenger visits and about US$21.5 billion in expenditures. While this may seem small in comparison to the world total, the fact is that the region's tourism arrivals and receipts command a disproportionately larger share of the global total than do their share in the world's population and GDP. CTO member countries with only 1 per cent of the world's population consistently attract about 3 per cent of global tourism arrivals and world tourism expenditure. (p. 2)*

According to the WTTC (2004), the top 25 nations ranked according to the contribution of tourism to GDP are all island destinations.

Table 3.1 exemplifies the dependency of these island states on tourism. In the British Virgin Islands, 95 per cent of their GDP is dependent on tourism. In the Bahamas, tourism is responsible for generating 74 per cent of household income and 58 per cent of government revenue (Caribbean Tourism Organization, 2001). In other Caribbean islands, tourism accounts for the majority share of jobs and GDP. Antigua and the Cayman Islands receive 75 per cent and 60 per cent respectively of visitor expenditure as a proportion of GDP (Silva, 2002). In Malta, over 25 per cent of GDP and 27 per cent of employment is from tourism (Dodds, 2007b). In the Pacific islands, tourism contributes as much income as the islands receive in foreign aid and contributes to over 12 per cent of all jobs in the region. Tourism's contribution to national economies is also far more pronounced in less developed countries (LDCs), especially islands (McElroy, 2006). Of the 31 countries in the world with more than 20 per cent of their GDP generated by tourism, 27 are islands states (WTTC, 2001 in Kerr, 2005; WTTC, 2004). Many island microstates

**Table 3.1** *GDP contribution to island nations*

| Rank | Country | Percentage of GDP |
|------|---------|-------------------|
| 1 | British Virgin Islands | 95.2 |
| 2 | Antigua and Barbuda | 82.1 |
| 3 | Maldives | 74.1 |
| 4 | Anguilla | 71.9 |
| 5 | Macau | 61.3 |
| 6 | Seychelles | 56.7 |
| 7 | Bahamas | 56.0 |
| 8 | Aruba | 54.5 |
| 9 | Vanautu | 52.4 |
| 10 | Barbados | 52.2 |
| 11 | Saint Lucia | 47.9 |
| 12 | Cayman Islands | 37.6 |
| 13 | Jamaica | 36.0 |
| 14 | St Vincent/Grenadines | 34.1 |
| 15 | Other Oceania | 32.1 |
| 16 | Virgin Islands | 31.9 |
| 17 | Mauritius | 31.0 |
| 18 | St Kitts and Nevis | 28.5 |
| 19 | Malta | 27.8 |
| 20 | Grenada | 27.6 |
| 21 | Cyprus | 27.5 |
| 22 | Kirbati | 27.5 |
| 23 | Fiji | 27.2 |
| 24 | Guadeloupe | 26.9 |
| 25 | Dominican Republic | 25.5 |

*Source:* WTTC 2004: 64

also have on average higher income and productivity than small states (Easterly and Kraay, 1993).

Many islands have recognized the potential contribution of tourism in overcoming economic disparities. A significant number of island destinations are dependent on tourism for their livelihood as a deliberate diversification away from agriculture to international tourism has helped them prosper. In many Caribbean islands, tourism is the only sector that has seen growth, as the real value of traditional primary exports has been declining/losing preferential markets (such as banana and sugar exports) (Scheyvens and Momsen, 2008). Conservation-related tourism has also been lucrative, 'creating many visitor-related livelihoods including operating tours, running accommodations and restaurants, and selling souvenirs' (Kelman, 2009: 15). As the Galápagos Islands (Kerr, 2005) and the Maldives (Ghina, 2003) have recognized, tourism must be controlled because too many tourists can harm the very attractions that tourists travel to see and enjoy. In the Galápagos Islands and Maldives, tourism has led to the destruction of precious wildlife and coral reefs as well as pristine beaches and cultures.

There is also a *hidden* dependency in tourism. Many governments suggest that tourism is worth more than it actually is as factors such as leakage and ownership are not taken into account and tourism is measured in gross rather than net terms. In Zanzibar for example, tourism is worth only approximately 20 per cent of GDP although the government has noted that tourism's contribution is around 80 per cent. This can be a difficult issue for governments as when disasters (such as the 9/11 attack or earthquakes) happen, often tourism revenues fall, thus leaving many people out of work. In the Bahamas, for example, many people did not have work due to layoffs post 9/11 as the Atlantis Hotel, one of the largest employers, let many staff go.

## Challenges of island tourism

The characteristic complexities of island destinations give rise to many resource management and governance issues (Douglas, 2006). Island communities offer rich and diverse languages, culture and history yet are isolated and restricted in dealing with social and environmental challenges that are aggravated by their location and attributes. Many of the services provided by tourism are resource-intensive, resulting in a significant environmental footprint, and island economies are particularly vulnerable due to their dependence on tourism (Briguglio, 1995; McElroy and Albuquerque, 1992; Selywyn, 1975). In addition, many 'warm-water' island destinations have historically focused on 'sun, sea and sand' tourism for development purposes and are dependent on this type of mass tourism for a large proportion of their GDP (Dodds, 2007a; Gössling and Wall, 2007).

**Figure 3.2** *Ratio of tourists often outnumber residents*

As the rapid growth of tourism in the last few decades has resulted in numerous facilities such as increased infrastructure in and around islands, this has often led to detrimental economic, social and ecological impacts such as water and soil pollution; lack of adequate infrastructure to cope with garbage and sewage; loss of habitat, marine and geological features; isolation or deterioration of local cultures; leakage; and disruption to traditional livelihoods. Islands are generally more susceptible to negative impacts of development as they often have limited natural and social resources and are more vulnerable to the market than the mainland. As a large percentage of islands' GDP is due to tourism, market fluctuations lead to more pronounced economic crises. These boom and bust cycles result in projects being abandoned and the loss of employment among a large proportion of island residents. Often an atmosphere of doubt has surrounded small islands in their ability to be self-determined or self-sufficient. Island countries dependent on tourism, such as Samoa for example, have gained 'least developed country' status due to their reliance on the tourism market (Scheyvens and Momsen, 2008).

Due to their size, islands often experience far greater excess of what continental counterparts usually experience (Lewis, 1999). For example, most of Montserrat's infrastructure in the Caribbean was destroyed and two-thirds of the population fled the island in the years following 1995 when the volcano started relatively minor rumbling. Meanwhile, island languages and cultures are being lost as their youth migrate to mainland cities and local island knowledge is devalued by the onslaught of cultural homogeneity (Kelman, 2009). Islands often have had to export staples, services and people in order not to perish.

As many islands have developed their tourism quickly and with little differentiation, it has forced them to compete with other islands or 'sun, sea and sand' destinations, 'often resulting in the neglect of historical, cultural and environmental impacts for the rest of the island. In addition, up/down turns in tourism numbers have rapid multiplier effects on the rest of the island economy and infrastructure strains are quickly felt as are the ratio of visitors to locals' (Dodds, 2007b: 48). Many islands face small populations and tax basis, therefore have limited productive capacities (Sharif and Hoti, 2005). For example, Antigua, the Seychelles and St Kitts and Nevis have less than 100,000 residents each. The smallness of islands mean that there is often little prospect of the island influencing the prices of its output (Kerr, 2005). As islands are often relatively undiversified in exports, they depend heavily on financial aid from the mainland or former colonies for infrastructure development and need a consistent flow of outside direct investment to maintain economic growth (Sharif and Hoti, 2005) or have to rely on external or foreign aid. In an increasingly free-trade and globalized environment, islands often cannot rely on guaranteed prices or markets for their traditional export earners (Scheyvens and Momsen, 2008). This is further exacerbated by the cost of substitutes, the ability of islands to reach their customers, and supply and price from competition – none of which is in the control of many islands. For small islands it is often difficult to borrow from international capital markets as they are perceived to be high risk due to their small economies. Furthermore, not only is their market small, their land area is small and their

**Table 3.2** *Leakage from tourism as a gross percentage of GDP*

| Leakage of foreign exchange from gross tourism receipts | Percentage |
| --- | --- |
| 1  Fiji | 56 |
| 2  Cook Islands | 50 |
| 3  Saint Lucia | 45 |
| 4  Mauritius | 43 |
| 5  Aruba | 41 |
| 6  Hong Kong | 41 |
| 7  Jamaica | 40 |
| 8  United States Virgin Islands | 36 |
| 9  Seychelles | 30 |
| 10  Sri Lanka | 27 |
| 11  Antigua and Barbuda | 25 |
| 12  Cyprus | 25 |
| 15  New Zealand | 12 |
| 17  Philippines | 11 |

*Source:* Travel and Tourism Analyst No. 3 (London, Economist Intelligence Unit, 1992)

resources are often limited (e.g. fresh water), meaning their production capacity is inadequate.

Leakage is also problematic (see Table 3.2). Due to distance and isolation of islands, many resources are imported, as they cannot be produced locally. For tourism the three main imports include:

- consumable or final goods and services such as foreign food and liquor, cigarettes, batteries, etc.
- capital goods and services such as machinery and equipment;
- intermediate inputs or raw materials such as fresh water, flour, fuel and meat. Many islands have an inability to develop infrastructure due to costs, lack of materials and skilled labour and therefore are often dependent on outside resources and financing to provide necessary facilities that tourists require (e.g. airports, hotels).

Power exerted by external business is also challenging. Small islands in the Mediterranean off the coast of Spain, Greece and Turkey show that they have suffered from a problematic supply-side relationship with tour operators and travel agencies from Northern European countries exercising power over the small island accommodation companies (Buhalis, 2000; Aguilo, Alegre et al, 2001).

It is often in islands, which depend heavily on tourism for their economic welfare, that governments have a large and active role, as illustrated in Bermuda, Malta, the Balearic Islands, Tasmania and the South Pacific, where a large portion of GDP and foreign exchange is generated through tourism. As Richter (1984) declares, government can often play a major role in providing infrastructure for the tourism industry. In other cases, governance is completely absent. Due to their distance from their mainland, some island governments may collect tax, but this does not provide enough of a base for funding infrastructure. Island tourism is also often focused on a monoculture for visitation such as wealthy customers from developed countries. Koh Phi Phi's visitors in Thailand are mainly English-speaking from the USA and Sweden (Dodds, Graci and Holmes, 2010) and very few Thais or friends and family visit the island. While high elasticity of demand is an issue, there is also a trend that many islands become destinations for one-off visits.

The natural appeal of an island as in any destination is typically one of its main tourism-related assets, yet the natural environment is also the feature most directly threatened by potential overexploitation (Butler, 1993 and 1998; Murphy, 1994). The Balearic Islands of Spain, such as Ibiza, have already experienced decline and have had to resort to rejuvenation strategies by focusing on wellness and yoga tourism (Lopez and Baum, 2004).

One issue that is particularly pertinent to islands is that their local infrastructure is not adequate. There are often inadequate sewage facilities and this has damaged mangroves, polluted lagoons and degraded fragile reef systems. Water shortages due to limited fresh water supply and electricity often come under pressure. Tourism construction can often be a major cause of beach erosion, silting of lagoons and reef damage (McElroy and Albuquerque, 2002). Construction of large-scale infrastructure projects such as marinas, golf courses, ship terminals and holiday resorts have impacted on coastlines and defaced delicate ecosystems. Transport, water, equipment and machinery are often costly and unreliable without adequate skills or maintenance facilities available. In Jamaica, for instance, the tourism industry has placed enormous pressure on fresh water and waste disposal systems (Thomas-Hope, 1998). Concern over the loss of market share has led islands such as the Bahamas to build a port to accommodate large cruise ships without regard to economic benefits that were not proportional to the level of visitations that resulted. In addition, in many islands, there is a current focus on new golf course and coastal hotel developments that provide short-term return that may not be sustainable because of impacts on the environment that supports them.

Lack of planning is also a challenge in many islands. Tofino on Canada's Vancouver Island has no strategic movement to protect the very resources that the industry depends upon. Although there have been specific instances of sustainability issues affecting tourism (such as the 2006 and 2009 water shortage), there seems to be no impeding change. Although tourism is the main contributor to the economy in Tofino, no formal plan or policy existed and few sustainable tourism practices were observed by stakeholders apart from the NGOs (Dodds and Basu, 2008). In other cases, the government does not plan for long-term sustainability and develops mass tourism with the aim of generating short-term gains. Cultural losses are increasing (such as on the islands of Thailand and Hawaii) as many islands have rapidly developed mass tourism without adequate planning. Often policy focuses on short-term economic benefits over long-term social and environmental sustainability and, in many cases, there is an absence of environmental protection or heritage of cultural appreciation. While stakeholders often lack a common consensus that 'tourism should be', there is often failure of policy-makers to manage growth within social and ecological limits (McElroy and Dodds, 2007).

Lim and Cooper (2009) outlines that small islands are often regarded as powerless as their political and economical power is often limited and unstable. The Seychelles and many small islands off Belize and Honduras are suffering from global environmental change such as coral bleaching, which may affect dive tourism, their main attraction. Worries of sea level rise from global climate change are also affecting islands. Many islands are at risk of losing their main product – beaches – while in some cases the entire country's population is at risk. The Maldives, for example, may have to relocate its population due to the issue that the island is barely over one metre above sea level.

It is not only environmental and economic degradation that islands face. Some of the most successful tourist destinations have also experienced social disruption. Malta experienced local antagonist behaviour towards tourists as by 1975 the number of visitors had exceeded the number of residents (Black, 1996; Mitchell, 1996). The Maldivian government has faced increasing pressure from pro-democracy campaigners in recent years (Scheyvens and Momsen, 2008) and bad publicity due to poor labour standards. 'Tourism development is not created exclusively by private commercial enterprise, but an adversarial attitude often inhibits tourism progress' (Gunn, 1994: 435). A desire to win votes and therefore favouring friends for construction contracts is common in many islands. For some islands, in the race to stay competitive with other destinations, accommodation sectors have built more four- and five-star hotels; however, although this might yield more income per room night, such facilities use a larger land area, are conspicuously sited, use more water and energy (air conditioning, pools, etc.) and often include some element of foreign management or ownership (Ioannides and Halcom, 2001). In Cyprus and many other Mediterranean islands, the dominance of foreign tour operators has created a self-induced problem owing to excessive hotel room supply in the island with limited demand. Foreign tour operators in the Balearic Islands and Malta were able to push prices down to such degrees that hotels were not receiving an adequate return on investment for the services rendered. In Malta, for example, rates offered by tour operators for four- and five-star properties were lower than many three-star rates in the resort area of Bugibba. This lack of long-term and/or strategic planning often results in lack of monitoring or implementation of policy. Although some policies exist, foreigners have been known to grease the politicians' hands to buy up land and build wherever and whenever they want. Boracay Island in the Philippines, for example, suffered from a lack of implementation of guidelines that led to zoning and environmental issues (Toursdale, 1999). In the Andaman and Nicobar islands, the lack of structure and management in different islands has also led to disparities in tourism employment salaries from island to island, and hotel owner, travel and tour operators are becoming wealthier and wealthier as they pay less and less to their employees (Reddy, 2008).

Some islands are vulnerable because their indigenous societies are rarely exposed to the outside world except through tourism and their lack of experience and expertise often makes them susceptible to foreign firms who develop tourism with little regard for local norms and cultures (Kerr, 2005). Displacement of communities also may result, as in the case of Hainan, China, where indigenous communities were moved to make way for a golf course.

As many islands are small in their economic scale, not to mention size, they often have little if any political and economic identity and are often overpowered by events beyond their control. As Kelman (2007a) outlines, the losses caused by Hurricane Ivan damage in Grenada in 2004 were valued at ten times the country's annual budget. The recent earthquake in Haiti had devastating effects as the entire island was affected. Islands tend to be more susceptible to higher incidences of natural disasters and structural difficulties perpetuate dependence.

## Strengths of island sustainability in tourism

In some islands, characteristics which breed challenges also yield to opportunities for tackling them (Scheyvens and Momsen, 2008). Isolated, small populations form tight kinship networks, a strong sense of identity helps develop bonds and leadership, and a unique cultural heritage often boosted by remittances from islanders overseas helps to diversify away from reliance on solely foreign tourists as visiting friends and relatives (VFRs) is strong.

Thousands of years of experience in dealing with social and environmental changes in isolation provides islanders some flexibility to adjust to contemporary changes such as human-caused climate change, improving Internet connectivity, and swifter transportation modes (Kelman, 2009). Despite the difficulties, islands present impressive advantages for building and maintaining healthy and prosperous communities.

Islands, due to their size and isolation, can also offer an enticing tourism product that is in high demand around the world (Butler, 1993; Gössling, 2003; Sheller, 2003). Rather than being a drawback, isolation tends to make the destination more attractive and exotic, especially in the case of small islands (Scheyvens and Momsen, 2008).

Tourism is a good economic development tool but diversification is also important and development of mass tourism tends to increase competitiveness and environmental degradation. Bermuda and the Channel Islands in the UK have combined tourism with becoming tax shelters, taking advantage of the global spread of offshore banking (McElroy and Dodds, 2007). Islands such as the British Virgin Islands and the Cayman Islands have avoided mass tourism and excessive development by also diversifying into other profitable economic activities like banking. 'Island planners are now seeking to diversify away from the attraction of "sun, sea and sand" that are typical of mass tourism, into special activity holidays etc.' (Lockhart, 1997: 4).

Islands must protect, preserve and manage their social and natural resources. Islands such as the Seychelles and Madagascar have a tradition of environmental conservation and offer a self-conscious, upscale tourism identity due to these efforts. The Galápagos Islands, through protection of wildlife, went from being a largely unpopulated volcanic outcrop to the richest department in Ecuador and has a higher GNP than mainland Ecuador (Kerr, 2005). Part of good conservation management of these islands is that the level of environmental awareness on the part of government is evident as they hold the power to check land encroachment by international developers, establish marine and national parks and implement controls over environmental management.

It is often the remoteness and traditional knowledge of dealing with environmental and social changes in isolation that have provided islanders with the skills to help them adjust to these changes. In some warm-water islands, tourism is restricted by limited transport, and this has allowed low-density or other eco-friendly tourism to develop. In St Barthélemy, in the Eastern Caribbean, a small airport has prevented the growth of mass tourism and has helped to develop an up-market destination for French cuisine (McElroy and Dodds, 2007).

Tourism must maintain the well-being and involvement of the local population or host community yet have economic benefit. Islands such as Newfoundland in Canada, Iceland and the Aland Islands in Finland are dominated by locally owned small operators across all sectors with almost a complete absence of external investment (Baum, 1999).

Governance can also be stronger in islands. Governments can exercise control over the conditions under which tourists are admitted to a country and they can influence the development of tourism in a specific area, set the conditions for investment and access, determine foreign enterprise concessions and legislate access (leases vs. freehold).

Some island communities have taken ownership and strong leadership to respect environmental and social issues. Islands may be more successful if prospects retained control over land and marine resources, have strong social institutions and a genuine sense of pride and cultural identity, and if natural capital is in good condition and has strong links to the diaspora (Scheyvens and Momsen, 2008). A multi-stakeholder approach that includes local islanders and recognizes the challenges that the individual island faces is imperative.

Seasonality also plays a role in controlling tourism development. In cold-water islands such as the Falklands, Nunavut in Canada, Antarctica and Greenland, tourism is controlled by a short season, expensive access and hard adventure exploration which is demanded only by few high-yield tourists rather than the masses. This has led to the preservation of these islands; however, due to climate change and the potential for melting seaways, this may open access to more tourists, thus leading to the greater potential for degradation.

## Conclusion

Small islands, large islands, island states and island nations all share physical–geographical and environmental characteristics that challenge sustainability. Both warm- and cold-water islands face issues of insular geography, fragile environmental and ecological characteristics, external global impacts and vulnerability to external change with increased demand for resources and low production abilities that make sustainability, let alone sustainable tourism development, testing. The very insularity of islands and apparent clarity of boundaries seem to make islands a clearly definable unit where all inputs and outputs can be measured (Kerr, 2005). Remoteness, smaller size, pace of life, distinct culture, exotic species and pristine environments are some of the basic characteristics of islands (Baum, 1997; Lockhart, 1997). Island communities have survived for hundreds of years; however, decades of haphazard tourism development can lead to severe degradation that can threaten the livelihoods of these islands.

> *Islands, by focusing exclusively on tourism as their main source of foreign exchange, without long-term planning for sustainable development, are potentially facing crises equal if not worse than their agricultural demise (Dodds and McElroy, 2008).*

Islands can provide insight into sustainable development, yet they are complex and difficult to define. There has been an overriding theme of island research that has focused on the susceptibility of islands to environmental problems and often a 'fatalistic' position has been taken (Baldacchino, 2007; Scheyvens and Momsen, 2008). There are, however, several examples of how island destinations have been able to rectify the impacts of development and plan tourism for the benefit of the island rather than lead to its demise.

**Figure 3.3** *Island tourism: susceptibility if sea levels rise?*

Island knowledge and experience does not apply just to themselves. Analogies and parallels appear with non-islands such as ski villages, Arctic communities and even cities, and thus this book seeks to illustrate examples and case studies to showcase both barriers to sustainable tourism development as well as successful innovative practices.

The key question for sustainable tourism in islands, therefore, is to explore how tourism investments and environmental and social quality preservation can ensure sustainable profitable tourism in the long term. Developing sustainable island tourism is complex as it is difficult to find any island tourism development model with universal relevance. The onus is on the tourism sector to be more open to alternative conceptualizations of development paths that focus on sustainable tourism and do not prioritize short-term economic growth but recognize social, cultural, political and environmental well-being as well. Optimization of tourism numbers while maintaining ecological and social balance is also challenging as sustainable tourism must enhance the quality of life of the population without damaging the environment and cultural capital of the island destination. An understanding of these dynamic relationships between infrastructure, environmental quality, socio-cultural preservation and policy issues is needed. This book will examine these dynamic relationships and provide a better understanding of the barriers to sustainable tourism development in islands and how these can be overcome.

# PART II

# CHALLENGES TO ACHIEVING SUSTAINABILITY IN ISLAND DESTINATIONS

# 4
# Challenges to Achieving Sustainable Tourism

## Introduction

Despite numerous discussions on sustainability in the tourism industry, there are numerous challenges that impede the development of sustainable tourism, especially in the context of islands. This chapter seeks to identify the challenges to sustainability, especially within the context of tourism. An overview of key literature identifying the challenges to sustainable tourism development is followed by a discussion contextualizing this in relation to islands. Challenges highlighted are issues of short-term vision, lack of environmental awareness, stakeholders with conflicting interests, lack of measurement, lack of resources, corruption, bureaucracy and impediments due to infrastructure. Three case study chapters will then follow, providing specific context about challenges to achieving the sustainability of tourism in island destinations.

## Identifying challenges to sustainable tourism

Most studies in tourism discuss what is needed to achieve sustainable tourism; however, it is important to also understand what inhibits sustainable tourism from being achieved so that one can understand what the challenges are and how they affect the goal of moving forward. (See also Sharpley, 2009, for a critique of sustainable tourism as it relates to tourism development and the environment.) There are a few studies that have been conducted that identify challenges, most often referred to as barriers to sustainable development. Most discussions define issues in achieving the notion of sustainability rather than specifically the sustainability in the tourism industry. However, as tourism is a multi-faceted and fragmented industry which depends on multiple other sectors, these challenges hold true. In the context of island tourism, an island has similar characteristics to an organization as it is an entity, comprised of stakeholders with specific limitations due to resources, space and revenue, and thus the barriers applicable to organizations in the general sense can also be applicable to islands.

Kirkland and Thompson (1999) examined challenges that affect the implementation of sustainability in an organization. They state that the implementation of an environmental management strategy involves several dynamic stages that may be affected by various issues. The specific challenges that may affect an organization depend on its size, corporate culture and formal and informal management styles, as well as the individuals involved in the process, and the stage of development of the organization's environmental programme (Kirkland and Thompson, 1999). Many of these challenges may be related to one another and often the presence of one challenge or barrier may increase the likelihood of, or lead to, the presence of another challenge. Lack of information, knowledge and resources; incompatibility with an organization's corporate culture; and the presence of multiple stakeholders with conflicting interests are the main setbacks identified by these authors.

Drawing upon the findings of an empirical study of corporate environmental policies in the UK, Ghobadian, Viney et al (1998) identified several factors that work with or against external pressures and determine the capability of the organization to implement sustainability strategies. The challenges identified by this study are technological requirements, opportunity and cost assessment, human resource availability, capital availability, organizational adaptability and organizational culture and leadership. Approaches to environmental issues are influenced by the attitudes held by managers, and an unsupportive manager can be a significant hindrance to the development of a sustainability programme (Ghobadian, Viney et al, 1998).

In a study of the Dutch dairy industry, Mauser (2001) identified variables important in determining the level of sustainability in an organization. These variables consist of the level of centralization of the authority to make environmental decisions and organizational culture. Organizations with a high level of centralization and an organizational culture open to sustainability will have a better level of environmental and social performance. Ownership structures incorporating multiple shareholders leads to conflicting interests and hinders the process of incorporating sustainability into an organization (Mauser, 2001). Although examining the dairy industry, many of these issues are similar to other organizations in varying industries.

Specifically relating to tourism, Ioannides (1996) discussed barriers to implementing sustainable tourism in Cyprus. He noted that there was a climate of mistrust between the government and the local communities. The local community was never approached about their opinions and was excluded from all stages of the planning process. Locals resented the capital city's 'bureaucrats backed by foreign consultants coming into their area, dictating what inhabitants can or cannot do with their land' (p. 590). Planners, on the other hand, believed that if planning or development was left in the locals' hands, it would result in chaos as they believed there were insufficient skills surrounding environmental protection. In addition to the local power struggles, there was no visible attempt to integrate regional goals for sustainable tourism development into the overall national tourism policy. Ioannides (1996) puts forth the idea that uncontrolled development in mass tourism leads to dire environmental and social consequences but that top-down attempts without the local communities' input are not successful.

Dodds (2005) reviewed tourism literature to identify barriers to implementing sustainable tourism policy in destinations. After reviewing 79 articles about coastal zone management, sustainable tourism and tourism policy and then testing barriers with academics and in the field, barriers identified included difficulties in human resources skills and accountability; lack of education, coordination and collaboration between agencies and authorities; as well as obstacles of adequate resources, political will, monitoring/control and economic priority over social and environmental issues. Dodds (2007a) determined that there were six barriers that were frequently encountered in achieving sustainability objectives. These six barriers are:

1 economic priority (short-term economic focus wins over long-term social and environmental concerns);
2 lack of planning (too much damage has already been done and sustainability initiatives are not strong enough to apply to already damaged areas);
3 lack of stakeholder involvement;
4 lack of integration with regional and national frameworks and policies;
5 lack of accountability of politicians (lack of political will);
6 lack of coordination with other government parties (political clash) (Dodds 2007a: 310).

Dodds (2007b: 55) also outlines similar barriers as well as additional issues in a study of Malta and its attempts to implement a sustainable tourism policy. Common barriers that were noted included:

1 non-coordination between ministries and authorities – power struggles;
2 more talk than action: efforts were implemented just to gain votes;
3 economic priority over social and environmental concerns;
4 short-term focus;
5 private sector power: pressure on politicians for development;
6 lack of commitment to sustainability: tourism not seen as priority;
7 lack of understanding/awareness of sustainable tourism;
8 lack of structure: no coherent strategic development plan;
9 lack of stakeholder 'buy-in' for sustainable tourism;
10 lack of integration into wider policy;
11 focus on tourism numbers rather than yield;
12 problems of insularity;
13 ambiguity of policy;
14 lack of participation by stakeholders;
15 lack of resources;
16 political clash between parties.

Dodds (2007b) supported Hunter's (1995) notion that a 'tourism-centric' approach will fail and that an integrated approach including all stakeholders is needed but noted that 'The case for an integrated framework may appear relatively straightforward in principle; yet, social and environmental agendas are often played off against each other; the links (rather than tensions) between them are rarely made explicit (pp. 62–63).

Altinay, Var, Hines and Hussain (2007) conducted a study that identified the barriers to sustainable tourism development in Jamaica. This study identified that the obstacles to this form of development are based on three themes: financial constraints, social instability and lack of coordinated tourism planning. The authors identified that several sustainable tourism initiatives are being implemented in the public and private sectors, but these lack management, cohesiveness and collaboration. In order for sustainability to be achieved, it requires effective financial management of industries and a focus on social issues. Jamaica is a prime example of an island that is over-dependent on tourism, and this has led to the under-development of other industries of sectors of the economy. In Jamaica, there is a growing trend towards large hotel developments undertaken by mostly foreign investors who appear to have little regard for social and environmental preservation of a developing destination. This focus on mass tourism has resulted in not only financial dependence but also in social impacts such as the evidence of cultural dilution due to American and European influences and increased prevalence of HIV/AIDS and prostitution in resort areas. Crime has also increased in Jamaica. With little emphasis on community-based and entrepreneurial forms of tourism it has led to leakage and stifled development of benefits for small tourism ventures such as crafts and restaurants. Despite the fact that the government of Jamaica was aware of the need for sustainability and understood the long-term impacts related to mass tourism development, there was a lack of coordinated effort and true collaboration among all the stakeholders on the island. Despite good initiatives being put forward such as a Tourism Master Plan (that outlined the role of the public and private sectors and proposes community-based tourism), the stakeholders deemed that tourism operates in a vacuum and lacks collaboration and integration. It was also identified that tourism development lacked importance, as it was not part of Jamaica's national plan.

Reid and Schwab (2006) identified, in a study that examined barriers to sustainable tourism development in Jordan, that unstable political systems and inept and highly centralized bureaucracies are problematic in achieving sustainable tourism development. This study concluded that despite the potential for written policies to be developed it is difficult to integrate these concepts if the culture of the destination has not embraced this form of change. The authors identified that challenges related to implementing sustainable development strategies are threefold:

1   gaining legitimacy for the new policies/changes, especially when their rationale is not fully understood or seen as incompatible with societal and cultural norms;
2   developing integration of the changes within a body of policy priorities;
3   developing the requisite capabilities to mobilize support and power resources to formulate and implement the new policies (Bressers and Rosenbaum, 2000: 532 as cited in Reid and Schwab, 2006).

This study also identified that the economic priority of tourism is emphasized over environmental and social impacts and there is a lack of community-based collaboration. The traditional players in Jordan's international tourism industry – large hotels, tour operators and airlines – benefit most from the emphasis placed on economic development. In the Tourism Master Plan developed by the Jordan Tourism Board, a community approach to tourism development was missing. Tourism development continues to be driven by the interests of the central government rather than the community (Reid and Schwab, 2006).

Ruhahen (2008) identified through her study of tourism development in Queensland, Australia, that it is difficult to achieve sustainable tourism development when the mandate of the public sector is to represent the whole population, not a particular interest group/stakeholder, and therefore it is often economic concerns which take priority over other elements (i.e. job creation or development of infrastructure). Due to this focus, there is often an absence of strong government planning and development controls as governments will often pay lip service to sustainability initiatives but will put priority on economic growth. There has also been little progress with sustainable tourism planning due to a lack of understanding by governments of the basic principles of sustainable tourism development. Government officials often change from one ministry to another or are appointed; however, they often do not have in-depth understanding about tourism, let alone the complexities of developing sustainable tourism. Another challenge identified in this study is that there is a grey area between sustainable principles and their translation into workable objectives and standards. It was identified that even though strategic sustainable tourism plans were in place, the majority of documents failed to include essential descriptive, baseline information on how to achieve such objectives. Long-term considerations were also not a feature in the majority of local government tourism planning processes and despite a discussion including all stakeholders, the local community was not included in the planning process. Vision and values were also not incorporated, and goals and objectives tended to be superficial and unsubstantiated. Despite the identification of objectives on paper, these were not supported with subsequent action strategies in the planning documents. Despite this study being conducted in Australia, and that the term sustainability is common in everyday use, it was determined that there is minimal understanding of the concept, which makes it difficult to apply in practice. The lack of tools such as sustainability indicators also contributes to the misuse of the concepts as there is no means of measuring efforts. In addition, local government planning did not have a long-term strategic view. The authors conclude the study by identifying that there is a need for education and knowledge about sustainability and its use in practice. Knowledge needs to be transferred into programmes tools, manuals and best-practice examples to overcome the identified barriers.

In a study conducted by McNamara and Gibson (2008), which examined on a macro scale the implementation of environmental management initiatives among the accommodation industry on Australia's East Coast, it was identified that large facilities were more likely to have formal mechanisms to implement sustainability initiatives. The most frequently identified challenges to implementing sustainable tourism development were high initial capital cost, impediments due to existing building structures, issues with facility age and location, lack of time and lack of incentives to implement sustainability initiatives. It is also important to identify that in this destination, as is often the case in many other destinations, smaller facilities did not believe that implementing sustainability initiatives were applicable to them as they felt that they did not affect the environment as much as larger facilities. It was identified in this study that smaller facilities required more information and incentives to assist them with knowledge on how to invest wisely in sustainability initiatives and facilitate the integration of practices into their daily operations. The key challenge identified in this study is the poor flow of information relating to sustainability from governments to businesses and communities.

Graci (2010), in a study that examined the factors that influence sustainability in the accommodation industry in Hainan, China, identified that despite political ideologies towards having a destination become eco-friendly, there are a number of barriers that impede this development. The main barriers to moving the sustainability agenda forward in this study are:

1   inadequate resources such as money, time and human capital;
2   incompatibility with corporate culture in an organization/destination;
3   government bureaucracy and corruption;
4   lack of environmental awareness in a community.

She noted that the lack of understanding for the need for sustainability principles impeded the adoption of such tactics in practice, and draws parallels to other barriers cited in organizational literature as well as identifying that these barriers are widespread and can be applied to multiple tourism destinations.

## Challenges to sustainable tourism development in islands

Through assessing the above-mentioned studies, a number of common barriers or challenges have been identified. In order to understand the relationship of these studies to the purpose of this book, it is pertinent to discuss barriers to sustainable tourism in an island context. The following are challenges that have been identified as specific to islands. Even though these can be applied in other contexts, tourism and otherwise, it is imperative to understand what hinders sustainable tourism in island destinations specifically. These barriers have been identified not only through other literature but also through the case study research that has been undertaken by the authors, and will be discussed in the following chapters.

### Challenge one: Physical and natural resources

One of the biggest challenges that islands face is that they are often limited by natural and physical resources. Due to their size, they often do not have large amounts of physical space or natural resources. Water is one such example as many small islands are unlikely to be able to rely on underground aquifers or catchments from large rivers for fresh water. This problem is often exacerbated as the smaller they are, the higher the ratio of circumference (i.e. potential beach or coastal attraction) to their area. Topography can also be a challenge: torrential rains and landslides have a much greater impact on a small island as much of the inhabitable land surface is affected. For example, Montserrat and Haiti were devastated by buildings collapsing during earthquakes and Sri Lanka and other islands in the Pacific were flooded from the Tsunami of 2004. Volcanic activity is also a concern as when an island volcano erupts, there is nowhere for the population to go to. Islands situated barely above sea level face increased threats from storms and sea level rise, while mountainous islands face challenges of mobility and landslides. For some islands, physical geography limits where tourism can be developed and hotels may be built on prime agricultural land or golf courses built on water-scarce islands.

Islands also often face problems of monoculture. Due to their location, size or topography, often they are export-dependent, and as outlined in Chapter 3, their limited physical and natural resources make them dependent on foreign aid or export of key resources. In addition, increasing populations on islands can put extreme pressure on often limited energy, and sustainable alternatives are not present due to cost, location or infrastructure issues. Solar power in some small islands may be a possible option; however, not all islands are blessed with plentiful sunshine, and alternative energy such as wind or geothermal may not be possible due to cost, governance or location. Physical and natural limitations can be a draw for tourism as unique ecosystems or natural features may attract visitors (e.g. The Faroe Islands' Vestmanna Cliffs for birdlife or the Galápagos Islands for the blue-footed booby); however, due to islands' limited physical geography, tourism development can threaten these areas easily, causing wildlife to move elsewhere or face extinction.

## Challenge two: Short-term thinking and lack of planning

It seems that the greatest challenge to developing sustainable tourism in island destinations is the fact that there is often a lack of long-term planning in terms of development. Islands are insular geographies that usually consist of small populations of unique people with traditional lifestyles and culture. Islands are not traditionally in tune with mainland ideologies as they have traditionally been governed without the assistance or involvement of the national government. Often due to their remote location, islands take control over their own affairs as historically they do not have as much power as the mainland government or are ignored or not considered important as they are far removed from the central government. In terms of nation state islands, these are also small in nature and boundaries and govern their own affairs. Island challenges are different in many ways from those of mainland tourism destinations and with a short-term vision that focuses much of its attention on economic gain, it is difficult to implement the principles of sustainability. Short-term thinking results in several other challenges, such as not investing in the required infrastructure, developing the skills and knowledge required, and stakeholder consultation. As tourism development is mainly on an ad hoc basis, especially in islands, and as islands have traditionally been of a lower economic stature than their mainland counterparts mostly due to their singular economic base (agriculture and then moving to tourism), planning does not occur at all, or for very short time frames. In Hainan, China, for example, the planning cycle of a business that is struggling economically due to continuous boom and bust cycles was one to two years. In other islands such as Malta that work on the electoral system, the planning cycle was for only two years and any implementation of policies or plans usually lasted only as long as the government was in power (four- to five-year cycles). This is detrimental to the destination as decisions are made with only short-term benefits in mind. Economic gain often takes priority over longer-term issues such as environmental conservation or cultural heritage because economic returns are often much shorter (rehabilitation of an area or addressing a water supply can often take upward of 10+ years). Destinations require planning that is longer term and focuses on the vision of sustainability at its core. Planning principles such as zoning and building by-laws are at a minimum required but also how growth will affect the carrying capacity of the destination in question is needed.

Islands have very limited resources with regard to their carrying capacity and instead of the 'build it and they will come' mentality commonly held in most islands that have rapidly developed tourism, there is a challenge to relate the ideas of development to what the ecosystem and community can withstand. This has not been the case in many islands as can be seen through rapid development such as in islands in the Mediterranean, where mass tourism has been the result. In Africa as well as the Caribbean, lack of planning has also resulted in adverse impacts. In the island of Zanzibar, for example, investment was often sought before land use zoning was put into place (Salima Sulaiman,

**Figure 4.1** *Overdevelopment due to lack of planning*

1996). This has also been the case in Maui, where development plans have primarily been based on economic profit rather than long-term viability (Farrell, 1994).

This dichotomy can also be seen with the development of cruise ship terminals. Small islands such as Roatan in Honduras or St Kitts in the Caribbean have spent much needed tax dollars on a new cruise ship terminal to attract bigger cruise ships. Governments are not aware of the full cost accounting of the impacts of cruise tourism as governments measure success in tourism through tourism arrivals rather than revenue per tourist. Cruise ships can place a huge strain on islands and their existing infrastructure. Thousands of cruise ship passengers come on shore on a daily basis in small islands (sometimes outnumbering the locals), and often contribute little to the local economy. As cruise ships encourage guests to not use local services at the ports they embark upon, and many of the stops are very short (under six hours), the economic gain from cruise ships is low in comparison to the environmental and social impacts related to waste, water and air pollution, not to mention acculturation and the demonstration effect that impacts on the local communities. Cruise lines have to take on water in several ports, vastly depleting precious water supplies. As many islands do not only focus on cruise ship tourism (Roatan, Jamaica, St Marten and Aruba to name a few), the impacts that result from degradation of the land and antagonism of the local people affect other aspects of their tourism economy in a detrimental way. In Roatan, for example, many brothels have cropped up with cruise passengers supplying the demand.

As economic gain is the priority for development in many islands, it is often that much needed tax dollars are allocated towards the development of transportation linkages such as airports and boat docks. As the only way to get to an island is through these methods, it is necessary to have development; however, frequently this is at the expense of much-needed infrastructure such as hospitals and schools. The thought is that through the development of transportation linkages more tourists will come, thus leading to further revenue gained for infrastructure such as facilities for the community. The reality is, however, that the expense of these transportation linkages is usually quite large and may only be used on a seasonal basis (depending on seasonality), not to mention that tourism growth is not always increasing, so it is possible for islands to place themselves in debt to foreign development banks or governments in order to build these superstructures.

Many islands cannot withstand rapid, unplanned development and this is affecting not only the natural environment on the islands but also the social and built environments. It has led to increased impacts such as water pollution, beach erosion, coral reef degradation, pressure on the electricity grids, development that does not heed to the local aesthetics of the place and antagonistic communities. The lack of planning results in the need for the wise use of resources and policies that examine development from a long-term perspective. The challenge, however, remains that even when a destination creates a longer-term plan, in a time of economic crisis, the focus switches to short-term economic gain and job creation rather than long-term viability.

When planning for a short-term scenario only, there is often very little priority or desire to hire expertise to aid in the development of sustainability programmes in a destination. Expertise is required to assist in raising knowledge about sustainability as it is not possible to raise awareness without empowering stakeholders with knowledge. Expertise is not always foreign, however. Although often outside consultants can be beneficial for providing best practices and expertise from other areas, many times locals have knowledge about impacts and can provide leadership in the island due to connections and past experience. Collaboration and consultation with all affected stakeholders are key not only in the planning stages but through development and implementation as well. Sustainability does not rank high on the agendas of many governments and private businesses and often environmental and social considerations do not take priority until negative and adverse effects are felt.

### Challenge three: Foreign ownership

Many tourism destinations and their resorts or accommodation facilities also happen to be owned largely by foreign-owned and multinational corporations. Foreign-owned investments often control a large majority of tourism facilities. In Cuba, for example, 20 per cent of hotels are owned by Sol Melia, a Spanish company, and although 49 per cent of hotels are now state-owned, 13 per cent are under joint ownership and a further 44 per cent are under international management (Sharpley and Knight, 2009). Cole (2006) identified that businesses that are owned by foreigners do not contribute to the local economy as they would have if they were owned by local residents. Carter (1991) also notes that foreign-owned airlines that operate in developing countries have a great influence on tourist arrivals, in turn influencing the potential for economic growth in certain areas. Having the involvement and potentially the majority of investment on the island as being foreign-owned results not only in leakage (where the majority of the revenue leaves the island and does not benefit the island in terms of the multiplier effect – in the Caribbean, for example, leakage can be as high as 40–50 per cent), but is influenced by foreign investors that have profit as their main priority as they often have no connection to the place. Some island economies are also dependent on foreign investment and ownership that can lead to a lack of control. The islands of Cape Verde, for example, have fewer than 100,000 tourists per annum and are promoting themselves as a second home destination for Europeans (UNCTAD, 2007 in Barrowclough, 2007). This dependency on foreign investment often leads to problems. First, with a dependency on this form of investment, islands often do not have a choice when or how foreign owners decide to develop, as they cannot afford to lose this investment. Often beach-based tourism development can result, leading not only to negative environmental impacts but also to a tourism product which cannot be differentiated from the next. If foreign owners or investors pull out, the island is left with development which will only further degrade and does not result in a competitive advantage. Second, reliance on foreign investment or ownership can increase an island's dependency on exports. For example, of the countries where tourism accounted for more than 50 per cent of total exports, all were small islands (Barrowclough, 2007). Islands also depend on other exports such as food, water and raw materials and often this demand fluctuates with seasonality and visitation of tourists, therefore making it difficult for islands to gain competitive pricing for such commodities.

## Challenge four: Lack of awareness about sustainability

The lack of planning in a destination and ad hoc development could be a result of the level of sustainability awareness among the government agencies, industry and local communities. The concept of sustainability is vague and does not mean much to destinations in a practical sense. For example, the definition of sustainable development discusses the idea that one must 'preserve for our future generations'; however, often many destinations do not know what is needed for the current generation, let alone the future ones. As most human beings are concerned about their day-to-day livelihoods there is often little thought about next year, let alone 20 years in the future.

Another element about awareness of sustainability is that different cultures embrace different environmental and social attitudes, therefore what one culture or country may consider to be responsible, another one may not. Tourism is also a soft industry compared to others such as mining or manufacturing and relatively new (the advent of air travel has only really turned tourism into a growth industry since the 1950s). For example, the pollution that results from tourism is not always as apparent as from manufacturing, so historically tourism has not been regulated as a polluting industry. It is much easier for governing bodies to develop policy on air emissions from stacks that pour out poisonous smoke than a hotel development that brings enjoyment to people. This can be a major challenge, as many governments, as well as other stakeholders, do not see the immediate need to manage tourism's impacts, or do not understand what the impacts of tourism are. Additionally, many governments or agencies responsible for tourism development limit their involvement to marketing, providing infrastructure, managing attractions or establishing a favourable political climate to enable foreign investment. These roles do not often touch on the cultural or environmental protection of the very assets that attract the tourists, nor consider the impacts of degradation. Many stakeholders claim that because of the non-regulatory nature of implementing sustainability initiatives, these actions are not a priority in the organization or destination and, therefore, resources such as money and employee time are not allocated to develop programmes, nor are politicians pushing for levels of sustainability in their terms of office. This is especially pertinent in destinations in decline where the market has fluctuated considerably over the years and many tourism organizations are struggling economically. In such cases, investments in sustainability are usually only considered when the economic viability of a destination is in decline.

Governments in many islands do not have a vision for the long term (past their own electoral regime) and therefore do not seek the opinions of their constituents in developing a vision. One must consider that some islands have an appointed government whereas for others it is elected. In an electoral system,

**Figure 4.2** *Clapboard accommodation: Whose responsibility is it for construction regulations?*

governing terms are often too short to consider long-term sustainability measures if such awareness even exists and are focused on mainly short-term economic gain or being re-elected. For governments that are appointed, often power takes priority over economic and social concerns and frequently there is neither education nor desire about the need to plan for sustainability. In both cases it is often the case that government and policy and planning are reactive rather than proactive. As several islands are located in less developed countries (LDCs), this is often exacerbated as the population is generally uneducated about the perils of rapid development as their primary concern is poverty alleviation. Governments usually do not hold the requisite skills and knowledge to incorporate sustainability principles into their destination or understand the importance of doing so. Guidance and assistance from experts in sustainable tourism development (not necessarily outsiders) is required to assist in identifying the principles of sustainability and how this can be integrated into development.

In addition, there is a lack of education among the local community. The local community is not normally aware of the term sustainability but may be aware of how to conserve resources and manage waste. However, they are not usually consulted on sustainability initiatives, policy development or the problems that may result on the island. Local communities are often only consulted after decisions are made. In several islands, due to a lack in environmental awareness, the local community is resistant to change despite the identified benefits associated with sustainable tourism initiatives (such as reducing health problems that have occurred from the burning of garbage or implementing fishing restrictions on detrimental fishing practices to protect fish stocks). Because there is limited education or awareness about such issues, many local people see such efforts as an infringement to their livelihoods or are sceptical about initiatives and are not willing to participate. This has been the case in many islands that have traditional livelihoods such as fishing.

Businesses are also not always environmentally aware nor understand the consequences of their impacts on the environment or need for long-term sustainability. Many businesses are not educated on sustainability, especially since they primarily focus on the financial bottom line benefits. As the primary objective of business is to make money, it is still not the norm to build a business for the good of the community or to support the concept of sustainability as this often requires some financial investment. Many businesses do not understand their impact and do not see past a short economic cycle despite the financial benefits that could result not only from resource conservation, but also from increased employee welfare, competitiveness and protecting the resources that sustain their business. There is often little assistance, let alone regulations or incentives, for business owners to become educated and more importantly take action in reducing their environmental footprint.

Tourists also impede sustainable tourism development in many cases. As businesses often say that they are demand-driven, they are waiting for tourists to demand sustainable tourism practices. Many tourists, however, are not necessarily aware of environmental or social issues in a destination nor do they factor this into their motivations for visiting this destination. In addition, tourists are consumers, not anthropologists (McKercher, 1993) and they also are only focused on self-pleasure in many cases. Compared with a few decades ago, tourism has become a right rather than a privilege and often the tourist is going on holiday to 'escape', 'relax', 'unwind' and therefore does not pay attention to much beyond the cocktail in their hand or the view from their hotel room.

In addition, there is usually a disconnect on the island as tourists are not exposed to the local community and do not see the perils that affect society. Many tourists also do not interact with the locals and stay in the tourist areas. This is evident in many islands that have developed hotel strips a distance away from the local community. In Puerto Plata in the Dominican Republic, hotels are built in a walled complex and the locals only have access to the area if they are employees. In Jamaica, locals are barred access to the beaches which are privately owned by resorts. Often tourists are hedonistic in their behaviour while on holiday and feel that they 'deserve' to be wasteful. For example, a hotel often uses as much water as a local village does and tourists expect such things as white towels, frequent showers, bottled water and certain foods (often imported). In Singapore, where water is not always plentiful, a high-end luxury hotel noted that water consumption was approximately 1800 litres per person, per day. This can be a difficult situation for many tourism providers. Not wanting to pressure tourists to restrict themselves, they often do not provide the necessary education about the vulnerabilities an island may face and many tourism businesses, afraid to lose customers, pander to tourists' wants rather than educate tourists about their impacts.

## Challenge five: Lack of measurement

A major challenge to sustainable tourism development is that many destinations do not measure or benchmark their performance or make decisions with adequate awareness of how actions will affect their destination. Without monitoring the state of the environment and measuring how many tourists visit their destination, during what time of the year and what they do there, it is hard to develop long-term strategies for tourism development and maintenance. As many destinations do not measure their tourism numbers or usage of resources or local host perceptions and issues, they do not have the information to develop a tourism master plan or develop a vision and strategy for tourism development. It is therefore not surprising that a lack of planning is the result. For example, in Malta, there was a lack of understanding about what sustainability is. The Ministry for Environment and Planning resisted a golf course development for 15 years, but the Prime Minister overrode this and now two sites are identified for development. According to local officials, there has never been a study done on the impact of golf courses (Dodds, 2007b). Many island destinations find it difficult to measure tourism arrivals and impacts as they are not skilled in measurement and monitoring techniques. Despite guidance that may be available on tourism indicators or benchmarking, it is pertinent to develop indicators with stakeholder consultation so they are applicable and meaningful specifically to the destination. Indicators need to be developed to identify warning signals, stress, the state of the resource base, impacts and consequences and efforts of management (Howie, 2002). Without measurement, unplanned growth and the challenges as identified are the result.

It is also challenging for many islands to use existing measurement tools. For example, the United Nations World Tourism Organization has developed a list of indicators for sustainable tourism. However, there are hundreds, and deciphering which indicators are relevant and applicable can be challenging. Indicators are only useful in the context of appropriately framed questions and must be related to clear management goals.

In many islands, as there is no vision for tourism development or measurement of the current carrying capacity, infrastructure is challenging. Without knowing what the initial impacts of tourism are in terms of resource usage, number of tourists, and so on, how does a small island state build an incinerator, waste treatment plant or other much-needed facilities? A challenge of this is also about scale. Spatial and temporal scale is a challenge for many approaches as often data are not available for different regions and funding studies to determine such data are often expensive.

## Challenge six: Multiple stakeholders with conflicting interests

In a destination, there are often multiple stakeholders involved in tourism development. These stakeholders can consist of the government of all levels, local and international businesses, the local community, employees, the destination marketing association (if it exists) and the tourists. Each stakeholder has its own, often unique, well-being and vision for the tourism destination. In an island context, these stakeholders work in close conjunction with each

**Figure 4.3** *Beach erosion*

other and due to the insularity of islands, a decision made by one stakeholder in power (i.e. the government) greatly affects the livelihoods of all other stakeholders. Unfortunately, often the values and ideals of stakeholders conflict and in many instances, there is a power struggle between stakeholders. Different areas of government, for example, compete for jurisdiction and the revenue from the tax base, and often policies made conflict with each other. Generally, the island's local government would be the one to govern the affairs of their jurisdiction, but in many instances, depending on the location and economic viability of the destination, the state or federal governments may intervene in the affairs of the island. In a small island state or nations, different industries on the island compete for the same pool of resources. Governments also have conflicting interests and a lack of coordination between different government bodies, and this has been noted as a challenge to sustainable tourism development by Dodds (2007 a,b), Graci (2010), Hall (1994), Hall (2008), Lickorish (1991) and Singh and Singh (1999). Politics and programmes of different levels of governments are often poorly coordinated, and actions and policies of one level may contradict policies or plans at another level, with little consultation between levels or departments. The often expansionist economic interests of governments can sometimes clash with local desires to limit tourism's impacts (Williams and Shaw, 1998). An island's desire to develop tourism may conflict with government ideas for conservation. This can be noted in islands that have been designated marine parks (such as Gili Trawangan, Indonesia, and Koh Phi Phi, Thailand). The marine park designation is a state or national initiative but unless the island knows and agrees with this designation, it can often be largely ignored by all stakeholders on the island. In Gili Trawangan for example, the stakeholders on the island were not even aware of the marine park status as this was not promoted or enforced by the local government. As Andriotis (2001) noted in the island of Crete in Greece, often policies and plans are devised outside the actual area in question and not focused on stakeholder needs. This is the case when governments develop policies without integrating the views of the stakeholders that will be affected.

There may also be conflicting interests in terms of sustainable tourism development on an inter-governmental level as well. Policies for sustainable tourism require close coordination with other sectors including taxation, transportation, housing, social development, environmental conservation and protection and resource management. As policy is often subject to change during implementation, these other sectors need to be aware of each other and communicate their needs and concerns in order to achieve progress in policy implementation (Younis, 1990). There is a problem with government departments working independently of each other in many governments and different agencies do not collaborate with each other or understand the pertinence of working together to solve sustainability issues. As sustainability does not occur in a vacuum and the issues affecting tourism greatly affect all other industries and the environment in general on an island, it is pertinent for government agencies to coordinate and collaborate on policy initiatives. This has not been the case in many areas of the world. For example, in Hainan, China, a tourism business has to receive approvals for a new project or initiative from five to six different government agencies. Many tourism businesses feel that since the government is unable to coordinate their vision and action in relation to permits for environmental improvements, it is easier to remain with the status quo (Graci, 2010). Boissevain and Theuma (1998) also illustrated this: 'In a country as small as Malta, ties linking people to each other are frequent and unavoidable. We have already noted that the legal consultant of the Planning Authority was also the legal advisor to the Hilton project' (p. 112).

There are often power struggles between stakeholders, but this is especially pertinent among for-profit businesses, government and the local community. The businesses, and in many cases the government, develop tourism strictly for profit and, as discussed, with a short-term vision. Local communities may be resistant to rapid changes and seen to be hindering the development of tourism. At Nggela (Florida island) in the central Solomon Islands, unresolved grievances between customary local landowners and foreign managers led to forced entry, burning and eventual closure of the Anuha Island Resort in 1992 (Sofield, 1996). According to Cole (2006) the barriers to sustainable tourism development in less developed countries or less developed islands stem from the belief that local people are too uneducated and ignorant to be involved in tourism development and that knowledge among the local people is lacking and therefore they are unable to participate. This is not just the case in developing nations. Often involvement of all stakeholders is seen as a token gesture (Ruhanen, 2009) and often, even when public participation has occurred, goals for development have remained centred on commercial interests (Sharpley, 2000).

In terms of businesses, even if there is a belief that current practices are inadequate and that action needs to be taken to protect the environment of the island or the cultural diversity, often responsibility is passed on. This 'pass the buck' mentality and blame placed on other stakeholders (other businesses, tourists, locals or the government) is the reason for inaction. Often it is common to see one business or home on an island as well maintained, but this effort only extends to their property line. In addition NIMBY (not in my backyard) syndrome often occurs as despite the fact that stakeholders may want a waste treatment facility on their island it cannot be in close proximity to their property. In islands with limited space, this turns out to be an issue, as siting of undesirable infrastructure cannot occur. Despite the concern that the environment may be degraded, stakeholders in general do not want to take responsibility for managing the implementation of the initiatives, especially when it involves time and money.

## Challenge seven: Lack of skills and funding
Challenges such as high costs, as well as the lack of information, skills, knowledge, expertise and time, are often encountered in trying to move towards sustainable tourism development (Dodds, 2007a,b; Graci, 2009; Graci, 2010; Salina Sulaiman, 1996; Wilkinson, 1997). As many islands have turned to tourism from agriculture or other industries, funding and skills are often inadequate in tourism as this has not been their traditional form of livelihood. Additionally, there has been a general lack of knowledge or skills in environmental management, which has led to the slow uptake of sustainability initiatives. Working collaboratively has also not been the traditional format of capitalism and individualism often triumphs over collaboration. The tragedy of the commons (Hardin, 1968) often prevails as the lack of knowledge and skills of sustainable long-term holistic management is absent, which results in common areas being degraded. In Hardin's tragedy of the commons theory, he examines population growth and its effects on the earth's finite resources. Commons can be defined as any resource held communally by a group of people, all of whom have access and who gain benefit with increasing access. Each resource has a limited amount of use it can support – or carrying capacity. Once a resource is being used near its capacity, additional use will degrade its value to its present users. Users typically enter a cycle of additional use to gain personally as others use the resource. Over-exploitation of resources leading to a breakdown or collapse of a natural resource base and ecosystem reliance is often termed 'tragedies' (Brunckhorst and Coop, 2003). Since all users tend to behave in this manner, the resource is ultimately doomed. When analysing common pool resources in a tourism concept, Healy (1994), suggests that

scenic and historic landscapes and other elements such as beaches are often susceptible to overuse because of the lack of 'incentive for productivity-enhancing investment' (p. 596). Agrawal (2001) reviews Hardin's (1968) theory and looks at the problems and conditions most likely to favour sustainable use of common pool resources such as green/public space and pollution. Common spaces such as beaches are usually open to all, without limit. The collective resource is overused by individuals concerned with their own interests over the interests of the entire group. The experience one may hope for when visiting a beach or park is diminished by the vast numbers of other visitors, each hoping for their own unique experience.

Many local governments are not trained in sustainable tourism principles such as planning, policy, measurement and indicator development, so it is difficult to anticipate that these principles will be implemented. As tourism development has been rapid and uncontrolled in many islands, it is usually after the fact that experts are called in for assistance. Despite the number of guidance documents provided by agencies such as the UNWTO on how to develop and manage tourism in a sustainable manner, many island destinations do not have the funds to attend international conferences where sharing of best practices takes place, or even have access to high speed Internet to download the documents. Many documents are also very theoretical or prescriptive in nature and not practical in terms of implementation or applicable in many unique circumstances. In order to adapt such documents and apply learning from other destinations, it first requires a general understanding of the concepts among the stakeholders in a destination to carry out the principles identified in guidance documents. In addition, due to the lack of consultation among stakeholders, several local best practices are not shared that could result in sustainable initiatives that cost very little to implement.

### Challenge eight: Corruption and bureaucracy

Government bureaucracy and corruption are also common challenges to sustainable tourism in island destinations. Many different government agencies are often responsible for various regulations associated with environmental and social aspects of planning and often the processes to gain such documentation are slow and not transparent in their practices. For example, Dodds (2007b) noted that Malta attempted to pass a tourism policy in 1996 but was unable to pass it through parliament due to time. Andriotis (2001), in his study of Crete in Greece, noted that there was a lack of autonomous decision-making and complex administrative systems which hindered more sustainable tourism being achieved. Wilkinson (1997) noted that there is often over-complex and confusing procedures for obtaining planning permissions and these also hinder such measures taking place.

Government corruption is also a challenge. In some destinations, government officials responsible for the development and maintenance of the island tend to take bribes to expedite development (or have development that does not follow the rules of the island). Officials commonly accept bribes to build in unauthorized areas such as beachfront areas and this has caused several environmental and social problems such as erosion of the coastline, sedimentation in the ocean and barring access to a public resource. Even though destroying and removing mangroves from coastlines is known to increase erosion, and legislation exists to ensure buildings are built well back from the high tide line, there are many examples of this being ignored (Singh and Singh, 1999). In islands which are part of countries, many governments at the provincial/state or national levels consistently collect taxes from their county's island without any return on investment in infrastructure or development of policy. Some governments both in island states and nation islands have consistently collected taxes and then dictated a top-down approach at governance without any consideration for the islands' needs or wants. As Wilkinson (1997) outlines, in the Caribbean, often government policy-makers and planners are not in control of the total area affected by tourism.

Corruption also occurs through charging with random pricing structures for services such as waste management (i.e. in some islands, foreign-owned businesses are charged more than local businesses, or 'friends' of officials are given advantageous rates). This is also apparent in relationship-building (where the government provides favours to businesses they have developed a relationship with). The disparity of policies and governance on islands can also be dependent upon personal relationships, bribes and government corruption. Bianchi (2004) noted in the Canary Islands off Spain that multiple corruption scandals with disregard for planning regulations were influenced by powerful families. Graci (2010) indicated that corruption was apparent through the guise of *guanxi* (relationship building) in Hainan to allow for certain businesses to receive building permits. In Mallorca, the private sector often bent the rules when building new hotels by paying bribes to have more rooms (Dodds, 2007a). Corruption is commonplace in many island states and although many countries have different ways of doing business, backhanded bribes, blatant disregard for legislation or greed can hinder the achievement of sustainable tourism development. Duffy (2000), who studied corruption and its impact on eco-tourism development in Belize, identified that in Amberigis Caye, despite environmental legislation, prosecutions for breaches have faced opposition from powerful interest groups on the island, most importantly the foreign-owned businesses that have ties to the government. Destruction of coral reefs through careless management regardless of legislation was indicated due to the corrupt decision-making process underway in Belize. This indicated an awareness that violates environmental legislation. Broader issues such as criminality among foreign and local elites were either ignored, endured or supported and encouraged by key members of state agencies, because parts of the state apparatus had been co-opted by these powerful networks of elites (Duffy, 2000).

Corruption has also led to frustration on many islands, especially since there are a number of stakeholders that look to the government for good governance. Stakeholder groups who do not participate in bribery or relationship-building do not receive the same level of treatment. This hinders sustainable tourism development as environmental legislation and planning laws can be largely ignored and there are not many avenues to take in terms of justice. Many business owners who wish to do good in terms of the environment find it difficult to speak out and feel powerless to oppose the current government structure for fear of making their own lives difficult and negatively affecting their business.

### Challenge nine: Lack of infrastructure

Physical attributes such as infrastructure are also impediments to developing sustainable tourism on an island. As islands are insular, they are also often limited by space. As many islands also have a low tax base due to a small population, the infrastructure on the island is usually minimal. Installing sewage treatment plants needs space and technological skills and many islands lack both of these. Fresh water is sometimes shipped into islands due to lack of fresh water at source and if such infrastructure does exist, it is often minimal and susceptible to wear and tear due to the constant proximity to salt water. Therefore, the infrastructure on islands may not last very long and can be old in its technology. Therefore in many islands sewage is usually disposed of in septic tanks that are privately owned and maintained or flushed straight into the ocean. Many innovative initiatives such as solar or wind power have been discussed as potential solutions on islands, especially in warm weather countries; however, these can lead to difficulties due to the distance of islands from the mainland where parts are manufactured and/or lack of skilled personnel who have the technological skills and training. In islands, electrical and water shortages may thus be more common and sewage treatment often basic. In the Cayman Islands (Wilkinson, 1997) issues for moving towards more sustainable measures included a shortage of qualified staff as well as a lack of modern aids for efficient operation.

**Figure 4.4** *Garbage dump on island*

## Challenge ten: Climate change

Although a much larger global issue, tourism is particularly vulnerable to the impacts of climate change (UNWTO, 2007, 2008) and this is especially true for islands. As tourism is dependent on its customers flying to their point of consumption, islands may face a loss of tourists due to increased legislation on flying in addition to the possible warming or cooling effects that a changing climate may bring about. Climate change can be defined as 'statistically significant variations that persist for an extended period, typically decades or longer, in classical measures of climate (e.g. temperature, precipitation, sea level, plus extreme events including floods, droughts, and storms)' (Intergovernmental Panel on Climate Change (IPCC), 2001). The UNWTO (2008) report's key conclusions are that carbon dioxide emissions from tourism activities (transport, accommodation, activities) account for an estimated four and six per cent of total emissions worldwide. This report estimates that if mitigation measures are not implemented, tourism's contribution to carbon dioxide emissions could grow by 150 per cent in the next 30 years (UNWTO, 2008). For islands, the effects could be catastrophic. Already islands such as Tuvalu have lost land due to sea level rise and they are seeing their potable water sources becoming salinated.

In addition to tourism being consumptive of natural resources such as water and energy (Alvarez Gil et al, 2001; Bohdanowicz, 2005; Dodds and Kelman, 2008; Gössling et al, 2006; Graci and Dodds, 2008; Kirk, 1995), climate also has an important influence on operating costs such as heating or cooling, irrigation, food, water supply and insurance costs. The IPCC (2001) has forecast that weather patterns are likely to become both more extreme and less predictable with an increase in storm intensity, hotter days, intense precipitation and severe droughts in mid-latitude continental interiors. As a consequence, 'the tourism industry will face increased costs associated with the repair of infrastructure damage, emergency preparedness, insurance costs, backup water and power systems and business interruptions' (Dodds and Graci, 2009). For islands which often already face challenging transport, infrastructure and supply problems, climate change only exacerbates the problem.

As Dodds and Kelman (2008) outline, placing climate change into wider contexts reveals that some aspects of tourism might not be sustainable for small islands. The authors state three challenges. First, if climate change projections manifest for precipitation, then in the absence of cheap desalination, meeting tourists' water expectations could be challenging. Second, many tourist islands are reached principally by commercial jet flights which are an intensive use of fossil fuels, contributing to climate change. Encouraging people to travel by boat in order to avoid air travel for islands that are within reach might be counterproductive from energy and safety standpoints if long distances are driven to and from the mainland ferry terminal and if that increases private car use on the islands. Third, tourism dependency is a concern for any location, because it means that livelihoods are dependent on outside interests. 'For example, Malta's dependence on British tourists means that if climate change warms the UK's weather sufficiently to discourage Mediterranean tourism, then Malta's tourism industry could potentially be affected to an extent similar to a decline in the British economy or an increase in European air travel costs' (Dodds and Kelman, 2008: 68).

Although climate change is perhaps not a detailed management issue, it relates to many of the above challenges as governments may be slow to take action, lack of education about effects may exist or there may be an overall lack of preparedness for adaptation and mitigation. Climate change should therefore be considered alongside sustainable tourism, providing impetus for strategies which also have other reasons to be pursued.

## Conclusion

The first nine challenges identified in this chapter provide a framework as to why there has been limited movement in island destinations towards a sustainable tourism agenda. The last challenge, although different from the others, is important to note and as many tourism industries in islands depend upon transport, it should not be overlooked. To illustrate these challenges, the following three chapters provide case study examples. The island of Hainan in China identifies that without a multi-stakeholder participation and understanding of what sustainability is, it is difficult to implement written policies that focus on environmental protection. The Cayos Cochinos islands in Honduras illustrate lack of stakeholder accountability and coordination across government and NGOs and how the lack of consultation with locals leads to the development of a plan that does not fit or meet the needs of the local community. The island of Koh Phi Phi, Thailand, illustrates the lack of planning and resource management issues as well as the power of a few landowners in the development process. St Kitts identifies how short-term planning and the need to copy other destinations lead to a lack of competitiveness in island destinations and impacts from development that does not incorporate sustainability.

# 5
# Lack of Stakeholder Awareness and Education in Sanya, Hainan, China

## Introduction

China has been undergoing economic reform since 1979, and this has led to a shift from a command economy towards a free market economy (Graci, 2010). During this time, China's tourism industry has experienced dramatic growth, which has resulted in a major increase in foreign investment, ownership and management in the tourism industry (Child and Tse, 2001; Yu and Huat, 1995). Further, it has been projected that by 2020, China will be the world's foremost tourist destination, with annual arrivals of 130 million visitors, thus leading to an increase in foreign investment in the accommodation industry (Pine, 2002).

Due to this rapid economic expansion, there is concern that the environment will become damaged. As the environment is the core asset of the tourism industry, China has a vested interest in protecting its natural and cultural assets (Pryce, 2001). To address this, China designated the Province of Hainan as its first eco-province. Eco-provincial designation was developed to attract economically productive and ecologically efficient industries to the area while protecting the culture and physical beauty (Xie and Wall, 1999). Sanya, located on the southern tip of Hainan Island, is an important tourism destination in Hainan due to its natural and cultural attractions and growing accommodation industry (Xie and Wall, 1999). Despite the status as an eco-province, however, environmental issues remain in Sanya such as water pollution, waste, dirty beaches, rapid expansion without proper planning, spitting and littering by the local people and vermin.

## Background

Hainan Island is a tropical island located in the South China Sea, off the Southwest coast of Guangdong Province (see Figure 5.1). Hainan is the

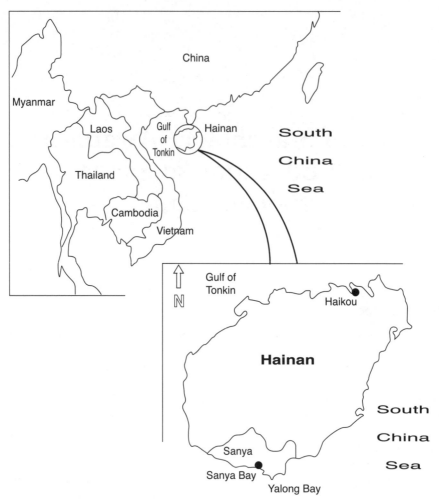

**Figure 5.1** *Map of Hainan, China*

smallest province in the People's Republic of China. It has an area of 33,920 square kilometres and is China's southernmost province. There are eight major cities on Hainan Island, but the biggest and most popular tourist destinations are Sanya and Haikou, which is the capital. Established in 1988 as a province, Hainan Island is endowed with natural resources that include tropical forests, mountains, mangroves and beaches. Due to its unique ecosystem, Hainan is recognized as one of the most biologically diverse regions in the world (Stone and Wall, 2003). It is also among the most popular tourism destinations in China, offering sun, sand, sea and sex attractions (Xie and Wall, 2002). Growth of tourism has been rapid and the island received approximately 2.5 million tourists in 1992, increasing to 7.9 million in 1997 (Stone and Wall, 2003). In 2002, the total number of tourists received by Hainan increased to 12.5 million (Guide, 2003). The vast majority of tourism occurs in coastal areas and Sanya, one of Hainan's largest cities, is located on the southern tip and is its most popular tourist destination. The rest of the province, with the exception of Haikou, the capital, is mainly underdeveloped and home to several indigenous populations. Sanya, as a tourist destination, has rapidly been developed over the last decade for mainly mass tourism for package tourists. Despite its resources and numerous accommodation facilities, Hainan remains one of China's most economically underdeveloped provinces (Stone and Wall, 2003).

## Stage of the life cycle

Sanya, Hainan, could be considered to be at the development stage of its life cycle, moving towards consolidation. In Sanya it is rapidly expanding to include more facilities and tourists. Outside investment is attracted to the destination and there is the beginning of antagonism among the local community.

## Issues in Sanya

Immediately after establishment as a province and the fifth Special Economic Zone (SEZ) in 1988, Hainan experienced rapid growth, particularly in tourism, with inflows of capital and population from Mainland China, Hong Kong and other regions and countries. The SEZ allowed Hainan to offer foreign investors an attractive package of tax exemptions and duty-free status for

Figure 5.2 *Beach view of Sanya*

**Figure 5.3** *Hotel developments in Sanya*

production inputs. In addition, Beijing declared its intention to make Hainan a special area that would go beyond the other SEZs in system reform. Hainan was meant to be a province that focused on moving from a command economy to a free market economy and allowed foreign investments. Hainan was to have minimal detailed government intervention in the economy and few state-operated enterprises (Xie and Wall, 2002). Although tourism grew rapidly from 1992, growth slowed after 1994 when investment was redirected to SEZs on the mainland (Ouyang 1999). Since 2000, foreign investment has been revived, making Hainan, and more specifically Sanya, one of China's more popular tourist destinations.

Due to Sanya's location and tropical weather, it is considered a premier tourist destination in China and has hosted international events such as the Miss World and Strong Man competitions and several international conferences. Tourism is the leading industry in Sanya and tourism development is rapidly increasing. In 2002, there were 74 hotels in Sanya and by 2004, there were 129 hotels with approximately 30 more hotels in the four- and five-star category under construction (Sanya Tourism Bureau, 2004; Statistical Yearbook, 2002).

Most of the tourists to Sanya come from mainland China. This may rapidly change with the influx of international chain affiliated hotels being built and the hosting of international events. Although currently popular, there are many issues in Sanya that hinder its popularity among international travellers. As China is new to the tourism industry (and especially Hainan) there is a lack of understanding of the needs and desires of foreign tourists. Service in hospitality is not a concept that has been largely grasped in Sanya and even the five-star luxury hotels struggle with the concept of service. The tourism infrastructure in Sanya is also lacking. The transportation system is dirty and crowded with many Chinese still smoking in the small confines of a bus. The streets are littered with garbage and there are many food vendors pouring cooking oil directly on to the pavements. The cooking vendors also use fuel that makes it very hard for the people passing to breathe. Many areas are infested with rats and the beaches are at times covered with sewage or hospital waste. For example, a tourist on their first visit was excited to walk on the beach but immediately encountered a used syringe. At night, Sanya is a city that offers prostitution. Sanya also has not adapted to the needs of many foreigners – most signs are in Chinese only and most locals speak no other language, thus affecting the ability of international travellers to move around the city. Local practices such as spitting and littering have also made it unattractive for international visitors but Sanya remains a popular destination for Mainland Chinese.

## Challenges to sustainable tourism development

It is evident that Hainan Island is undergoing rapid economic development. Much of the development has been implemented without proper planning, leading to the influx of infrastructure, buildings and tourists that puts a strain on the current system. Despite the self-proclamation that Sanya is a destination with a high level of environmental quality; waste management, water quality, congestion, improper planning and development are potential problems for this tourist destination. Sanya is a typical mass tourism destination

Figure 5.4 *Garbage in Sanya*

with poorly managed infrastructure and services that are undergoing an increasing amount of development without acknowledgement of any adverse consequences.

The consequences of tourism development in Hainan, and more specifically Sanya, are quite evident. Tourism development is expected to continue to increase as it has been projected that by 2020, China will be the world's foremost tourist destination with annual arrivals of 130 million visitors, thus leading to further foreign investment in the accommodation industry (Pine, 2002).

As economic expansion and an increase in tourism visitors are projected to be directed at an island that up until the 1980s has mainly been a farming community and home to several indigenous Chinese people, it has been a steep learning curve for the people in Sanya to be part of the tourism industry. This has resulted in several impediments such as lack of service, high turnaround rates in the tourism industry and lack of cooperation from the local community. Due to tourism, Sanya has had an influx of mainland Chinese in order to work in the industry. This has caused irritation among the local population. One of the major impediments is the lack of cleanliness in Sanya, and Hainan in general, and this is due to the rapid and mismanaged infrastructure development and lack of environmental awareness among the community.

There is little knowledge about what sustainability is and why it should be considered for the future viability of this tourist destination and many sustainability initiatives have either not been presented or have been haphazardly developed and implemented. Due to the lack of cohesion in terms of vision,

**Figure 5.5** *Water pollution on the beach*

goals, objectives and policies among all stakeholders, but especially in the levels of government, many of the tourism organizations claim that sustainability is not a priority for them. This is problematic as Hainan was named China's first eco-province, the expectation being that it would be managed accordingly. There are several challenges with this expectation. The first is that the local and provincial governments in Hainan are not entirely certain what sustainability means in a practical sense, therefore the environment is not the focus. The governments believe that being a province with very little industry and new to development with less pollution than in other areas of mainland China is enough to be considered an eco-province.

From the tourism industry perspective, some efforts in environmental management in Sanya were implemented; however, they have been haphazard in their approach. For example, the Sanya Tourism Association has tried to take the lead in Sanya by implementing a battery recycling programme, but as there is nowhere for the batteries to be recycled once they are collected, the initiative has not continued. Individual hotels have also tried to implement solar energy in their hotels or have tried to educate guests about waste management and the conservation of water and energy. As there is a high turnover rate in employees, and as the culture in Sanya is not one of conservation due to the mentality that they are in a land abundant in resources, it has been difficult to make these initiatives commonplace in the industry.

## Discussion

The major problem in Sanya is that there is short-term thinking at the industry and government levels. The practice in the Sanya tourism industry is to plan on six-month to one-year business cycles. This practice has a focus on generating short-term revenue rather than long-term gain. This is evident by the number of hotels that went bankrupt in Sanya in the last decade. Numerous empty hotels or shells of buildings were visible in 2004 as a result of the economy going bust. The short-term thinking led very much to a 'field of dreams' mentality, without thought to infrastructure support, human resources or the number of tourists coming to the island. This same lack of planning applies to the development of sustainable tourism. There has been a high turnover rate of employees as they stay employed by a facility for only one year on average. This high turnover rate has led to a loss of information, skills and expertise in the facility and any attempts at environmental management or sustainable tourism are lost when employees leave. In addition, the momentum to implement sustainability initiatives that are for the most part voluntary is slow due to the lack of long-term thinking. From a management perspective, there is also a lack of effort. As many managers have employed a short-term vision focused solely on economic growth, there is a lack of capital to hire outside expertise to aid in the development of a sustainability programme.

As the tourism industry has limited environmental awareness, their expertise on this subject is minimal, and the government has not provided much direction or leadership in terms of achieving sustainability initiatives.

However, as there is currently little profit to be made in the accommodation industry from tourists in Sanya, facilities often consider only short-term gain and the necessary funds required to implement other technological advancements. Several of the tourism organizations or businesses were doubtful that adopting sustainability initiatives would increase the profitability of their organization.

There is also a challenge of cohesive unified decision-making. As Sanya is a relatively new island in terms of development, the majority of tourism organizations consist of small, locally owned or Chinese-owned business chains. In China, there are numerous ownership structures which are quite complicated and lead to having a number of shareholders that participate in the decision-making structure for the organization. Many hotels in Sanya were owned by governments in other parts of the country and primarily used for short-term investment or as a place to house government bureaucrats when they stayed in Sanya. Many of the hotels were undergoing changes in their investors and because of the laws in China, even multinational corporations such as the Sheraton and Holiday Inn were franchised or property-managed, resulting in a number of investors being involved in the business of the facility. With a number of conflicting stakeholder perceptions on the management of the tourism organizations in Sanya, it is difficult to implement initiatives, even as small as changing a light bulb. For example, to change a light bulb in a hotel takes the approval of six to eight managers, and upwards of one month to do. The amount of bureaucracy in several of the organizations is difficult to overcome, especially in relation to investment for sustainability purposes. If it is that difficult to change a light bulb, initiatives that require investment and funding are extremely difficult to gain approval for.

Governance is also an issue. As China is moving from a command economy to a free market economy, it still is influenced by old regimes in government. The municipal government in Sanya is composed of several agencies and on a local level, the tourism industry has to work with five different agencies on a similar issue. There is also no indication to the tourism industry what specific taxes are being collected for and no guidance on how to increase efficiency so that fees are not as great for resource management such as garbage and sewage disposal. This leads to many small hotels, for example, unhooking the government-regulated sewage system from their facility and pumping directly into the ocean. This enables them to save money by not being on the government system.

## Conclusion

It is evident that there are a number of barriers that affect sustainability in the island of Hainan, China. The lack of environmental awareness in the Sanya community has been determined to be a key impediment (Graci, 2010). It is difficult to discuss sustainability in a community where the notion of environmental management for the majority of the population is defined as cleanliness. Despite the claims to being an eco-province, Hainan has a lower level of environmental awareness in comparison to other provinces in China as the province has recently converted to tourism from a rural, agricultural economy. Increased awareness is necessary so that the community keeps Sanya clean as spitting, littering and improper disposal of hazardous waste is a normal occurrence. In addition, as Sanya is a new tourist destination on an island rich in natural resources, there is no immediate demand for energy and water conservation, as they are not faced with an urgent crisis. It is not enough for destinations to designate themselves as eco-provinces. Without having goals, objectives and policies to establish what this eco-provincial designation means and without the required support from governments through enforcement and education to ensure that legislation is being implemented, this is just a statement on paper. The government and tourism industry must work together to overcome the identified barriers and begin dialogue to move the agenda forward.

# 6
# Lack of Consideration for the Local Community in the Cayos Cochinos Islands, Honduras

## Introduction

The Northern coast of Honduras is surrounded by 14 small cays in an area called the Cayos Cochinos, located at the southernmost point of the Meso-American Barrier Reef, the second largest in the world. The indigenous people of the area are the Garifuna, who traditionally rely on fishing as their main source of income and have utilized this area for such purposes since the early 1800s. To protect this fragile area, the Cayos Cochinos was designated as a Marine Protected Area (MPA) and with its managing body, the Honduran Coral Reef Foundation (HCRF) and the assistance of the WWF, a resource management plan was developed in 2005. The plan included regulations dealing with the extraction of marine sources, which eliminated the option for the Garifuna to continue fishing as a source of livelihood, opening up the opportunity to develop tourism as an alternate source of income.

Tourism in the case of the Cayos Cochinos and its designation as a Marine Protected Area has severely impoverished the entire area, and this has resulted in a decrease in the quality of life of its inhabitants. Tourism is being developed to bring in much-needed income for these communities, with one major oversight: many tourism products are being developed on an ad hoc basis, with a focus on bringing in as many tourists as possible without considering the long-term implications. In many cases, income is provided only to a select number of people and the economic benefits of tourism are not circulated among the communities.

## Background

The government of Honduras has designated the tourism industry as a national development priority, expecting to generate 70,000 new direct and indirect jobs, as it has become the country's second largest source of foreign

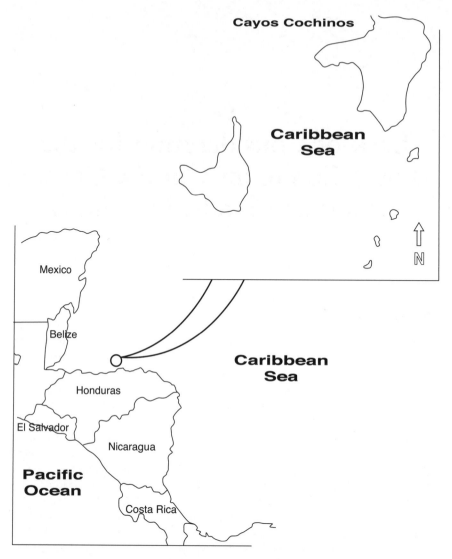

**Figure 6.1** *Map of Cayos Cochinos*

exchange (Thorne, 2005). Honduras is the second poorest country in Central America, where a tremendously unequal distribution of income has contributed to 51 per cent of the population living below the poverty line (The World Factbook, 2008).

The Cayos Cochinos islands are located 19 miles northeast of La Ceiba on the northern Honduran coast, and at the southernmost point of the Meso-American Barrier Reef (see Figure 6.1). The Cayos Cochinos was declared a Marine Protected Area (MPA) in 1993 and the management of the area's resources is overseen by the Honduran Coral Reef Foundation (HCRF), an organization formed by Honduran business leaders, and funded by international non governmental organizations (e.g. AVINA, WWF) and research organizations. In 2003, Legislative decree 114-2003 designated the Cayos Cochinos as a Marine Natural Monument and the HCRF as the managing agency responsible for the conservation of the islands for the following 10 years (2004–14). In 2004, the HCRF and the WWF developed a five-year management plan for the MPA. The 2004 Cayos Cochinos Marine Protected Area management plan established restrictions on fishing and development activities in an effort to conserve the southern end of the Meso-American Barrier Reef. Eco-tourism has been suggested in the management plan as a means to replace lost income from fishing (Brondo and Woods, 2006).

The Afro-indigenous Garifuna are the earliest occupants of the Cayos Cochinos islands. They are descendants of Africans and Amerindians (i.e., Carib and Arawak Indians) who settled along the Central American coastline more than 200 years ago. Many of the Garifuna who remain on the coast continue to practise subsistence fishing and cassava farming. The two Garifuna settlements within the MPA are Chachahuate and East End. Rio Esteban and Nueva Armenia are also important communities in close proximity to the Cayos Cochinos islands. Chachahuate is an island without water, sanitation or electricity; and East End is a small settlement on Cayo Mayor. Mainland Garifuna communities have temporary dwellings on other cays for fishermen to stay overnight and thus are also dependent on the Cayos Cochinos for their livelihood. These communities are Nueva Armenia, Rio Esteban, Sambo Creek and Corozal. Nueva Armenia (and its Cayos Cochinos sister settlement, East

**Figure 6.2** *Boat dock at Cayos Cochinos*

End) and Rio Esteban (and its Cayos Cochinos settlement, Chachahuate) are particularly affected by MPA regulations because many residents rely on fishing for subsistence and sale.

Chachahuate has approximately 40–80 permanent residents and is one of the most frequently visited cays. It has been supported by development organizations to develop small tourism businesses. East End is the sister community to Rio Esteban and has seen very little tourism or development. With only approximately 20 permanent residents, they traditionally fish to maintain their livelihood. Only recently has tourism been increasing and has resulted in the development of community-operated accommodation with 20 beds and a restaurant. Many other Garifuna communities in the area rely on the Cayos Cochinos for fishing. While the Cayos Cochinos are being promoted (at least in the management plan) as an eco-tourism destination, there is a wide range of tourist 'types' who currently visit the Cayos Cochinos but the majority of visitors are research and day tourists, most of whom are snorkeling or diving (Brondo and Woods, 2006).

## Stage of the life cycle

The Cayos Cochinos are in the exploration moving to involvement stage of the tourism life cycle. It is initially being discovered as a tourist area with basic, limited accommodation and restaurants being developed. It has not really established itself as a tourist destination but one that has one or two

Figure 6.3 *Fisherman in Cayos Cochinos*

private accommodations that specialize currently in dive tourism. The local community is attempting to become involved in tourism; however, they have not yet established an approach.

## Challenges to sustainable tourism development

With the implementation of the Marine Protected Area, fishing has been prohibited with the exception of a few designated areas. Fishermen are no longer allowed to use nets and most of them only have access to Cayucos (small dugout boats like a canoe) to take them to the designated fishing zones. As most of these fishermen are over 50 years of age, expecting them to travel such a great distance without their usual equipment and without a motor has instigated protest and general objections against the HCRF. This conflict has caused distrust and a lack of cooperation between the HCRF and members of the communities since the fishermen have such a dominant presence in the communities. The fisherman indicated that they simply wished to be left alone and allowed to fish since it is their way of life. The different conservation organizations involved such as the WWF and AVINA do not understand that the fishing ban has been a great detriment to the community and has negatively impacted on any progress for any sort of development in the community. Not being allowed to fish and telling the community that they can participate in tourism has led to a lack of cooperation from the community.

The lack of community involvement is a major barrier to sustainable tourism development in the Cayos Cochinos. As the local community has not been consulted on the plans for tourism, there is a general lack of enthusiasm in being involved in development. There is resentment that certain communities such as Nueva Armenia on the mainland have been paid far more attention than the communities on the Cayos Cochinos. Communities do not cooperate with each other in this area and the antagonism surrounding the conservation organizations and communities that appear to be favoured do not make for a collaborative working environment. The people on the Cayos Cochinos islands feel very cheated and this exacerbates existing historical feuds with other communities. For example, a person from the mainland was hired to be a coast guard for the HCRF. According to the coastguard, the HCRF wanted to hire a local person to demonstrate that they are willing to have local representation within the organization to help with conservation efforts. However, due to poor relations between the HCRF and the fisherman in the Cayos as a result of the fishing ban, this person, who was from the mainland, was looked upon as a traitor by the community.

Corruption is also an issue in the Cayos Cochinos islands, particularly in reference to the HCRF and the organizations that work with it. For example, the HCRF allowed a Spanish reality show to be filmed on the cays in the Marine Protected Area. Despite the fact that the development of any permanent structures are not allowed on any of the cays, the reality show was able to build pyramid-like structures which have now been left behind along with other equipment and garbage. The only penalty they faced was a fee that was paid to the HCRF. The funds that were collected from this venture were not shared with the local community, thus causing resentment and tension between the two stakeholders. In addition, the community does not trust the HCRF as when the community is provided funding from organizations such as the WWF for initiatives such as composting toilets, they have failed to see this implemented.

Many of the organizations that are working in the Cayos Cochinos islands, such as USAID, WWF and NAPENTHES, all have their own reasons for involving themselves in tourism development. Despite the fact that the intentions are generally positive and the purpose is conservation, the communities have suffered on more than one occasion by the involvement of these organizations. The Smithsonian was one of the first organizations to approach the landowners of the Cays to create the Marine Protected Area. With conservation and preservation at the forefront of their decision-making, the local people living in the surrounding communities were not consulted and were completely eliminated from the decision-making process. The Smithsonian went so far as to recommend the removal of the Garifuna people from the Cays to somewhere on the mainland so that conservation efforts could take place. This recommendation instilled fear in the local people that still resonates among the communities.

When projects are developed with a commitment made by the community members, a major problem that exists is the duration of the commitment by the organizations. The unsuccessful projects that were developed by different organizations had one major flaw: they built the project but they did not stay in the communities long enough to ensure that the local people had the capacity to operate it. This creates additional tension within the community as the hope for a better existence is lost once the organization leaves and the project fails. This leads to a lack of enthusiasm in communities for further projects. In addition, the funding organizations do not try to build capacity and skills in the community, rather than support members of the community who are without income. The handout mechanism of these organizations creates a culture of dependency.

Along with the barriers related to stakeholders with conflicting interest and the lack of community-based tourism development, and despite the marine park status, there is still destruction to the area. Educating the local people and the organizations about the different levels of involvement in tourism development seems to be lacking. From the restaurant operator in Chachahuate to the fishermen in the communities, concepts related to conservation, environment and tourism are not clearly communicated. Even those who do realize the benefits associated with preserving the environment, food and water shortages occur at times, which means that locals will eat anything they are able to find, which can include protected species. The CURLA University, with a programme in sustainable tourism development, is training students about the concepts of conservation and tourism that are being passed along to the members of the community. There are still, however, many locals who do not understand conservation, which makes it very difficult to implement programmes such as waste management since most local people currently burn all of their garbage.

**Figure 6.4** *Tourism accommodation on Cayos Cochinos*

## Discussion/conclusion

The communities have been fishing as a livelihood and cultural activity for generations. As commendable as the initiatives of the HCRF and other conservation organizations to preserve the natural environment are, these fishermen have on numerous occasions voiced their opposition to the fishing restrictions. Without building capacity in terms of community-based tourism and opportunities for alternative livelihoods for entrepreneurs, the idea that the Cayos Cochinos will turn into an eco-tourism destination that will bring enough income to the local Garifuna people will not be possible. The local community currently wants to remain as fishermen and has not been consulted about other opportunities for income generation. The HCRF has invested countless resources to prevent fishing; however, the resources would be much better used in educating the youth about conservation, tourism and alternative livelihoods. The HCRF could also work with the fishermen to identify more sustainable methods of fishing and identify the carrying capacity of the marine park to withstand small fishing operations.

The youth in the communities have shown an interest in tourism and have the capacity to understand the importance of conserving their surroundings. There are fishermen who are interested in taking tourists out on their fishing boats and earning an income in that manner. These fishermen will set an example for all others that it is possible to live in this way without compromising the marine life of the area. The organizations that contribute funding and training should also ensure that the local schools are integrating sustainability into the curriculum and teaching the young children about conservation and the reasons behind the implementation of the Marine Protected Area.

A development organization that wants to create tourism projects as an alternative livelihood should consider the way in which it approaches the local

**Figure 6.5** *Fisherman turned entrepreneur*

people with the project idea. There are many locals who already have ideas they want to develop, such as on the mainland with the development of a community-based restaurant. Funding should be provided to those who already have an idea but not in the form of a grant. It should be a loan with low interest that needs to be paid back after a mutually agreed-upon time so that there is a sense of connection and a need to succeed with the project. Entrepreneurs should be supported and allowed to take part in the development of projects; they should not be eliminated from the potential of gaining funding due to the fact they already have a business.

This chapter identifies the fact that without the involvement of the local community and the ability to build community capacity in an area, many initiatives fail. Despite the abundance of resources through the NGOs present in the area, and the development of the HCRF, the communities in the Cayos Cochinos islands are suffering. They are continuing to be in conflict with the conservation organizations and initiatives and are not willing to work with organizations that have disappointed them in the past. The support and involvement of local people are required for tourism development to occur in the Cayos Cochinos.

## Acknowledgement

Special thank you to Mirjana Micic for her research on the Cayos Cochinos that contributed to this case study.

# 7

# Unsustainable Development in Koh Phi Phi, Thailand

## Introduction

Tourism is a key industry and heavily promoted in Thailand; however, social and environmental costs are not always considered alongside the economic and monetary gains. International arrivals to the Kingdom of Thailand have been growing steadily since 2006 and are projected to continue growing positively in the next few years. In 2006, tourism contributed 14.3 per cent of Thailand's GDP (World Travel and Tourism Council, 2006) with estimated target revenues of 547.5 billion baht, or the equivalent of US$17.29 billion (Tourism Authority of Thailand, 2007). Although indigenous and city tourism is offered, the majority of tourism comes from sun, sea, sand and sex tourism. According to Cushman, Barry, Field et al (2004), the earnings from tourism have come disproportionately from the beach resorts on Thailand's southern islands. In 2000, roughly 45 per cent of visitors stayed on the southern islands, including Koh Phi Phi. Many small islands such as Koh Phi Phi are dependent on tourism for a major portion of their income as they are often remote, small in size and have limited alternative livelihoods. Islands, particularly those with warm climates, depend heavily on sun, sea and sand as their main attractions and it is these resources their industries have traditionally been based upon. As a result of lack of planning, over-dependence on limited resources and insufficient infrastructure, the island of Koh Phi Phi has experienced substantial overbuilding, congestion and resource degradation.

## Background

The islands of Koh Phi Phi Don and Koh Phi Phi Ley are located in the Andaman Sea, a two-hour ferry ride from the island of Phuket in southeastern Thailand. Both islands are located in Thailand's National Marine Park; however, Koh Phi Phi Don is the only island with development. Governance on the island consists of a local mayor and a governing head (called the

**Figure 7.1** *View of Koh Phi Phi Don Tongsai © Nick Palin*

OrBorTor in Thailand) who is located in Aonang/Krabi province which Koh Phi Phi is under the regulation of (Aonang/Krabi province is located just to the east of the island as part of the mainland). Although there are a few international resorts on the island, the majority of development exists in Tongsai, the main town (see Figure 7.2).

Koh Phi Phi Don first became known as a backpacker destination in the late 1980s/early 1990s but gained immense popularity and underwent rapid development after 'The Beach' starring Leonardo Di Caprio was filmed on neighbouring Phi Phi Leh in 2000. Flimsy beach huts as well as quickly erected hotels became the norm and tourism numbers grew from a few hundred a year to 1.2 million per year up until 2004. In December 2004, a Tsunami struck Southeast Asia and devastated many areas of Indonesia and Thailand, Koh Phi Phi being one of the hardest hit. Major sections of the coral reef were destroyed, and a large portion of infrastructure such as hotels and other buildings were flattened or seriously damaged. The government shut down the island for over three months and Koh Phi Phi became a focal point of discussions for more sustainable development due to the number of tourists and locals that died in the disaster. Tourism numbers decreased from 1.2 million to approximately 500,000 visitors in 2005–2006. Due to the devastation, many stakeholders such as businesses, NGOs and government discussed the need for Koh Phi Phi to be redeveloped in a more sustainable way. Reasons for these discussions were numerous. First, the island is in a national marine park and therefore it was questioned if any new development should occur or if the area should be protected. Second, many buildings were not built to code and collapsed during or after the Tsunami, therefore

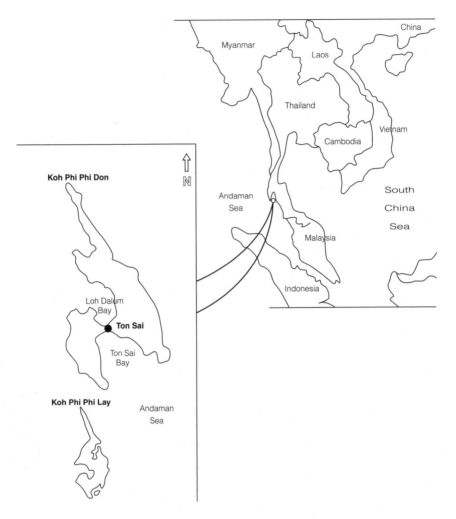

**Figure 7.2** *Map of Koh Phi Phi, Thailand*

discussions on the future sustainability of buildings and development were explored. Third, land ownership was debated as many local people who had lived on the island did not have title to the land and there were claims of ownership and threats of moving people off the land to make way for 'high-end' development. Discussions for a sustainable tourism development plan, policy and repositioning happened for approximately six months, however nothing was ever agreed upon and the island redeveloped much as before. Tourism numbers are now back to almost their former levels and each year new buildings are erected. The majority of development has occurred in Tongsai, the narrowest strip of the island which houses 90 per cent of the 2000 existing hotel rooms. There are approximately 2000–3000 workers on the island and approximately 600 locals.

## Stage of the life cycle

Koh Phi Phi Don could be considered in the maturity stage of the life cycle, approaching decline. Although as this chapter outlines, tourism was wiped out by the Tsunami, it has been rebuilt quickly and the issues that the island are now facing are threatening its long-term viability as a 'paradise' destination. Koh Phi Phi Don's sister island, Koh Phi Phi Leh, would be considered to be in the introduction stage of its life cycle but that is because it is a no-building zone and designated park. It should be noted, however, that due to the sheer number of tourist boats that visit 'the Beach', this island is facing issues of unbalance.

## Issues in Koh Phi Phi

Tourism arrivals in Koh Phi Phi increases at times to 5000 tourists per day. During the busy season, day visitors can make up to 40 per cent of this number (approximately 2000 day visitors) coming on jet boats and ferries from Phuket or Krabi, the two main launching points. Koh Phi Phi has global recognition, especially since the Tsunami and numerous marketing agencies proudly boast the island as 'paradise'. Development since the Tsunami has not relented and multiple social and environmental issues are increasingly common; basic amenities such as water, waste disposal and electricity are in a critical state. Water prices are up to 380 Baht per unit from 100 Baht per unit (approximately 1158 Baht per family) (1 US$ = 33 Baht) on the mainland and drinking water is often shipped in for tourist consumption. Water is so critical that in February/March of 2007, the island ran out of fresh water and shortages have threatened since. Although a new water treatment plant was being built on a local hilltop in late 2007, water shortages have primarily been due to an increased demand for concrete mixing post-Tsunami. In addition, the water plant is rumoured to be owned by one landowner who is planning to charge higher-than-average rates for water. In the early aftermath of the Tsunami, a desalinization plant was discussed but the landowner who offered his land for construction withdrew because the mainland government took too long to make a decision.

There is also a problem on the island of 'grey water'. Phosphates from shampoos, washing and effluents go straight into the ocean and are thought to be upsetting the pH balance of the water and marine life. Although a new sewage treatment plant was built post-2004, only 200–400 litres are pumped through the plant daily as it only serves buildings nearby and is not large enough to service all buildings on the island. In addition, many smaller buildings or restaurants are not hooked up to the treatment plant or do not even have sewage tanks, and thus continue to pump waste out to sea. According to Hansen (2006), the residents faced appalling conditions: standing wastewater, strong odours and groundwater pollution from overflowing septic tanks. Waste management on the island is also an issue. Almost everything is imported to the island and tourists also use enormous quantities of water bottles and alcoholic drinks in cans; however, there is no recycling or waste plant

*Source:* © Nick Palin

**Figure 7.3** *Increasing numbers of tourists on Koh Phi Phi Don*

on the island so everything must be shipped off the island. The cost to dispose of waste is 10 Baht per bag (compared to 1 Baht per bag on the mainland) and increasing incidents of illegal dumping have been reported. In an effort to move towards better waste management, a local business owner attempted to start a recycling programme but stopped after local residents continuously threw fish bones into the recycling containers.

Electricity on the island is also incredibly costly; as it is six times more expensive than on the mainland (5 Baht in Krabi and 30 Baht in Koh Phi Phi) and blackouts are common in the high tourism season due to over-consumption. Currently all electricity is privately owned although a new electricity line is soon to be installed on the island. The shortage, however, has not led to alternative energy although one initiative – a new solar-lit walkway – is now operational. There is little effort by large hotels to use solar energy. There is no systematic collection of rainwater and there is increasingly little space for rainwater barrels due to the high density of buildings in Tongsai. A new reservoir is being built on the island but there is talk of charging for the water gathered from it, and that it will only be for the new village of residents that have been relocated from Tongsai. Water and sewage infrastructure are inadequate and there is also concern about new infrastructure. For example, due to the devastation of the main pier of Koh Phi Phi from the Tsunami, the central Thai government funded the building of a new one. Construction, however, only started in December 2007 and has been delayed continuously due to environmental concerns and although many studies have been conducted, few decisions or agreements have been reached.

**Figure 7.4** *Illegal dumping of garbage*

**Figure 7.5** *New pier construction on Koh Phi Phi Don*

Marine issues are also escalating. The government funded anchor blocks for boats to protect the reef; however, these were made of concrete and because of their construction (concrete has air bubbles), these blocks have been dragged along the ocean floor, causing even more harm to the reef. There is also damage to the reef from the sheer number of boats visiting. There are, however, some examples of leadership to preserve marine environments, such as those of the Adventure Dive Centre dive shop that has implemented reef protection initiatives and started numerous educational programmes, but boating regulations that should help protect the environment continue to be absent. Many long-tail boats continue to dump fuel into the ocean against the regulations, and this has resulted in a visible film across the bay area. In neighbouring Koh Phi Phi Ley, where 'The Beach' was filmed, there are hundreds of people who visit the bay daily. Often up to 30 boats are in the bay at the same time (which can double during high season) and there is a constant film of diesel fuel on the surface. There is no one anchor so boats throw down anchors at will and the coral below is lifeless. Often the bay is swimming with discarded cigarette butts, empty cups and fruit peel from the tourists.

Social issues and problems are also evident within the island community. There are currently no wage standards and there is little material/collateral ownership by residents of the island. As a few main landowners control the majority of Tongsai, most people rent or lease their businesses for 10 million Baht for 10 years. Since the Tsunami, rent has reportedly increased fivefold, and due to majority land ownership (there are five main landowners although there are approximately 600 locals with registered homes), there is little perceived responsibility for ensuring responsible use of resources. Safety standards within the community are also a problem. For example, there are no mandated safety standards for boats or fire. Following a recent fire on the island, many stakeholders expressed concerns regarding safety regulations.

## Challenges to sustainable tourism development

The island suffers from numerous challenges including depleting fresh water resources, dependence on expensive generator-produced electricity, ineffective waste management practices, beach degradation, and rapid development with no formal planning.

Issues that have prevented the sustainable re-development of the island include lack of planning and ad hoc development, economic priority, lack of education about sustainability and power issues. Even though the life cycle of Koh Phi Phi was essentially renewed after the Tsunami, there is still no substantial movement towards sustainability. A general lack of education surrounding issues of sustainability is part of the problem (e.g. boat owners' lack of knowledge or awareness about safety or fire issues). There also exists a general lack of trust in politicians, especially once local stakeholders realized that potential new development plans and the desire of the five powerful landowners to build bigger and more intensely proved their priority of economic growth over social and environmental concerns. The priority of economic growth was public news as newspapers around the world discussed the potential of Koh Phi Phi to attract high-income tourists. Deputy Prime Minister Pinit Jarusombat was quoted as saying 'accommodation charges could be raised to between 5000 Baht and 30,000 Baht per night from the current 200–1000 Baht now', (*The Standard*, 2005). This resulted in many local businesses feeling threatened and as soon as was possible, buildings were erected to protect their livelihoods. Increasing power struggles between the landowners and the government became evident and many hotel owners who were allowed to 'repair' their buildings after the Tsunami, used this as an excuse to expand them. Lack of leadership was also a problem. Although some local businesses, such as the Western-owned Adventure Dive Centre, tried to initiate sustainability practices, they are not the majority landowners and therefore do not have the power to influence. Additionally, due to the layout of the island, it was difficult to regulate building. New regulations were proposed for all buildings to be set 100 metres back from the high tide line, then they were reduced to 50 metres and ended up being 30 metres. This is difficult, however, as the peninsula is hardly more than 30 metres wide at its narrowest point.

Another challenge to sustainable tourism development on the island was the lack of policy and planning. There was no overall tourism development policy for the development of the island before or after the Tsunami. Although many government officials came to the island and the sustainable re-development of Koh Phi Phi was on the federal agenda for three months after the Tsunami, no final policy agreement was ever achieved or mandated. Multiple meetings were held but as many different stakeholders had various visions for development, no consensus was agreed upon and the landowners who were present on the island started re-building. An example of this was reported by a local French initiative (Phi Phi Releve Toi, 2006), who noted the continued lack of progress. Phankam Kitithorakul, the local authority representative for the islands, told the press 'it was the same as all the previous meetings held to discuss Phi Phi, [a] lot of talk but no decisions'.

From the 1980s when tourism first started as an industry on the island, building development had been ad hoc at best and many clapboard and unstable wooden buildings had been erected. In addition to no planning, little, if any, regulations existed. Post-Tsunami, legislations were put into place and environmental impact assessments (EIAs) are now required for new developments. Legislations, however, are not generally enforced. One reason for this failure is that not all stakeholders were involved in the re-planning process post-Tsunami and some believe that 'the rules are only to benefit the rich'. According to the Thailand Environmental Institute, only 50 per cent of those who have actually received an official EIA have followed them. In one area of Tongsai, a new hotel is being developed on top of a swamp area.

Another challenge to moving towards sustainable tourism is the lack of ownership within the island community. One such issue is land tenure in Thailand. Although there are five main landowners in Tongsai, it was reported that many sea gypsies had historically lived and owned land along Thailand's coast (see Kaewkuntee (2006) for more information). Land tenure is complex in Thailand. Many nations in Southeast Asia have reformed their land administration system to provide sufficient tenure security to support any land market (Dalrymple, Wallace, and Williamson, 2004). In Thailand, the Land Titling Project was implemented by the Department of Lands from 1984 and the 'traditional or customary' tenure is no longer recognized (United Nations University, 2005). These five major landowners in Tongsai (who own the majority of the 2000 hotel rooms in Tongsai) also own and control the majority of the area (80 per cent of the land). Two of these five are from Aonang/Krabi province and the governing head (called the OrBorTor in Thailand who currently resides in Krabi) is heavily influenced by the main landowners. Although Koh Phi Phi is part of Krabi province and under their legislation, the island operates and runs on a different mentality in that certain laws do not apply to them due to their insularity. Businesses and community members note that little governance from the mainland is enforced because they 'are far away'. Although the island archipelago was declared a marine national park in approximately 1990, villagers and some mainlanders from powerful political families obtained coveted land-ownership documents for the narrow sandbar between the two bays, which excluded the spectacular area from park protection. In keeping with Thailand's freewheeling capitalist tradition, the landowners, or their tenants, built without restraint: bungalows, multi-storied hotels, shops, restaurants and bars (*The Standard*, 2005: 17). This, coupled with lack of planning and reports of bribes, made contesting new building decisions difficult with the exception of building height. Most buildings have remained under four storeys, because any building fewer than three storeys falls into local jurisdiction.

Possibly the biggest challenge to achieving sustainable tourism in Koh Phi Phi is economic growth taking priority over social and environmental concerns. Although many stakeholders after and before the Tsunami agreed an overall land management plan would be beneficial, there was no clear direction or leadership developed in this regard.

## Discussion/conclusion

While island environments generally have already been altered in the past, tourism is now often cited as one of the major factors contributing to environmental change in islands (Gössling and Wall, 2007: 4). Too many tourists were introduced to pristine tourism resources before appropriate investments for supporting management, infrastructure and amenities had been established. Economic development in islands that is evident in Koh Phi Phi is constrained by the lack of local community capacity, high transport costs and poor infrastructure.

In Koh Phi Phi, although multiple island residents and business owners are involved in tourism, it is rare that the locals have a substantial impact on decision-making (Dalrymple, Wallace and Williamson, 2004 in Mekong Update and Dialogue (2006)). Multiple issues still exist for the local people such as water shortages, electricity outages and sewage management problems. The mainland government of Thailand has little influence on the island and power is distributed into the hands of the few large landowners of Koh Phi Phi.

Source: © Nick Palin

**Figure 7.6** *Koh Phi Phi: an island paradise or is sewage in this ocean?*

Thailand's decentralization scheme has recently delegated more power to local governments, but little change has happened for Koh Phi Phi because there was no original master plan for the island, nor has one been agreed upon by all stakeholders. The mechanism to implement a plan was not evident and there was little coordination between local, provincial and federal levels of government.

As Koh Phi Phi developed, economic growth took priority over social and environmental considerations. Even after the Tsunami of 2004, when social and environmental issues were brought to the forefront of discussions and proposed as the core for redevelopment, economic growth and private sector pressure still won out. As a destination's economy develops (for example, growth through infrastructure development or increased tourism arrivals), social and environmental considerations are often not deemed as important as economic ones and are sacrificed for monetary gains. Tourism development is not created exclusively by private commercial enterprise, but an adversarial attitude often inhibits tourism progress. Different stakeholders have varying agendas and there is often a disconnect between ideal policy goals and achievable outcomes.

Sustainability may be achieved in some cases where the local population participates and is involved in the tourism-related development process (Gössling and Wall, 2007); however, this depends on the extent and level of participation. As power, legitimacy and urgency play a part in stakeholder roles, one must examine these issues when considering the implementation of more sustainable tourism initiatives. 'Even when the elements and processes of sustainability are identified and understood, there is still no guarantee that it will be practiced in destination areas' (Butler, 1999: 20).

# 8
# Lack of Long-Term Planning and Copycat Tourism in St Kitts

## Introduction

Similar to many other island economies, especially in the Caribbean, St Kitts has moved from an agricultural-based economy (sugar cane) to tourism over the recent years. For many island economies, this has become the reality and in a scramble to retain its economy, St Kitts has rapidly moved towards tourism development. This shift to tourism, however, has led to issues such as rapid and at times unplanned development, a lack of a cohesive vision and long-term planning, the disregard for sustainability principles in tourism development, a focus on tourist numbers rather than yield and the development of copycat development strategies that focus on traditional mass tourism rather than diversifying the tourism product to provide a unique and differentiated experience. These management and governance strategies have led to environmental and social impacts on the island resulting in a decrease in the tourism economy and related benefits to islanders.

## Background

The Federation of St Kitts and Nevis is located in the Leeward Islands. They are a federal two-island nation in the West Indies and one of the smallest sovereign nations in the Americas, in both area and population (see Figure 8.1). St Kitts has a land area of 168km$^2$ with a population of approximately 39,000 inhabitants (CIA, 2007). Originally populated by Native Carib Indians, St Kitts was colonized by the British in 1623 and gained its independence in 1983. The capital city and headquarters of government for the federated state is Basseterre. St Kitts was among the first islands in the Caribbean to be settled by Europeans and was home to the first British and French colonies in the Caribbean.

The economy of St Kitts is characterized by its dominant tourism, agriculture and light manufacturing industries. Sugar was the primary export from the 1640s onward, but rising production costs, low world market prices and

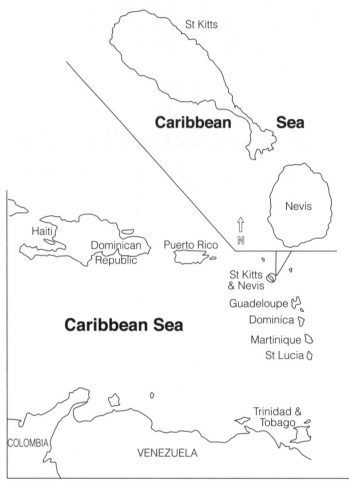

**Figure 8.1** *Map of St Kitts*

the government's efforts to reduce dependence have led to a growing diversification of the agricultural sector. In 2005, the government decided to close down the state-owned sugar company, which had experienced losses and was a significant contributor to the fiscal deficit. Former sugar plantations still dominate the St Kitts landscape; however, many of the cane fields are being burned to make room for land development, especially on the northern side of the island in the parishes of Saint John Capisterre and Christchurch. The agricultural, tourism, export-oriented manufacturing and offshore-banking sectors are being developed and are now taking larger roles in the country's economy. The growth of the tourism sector has become the main foreign exchange earner for St Kitts and neighbouring Nevis. The country has also developed a successful apparel assembly industry and one of the largest electronics assembly industries in the Caribbean. Tourism is now a major part of economic development in St Kitts and makes up 33 per cent of local GDP, employs 35 per cent of the workforce and accounts for 28 per cent of new investment and 43 per cent of exports.

For a number of years St Kitts has been dependent on tourism to drive its economy. One such current project driving the tourism of St Kitts is the new Ocean's Edge development although it is very focused on attracting foreign investment. As well as driving the economy through tourism, Ocean's Edge is also an approved project of the Citizenship by Investment Programme of the Federation of St Kitts and Nevis provided for in the Citizenship Act 1984. Purchasers who make a minimum investment of US$350,000 in a unit or a villa plot will be entitled to apply for Citizenship of the Federation of St Kitts and Nevis.

Economic growth is currently being supported by new programmes that are being developed to help improve the local communities in St Kitts although these are mainly focused on broader alternative livelihood approaches rather than tourism. By 2012, a development on Kittitian Hill will be a centre point for improving the economy by leading several new community programmes. These include:

- a hospitality institute that will train local people in the hospitality trade rather than simply importing skilled workers;
- an agricultural extension programme that will work with the local farming community to assist in the selection of sustainable crops and farming techniques such as organic farming. There will also be a regular Saturday Farmers' market, allowing direct trading between tourists and farmers;
- a computer and Internet access programme that will introduce the one-laptop-per-child programme in the surrounding communities and assist getting children broadband Internet access and suitable online training;
- a small business development programme that will encourage entrepreneurship in the immediate community and the development of small business.

Continued development from within St Kitts is planned and it will continue to support future economic growth of the island.

## Stage of the life cycle

St Kitts could be considered to be at the development phase moving to the consolidation or maturation phase of the tourism life cycle. St Kitts is developing more facilities, aiming to increase tourists. Accessibility is being enhanced to attract outside investment to the destination. Along with many other destinations at the intermediate level of development, St Kitts' tourism is characterized by growth volatility, intense pleasure from competitor destinations and planning challenges as resource conflicts emerge as land and labour migrate from traditional activities to the more lucrative tourism sector (Dodds and McElroy, 2007)

## Challenges to sustainable tourism development

Part of the problem in achieving sustainable tourism development in St Kitts is the inability to establish a brand identity beyond the traditional generic paradise image. St Kitts faces pressure from other nearby destinations and recent tourism trends suggest that some of the volatility and competitive pressures may be a result of events such as the 9/11 terrorist attacks in 2001. St Kitts did not fully recover from this event until 2004. Since then growth has been steady with the expansion of resort complexes and cricket stadiums; however, this has been more growth than a sustainable form of development. The island's dependence on tourism and particularly its dependence on arrivals from the US market have been hit by the recession. Hotel occupancy in 2008 declined by between 30 and 40 per cent and many airlines cut back operations. In March 2009, Windward Islands Airways International said it was considering ending its flights to St Kitts and Nevis. As tourism has been focused on increasing tourism numbers rather than differentiating products, St Kitts has not been able to establish a brand identity beyond the traditional generic paradise image of sun, sea and sand beach tourism. This does not leave it with a competitive edge as there are several competitors in the Eastern Caribbean that have chose to develop more sustainable forms of tourism and establish niche markets for themselves (for example diving in Bonaire, eco-tourism in Dominica, sailing in Antigua and St Vincent and the Grenadines, volcanic exploration in Montserrat and gastronomy in St Bartholemy (Dodds and McElroy, 2007). The island also does not offer the region's best beaches for price offered (the sand is not the bright white of islands such as Cuba or the Dominican Republic, which also are much more inexpensive) nor ease of access. Many other Caribbean islands offer direct access from major North American or European cities, while St Kitts is not always a direct route (although British Airways did start a direct service in 2007/8).

St Kitts has attempted to shift its focus to historical tourism through endeavours such as the scenic railway that mimics the original sugar transport and its heavy promotion of the historical Brimstone Hill Fortress, the only man-made UNESCO World Heritage Site in the Eastern Caribbean. The island has also tried to promote itself as an eco- and soft adventure destination by promoting products such as rainforest hikes and heritage tours of the island's sugar plantations but without much success as their product cannot compete with the likes of other destinations in terms of quantity, quality and/or unique features. There are stories of historical houses being appropriated by foreign investors and 'Disneyfied', and St Kitts has focused on large-scale resorts and casinos rather than eco-tourism-type attractions. Additionally, Nevis, its neighbour, tends to offer much more in terms of smaller-scale and eco-tourism offerings and has been much more successful at attracting this type of visitor.

Another attempt to diversify was through sports tourism. In 2007, St Kitts was a host venue for the ICC (International Cricket Council) Cricket World Cup; however, the benefit of this promotion was short-lived and other islands received more benefits than St Kitts. St Kitts markets its diving as a key attraction; however, there is no marine park or protected area and

Figure 8.2 *Brimstone Fort*

dumping of sewage and other waste in the ocean is a large concern for divers. In a recent National Geographic Traveler and National Geographic Center for Sustainable Destinations fourth annual Destination Scorecard survey with 522 sustainable tourism experts, St Kitts received a low 59/100 as a score for sustainability.

Like many other tourism destinations, concern over intense regional and international competition has led St Kitts to adopt a copycat strategy that is based on the development of new product offerings and the exploitation of local resources. For example, a port was built to accommodate large cruise ships without regard to economic benefits that were not proportional to the level of visitations that resulted. In addition, there was a focus on golf course and coastal hotel development that may provide short-term return but may not be sustainable due to the long-term impacts on the environment. These projects may prolong the inevitable journey into the decline stage of the life cycle but without long-term planning, this haphazard approach to development will result in a degraded tourism destination which will continue to lose its competitiveness. As Butler (1999) and Wall (1997) have identified, the effort to enhance competitiveness in a tourist destination mirrors the inability or unwillingness of policy-makers and politicians to promote and develop tourism based on a sustainable, long-term balanced approach.

In line with this short-term thinking, St Kitts has focused its growth strategy on numbers and not yield. With the development of cruise ship ports, the increase of day trippers has been the result. However, as identified in Tables 8.1 and 8.2 (Average spending per cruise passenger, 2002), St Kitts was one of the ports of call with the least average spending per passenger. Despite this

**Table 8.1** *Cruise and yacht arrivals 1995–2000*

| 1995 | 1996 | 1997 | 1998 | 1999 | 2000 | % Change '95-'00 |
|------|------|------|------|------|------|------------------|
| 120,912 | 85,778 | 102,738 | 154,107 | 137,329 | 187,081 | 118% |

*Source:* St Kitts & Nevis Ministry of Tourism (found in TDI, 2002)

**Table 8.2** *Average spending per cruise passenger*

| Ports of call | Average spending per passenger |
|---------------|-------------------------------|
| Antigua | $86.81 |
| Aruba | $82.02 |
| Bahamas | $77.90 |
| Barbados | $81.12 |
| Cayman Islands | $79.42 |
| Jamaica | $73.15 |
| Cozumel | $131.40 |
| Puerto Rico | $53.84 |
| St Kitts and Nevis | $56.22 |
| St Thomas | $173.24 |
| Average Spend | $103.83 |

*Source:* PricewaterhouseCoopers (found in TDI, 2002)

knowledge, there is still a push on the island to bring in more visitors through cruise ships rather than increase the amount of money and length of stay on the island.

The lack of long-term planning and commitment to sustainability is evident on St Kitts. There is a lack of legislation to protect valuable areas for tourism (such as marine and national parks). The level of environmental awareness on the part of government is evident in the failure to hold in check land encroachment by international developers, the reluctance to establish a marine or national park and the absence of controls over the dumping of wastes. For example, currently there is no standard or policy for cleanup of the many rusted old vehicles which have been discarded in the rainforest and near abandoned sugar mills. In addition, there is no environmental plan for the protection of marine areas. As dive tourism is one of the island's key attractions there is a need to ensure recognition as well as integration of environmental planning with tourism planning.

Although entrepreneurship is encouraged by the Tourist Board, there are few economic incentives or training programmes to assist new business development or community and rural development. In addition, the tourist attractions such as Brimstone Hill Fortress and other plantation and factories that are a legacy of the sugar industry are becoming old and decrepit and rather than focusing on restoration, there have been complaints of turning these into inauthentic tourist traps. Lodging on these plantations are often more expensive than newer foreign-owned hotels and their facilities need improvement and the quality of the service is low.

**Figure 8.3** *Plantation house on St Kitts*

Due to the development of St Kitts as a 'sun, sea and sand' tourism destination, there has been a failure by the government to identify resources for tourism and to designate areas for tourist visitation. Enabling development in all areas of the island is short-sighted and for tourism destinations the natural and cultural resources which attract the tourist needs to be protected. Tourism products could be developed from these resources and offered as an experience rather than just another 'sun, sea and sand' product.

## Discussion/conclusion

Although St Kitts is trying to increase and diversify its tourism offerings, most efforts have focused on attracting a higher-yield tourist without taking into consideration the increased impacts this may have on the island's resources. Developing four-star resorts has led to increased water and energy consumption, often at the expense of islanders. Measures of the effectiveness and success of tourism policy to date are invariably set according to the numbers of tourists that arrive at destinations rather than the net benefits that tourism brings to a destination, and there needs to be a change in the government's role from promotion to protection. Instead of focusing on sustainable tourism and developing a long-term strategy, St Kitts has attempted to copy other regions' successes in that they have developed new product offerings or exploited resources solely because their competitors have and they fear loss of competitiveness. This perhaps has not changed since tourism became a key focus; the island has just changed product focus to be competitive with other destinations (e.g. development of a casino). Sadly, destinations justify this by pointing out that development projects are vital to prevent the destination's decline and to maintain competitiveness rather than to implement long-term planning. Through the idea of up-scaling tourism in both destinations, the island has also up-scaled their consumption patterns.

The issues that St Kitts faces are a lack of long-term planning and policy implementation, focusing on short-term numbers rather than yield, and lacking the vision to develop a diversified tourism product to compete with other islands in the region. Measures of the effectiveness and success of tourism are set according to the numbers of tourists that arrive at a destination rather than the net benefits that tourism brings to a destination. There also needs to be a change in the government's role in tourism from solely promotion to long-term economic benefits as well as social and environmental protection and awareness (Dodds and McElroy, 2007).

In order to move towards long-term sustainability a number of key factors must be incorporated into the tourism strategy in St Kitts. These include educating the government, businesses, local community and tourists about sustainable tourism; developing synergies and partnerships with multiple stakeholders to develop a holistic vision and experience for tourism in St Kitts; and integrating environmental protection policies and protecting the resources that will continue to sustain the island. St Kitts needs to focus on sustaining livelihoods of its resident population rather than offering continued incentives for foreign investment, often without any parameters for protection and resource management. Experience from the life cycle literature suggests that sustainable destinations must constantly innovate to maintain and grow their position in a changing global marketplace. For islands like St Kitts in the consolidation stage of development – facing instability and intensifying competition at the crossroads between past reliance on the traditional sun lust formula and mounting new directions – means a strategic shift towards diversifying its product and focusing on sustainable long-term planning is key. To achieve sustainable tourism that is socially acceptable, economically viable and environmentally compatible requires serious effort and long-term commitment. It calls for a consistent set of policies, practices and programmes that move towards more sustainable tourism implementation. St Kitts, by focusing exclusively on tourism as their main source of foreign exchange, without long-term planning for sustainable development, is potentially facing a crisis equal if not worse than their agricultural demise.

# PART III

# SUCCESSES OF ACHIEVING SUSTAINABILITY IN ISLAND DESTINATIONS

# 9
# Successes in Island Tourism

*Achieving these elements, in whole or in part, will ensure islands are moving towards profitable tourism that is socially acceptable to the host population and environmentally sustainable for future generations. (McElroy and Dodds, 2007: 3)*

## Introduction

There is now little controversy about the adverse effect tourism has on the natural environment (Williams and Ponsford, 2009); however, the challenge for tourism is to have a beneficial industry while not exploiting or stressing the environment and culture the way it has done in the past. When discussing sustainable tourism, usually negative examples are put forward about what has not been done rather than offer practical or real examples of successes. As Scheyvens and Momsen (2008) argue, the narrow and frequently negative conceptualizations of islands as environmentally vulnerable and economically dependent are problematic for sustainable tourism development. Progress towards sustainable tourism must be supported by showcasing and sharing practical examples. This chapter will provide some examples of success, showcasing how islands have successfully developed alternative forms of tourism or worked to manage or diversify their industry. In an island context, this is especially important as supposed challenges of isolation, size and population have led to success.

## Pride

It is often claimed that islanders lose their social and cultural sense of identity when tourism is developed – as often it is foreign led and owned, thereby affecting the cultural and natural integrity of the island. The exposure of locals to tourists also leads to acculturation and the demonstration effect, where locals then wish to become more Western and lose their culture. In the Cook Islands, however, this is not the case. When residents felt like they had control over tourism, they were less likely to experience what others may see as negative cultural or social impacts (Berno, 2003). In Fiji, the villagers in

Vanuaso Tikina, Gau Island, collaborated with the University of the South Pacific to manage their environmental resources and have successfully developed a community initiative which has built capacity among the islanders and helped prepare them for the challenges of dealing with sea level rise and other issues (Veitayaki, 2006). The villagers are using their traditional practices and an iterative approach to safeguard their interests in their island environment. The project came together using the Participatory Learning and Action approach and the focus was on basic needs: take care of the environment that will then be able to take care of them in times of need. The villagers demonstrate their commitment to the initiatives and are encouraged to be consultative in trying to map their own course of action towards sustainable development (p. 249). On the islands of Moorea, French Polynesia, the local community stopped the development of a foreign-owned luxury resort as they felt it did not benefit them because they did not see that the financial gain was worth the social and environmental costs (Scheyvens and Momsen, 2008). The people in Moorea chose to retain the territories as they felt that the price paid by their aboriginal people was too high for the economic gains of the country.

## Size

Another challenge that is also stated about islands is that they are seen as vulnerable due to their small size. Dominica is a small island that has achieved success for this very characteristic. Due to its limited size, Dominica has not built a major airport nor does it have the capacity for large numbers of visitors. This has allowed facilities to stay locally owned and the government policy has promoted small facilities and eco-tourism. 'Larger facilities tend to demand economies of scale that are not available on Dominica... and therefore encourage the importation of goods to supply the industry' (Slinger-Friedman, 2009: 16). The locals are therefore able to supply most facilities and individual conservation efforts involved in the eco-tourism industry have been high. Eco-tourism on Dominica is also benefiting the local indigenous community through greater recognition, revival and maintenance of their culture. Traditional activities are symbiotic with the livelihood of eco-tourism (Slinger-Friedman, 2009: 16). Various reasons exist for this success. First, the government has had strong support to form policies and planning for eco-tourism as a form of tourism. Second, due to the island's size, impacts are easily observable and managed (Slinger-Friedman, 2009). Dominica avoided traditional tourism which often results in foreign ownership, profit repatriation, accentuation of regional disparities and environmental and cultural destruction (Klak, 1998).

## Control and power

Islands are also sometimes seen as powerless (Lim and Cooper, 2009) as they can lose political and economic identity being disconnected from the mainland. Island states are often under a larger country's legislation that does

**Figure 9.1** *Small is beautiful*

not necessarily 'jive' with their own society and islanders rarely have power to control situations. In some instances, however, it is the islands themselves that have taken control of a poor tourism situation and put in place practices to limit negative effects or curtail growth. For example, after noticing the effect of growth, Illes Meaes off the Spanish Costa Brava strictly enforced a policy to reduce capacity from 800 daily dive submersions in 1994 to 450 in 1995 (Priestly and Mundet, 1998). Local authorities in this area also displayed reluctance to promote the use of environmentally sensitive areas as tourist attractions until adequate legal protection was obtained. The island of Mallorca also decided to limit tourist arrivals by reducing the number of flights allowed on the island.

Ameland in the Netherlands has also regulated the tourism market (Krozer and Christensen-Redzepovic, 2006). Some efforts this island has undertaken included placing restrictions on accommodations, establishing nature reserves and putting in place environmental regulations, limiting several development projects and placing a cap on apartment building construction. These initiatives fostered an image of environmental quality. Success was due to cooperation between businesses and authorities to secure common goods and to innovate. 'A priority for more added value from tourism with new activities instead of attracting more tourists is widely supported' (Krozer and Christensen-Redzepovic, 2006: 119). In Roatan, Honduras, for example there has been an emphasis on how to use local knowledge to manage waste on the island (through methods of reuse that integrate the women in the community through micro enterprise initiatives). Many local communities have a culture of conservation and have ideas on how to ensure that resources such as energy and water are optimally used. Now when tropical islands use traditional wrapping such as banana leaves or other plants for food, it is considered authentic and interesting to tourists but the materials also naturally decompose, thereby eliminating the need for plastic bags.

## Policy and management

Setting policy and managing development and progress are key criteria to achieving sustainable tourism, as this is a proactive approach and can set limits of acceptable change. Management plans need to ensure that changes in land use are sympathetic within the milieu and the ecological value of the destination (Inskeep, 1994). Often islands and other tourism destinations are critiqued for either not having policy or the policy not being implemented. In the islands of the Maldives, they have not only set policy, they have created law. The Maldives established a tourism policy that focused on setting guidelines for environmental construction. The Maldives has a National Sustainable Tourism Law No 2/99 – National Environmental Action Plan (NEAP), which details guidelines for location and construction of coastal tourism resorts (UN, 2003a). NEAP was developed in 1996 for a six-year period to ensure environmental protection and sustainable development. The law detailed such measures as leasing land for tourism development, allocating maximum build (20 per cent with 80 per cent open land) and height, tree replacement and prohibition of coral and sand mining for construction. The government also implemented the resort island concept (to protect the mainly Muslim population) where tourism is concentrated on private islands where there is less host–guest interaction (Domroes, 2001).

The Bahamas also developed a sustainable tourism policy and guidelines in 1995 by the Environment of the Out Islands as they felt they were threatened by high tourist concentration. The policy document outlines that the Bahamas have made a substantial effort to protect their environment through the creation of a protected area system as well as encouraging eco-tourism and promoting good practices to the environmentally conscious visitor (Ecoplanet, 1995). The policy had a detailed action plan outlining such items as identification of stakeholder participation funding and public participation mechanisms, joint venture investment programmes, creation of a conservation area, completion of energy audits and reduction of hazardous waste and general waste.

Bermuda is also an example of an island that took a proactive stance to restrict tourism development. Bermuda was one of the first destinations to realize the danger of uncontrolled growth, and set policies such as a cap on bed numbers (maintenance and monitoring of a 10,000 bed ceiling accommodation), a hotel grading policy (cleanliness, upscale and attractiveness ratings), a restriction on timeshare development and a cruise ship policy to limit numbers and impacts (Conlin, 1995, 1996). Although the country may have faced other sustainability challenges in recent years, it should be considered a good example of pro-active policy formulation.

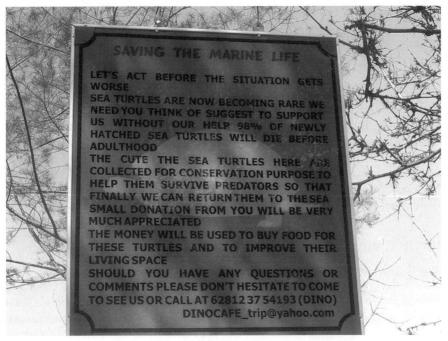

**Figure 9.2** *Education and conservation*

Crete in Greece has also attempted to implement sustainability policies and although there have been issues with implementation, policies on a regional and national level are moving towards a 'greener approach'. In Crete, laws were directed at protecting and restoring the environment (Law 1892) and environmental conservation (Laws 2160 and 2234) (Andriotis, 2001: 312).

Malta also developed a policy with several sustainability initiatives. Although the main 2002–4 and 2004–6 tourism policy of Malta was not exclusively focused on sustainable tourism there were a number of objectives within it that relate to the sustainability of tourism. The 2002–4 policy 'embraces the findings of the Carrying Capacity Study, central to government tourism policy, and requires stakeholders as well as strategic partners to coordinate efforts in an integrated approach to problem solving and proactive planning' (MTA, 2002–4 Strategic Plan: 5). The objectives set out in this plan mimicked the master plan originally proposed in 1989 by noting that markets must be diversified and that development of the product must be addressed in addition to marketing (Dodds, 2008). Due to the policy being developed and implemented, general awareness of issues of sustainability has been raised among stakeholders and Malta has started to focus on heritage tourism in an attempt to shift from the mainstream markets into another niche segment.

Green Island in Australia is also an example of a planned development with management influence. This resort was subject to strict controls by Cairns City Council and Queensland Department of Environment and Heritage to change from a busy day trip reef location to a luxury overnight destination. Measures legislated for the resort included: layout of resort, design details including materials and finishes, waste disposal methods and construction methods. The resort also has to abide by a code of Environmental Practice which provides advice on maintenance of flora, fauna and ecosystems, cultural heritage, groundwater use and working with the national and marine park (Pigram and Ding, 1999).

In order to protect the resources that sustain its dive tourism industry, Bonaire instituted a marine park strategy in 1979. The marine park was originally funded by a Dutch grant but is now self-funded due to the implementation of a US$10 annual user fee that is collected from all divers. The Bonaire Marine Park has implemented a strict policy called the Marine Environment Ordinance, which created a management regime of the marine protected area. This policy is strictly enforced by an NGO called STINAPA which is also responsible for the day-to-day management of the park (Parker, 2000).

## Integration

Sustainable tourism cannot operate in isolation and tourism must be integrated into the wider issue of sustainable development (Dodds, 2007a,b; Dodds and Butler, 2009; Godfrey, 1998; Hunter, 1992). Sustainable tourism will be more successful if there is greater integration of tourism in wider areas. As most development and management is in control of more than one authority or government ministry, communication and cooperation is needed to ensure a collaborative and transparent approach without creating silos and bureaucracy. In Barbados, this was illustrated when the Ministry of Physical Development and Environment collaborated with the Ministry of Health by putting forth new legislation 'that awarded hotels a tax deduction if they join an eco-certification programme (Greenhotelier, 2003: 6). This type of initiative allowed private industry to gain economically while implementing environmental and social practices.

In Thailand, Phuket and Koh Samui have realized some of the negative impacts of tourism and the resort areas have installed a waste-water treatment plant to reduce water pollution, and worked towards beach improvement, landscaping and re-nourishment and land reclamation. These islands learned from other degrading areas in Thailand and now are integrating these environmental initiatives into the larger management frameworks for the area (Wong, 1998). As these destinations rely almost entirely upon tourism, sustainability measures were introduced to try to upgrade the destination and regain market share (Dodds, 2008).

## Diversification

Tourism is often a monoculture in islands and there is a need to shift away from the historical focus on sun, sea and sand that can often lead to increased competitiveness and a dependency on a common pool of foreigners. Many islands in the Eastern Caribbean have successfully diversified away from the traditional sun, sea and sand market by establishing niche markets. Bonaire has a successful dive industry, Dominica has developed eco-tourism, Antigua,

St Vincent and the Grenadines offer sailing and St Bartholey is known for gastronomy (Dodds and McElroy, 2007).

The US islands of Hawaii are also trying to diversity. They have developed a competitive air transportation system with the plan to attract a number of different categories of tourists rather than relying solely on cruise ship tourism. Hawaii's development plan also has a number of important features including conservation efforts supported by local government, a focus on less beachfront development, and monitoring and evaluation of environmental issues, over-crowding and carrying-capacity (Bardolet and Sheldon, 2008).

## Alternative livelihoods

For islands to be more sustainable, there needs to be efforts to provide alter-native sources of livelihood and some islands have also increased alternative forms of income from tourism. In Barbados, there have been efforts to make and sell beauty products to tourists. Earth Mother Botanicals produces and sells products made with locally grown herbs to the Sandy Lane Hotel and Spa. In Antigua, efforts are being made to use local suppliers. Curtain Bluff Hotel maintains a list of suppliers of local produce. Before placing orders with larger suppliers who import food produce, the company first approaches the local suppliers to see whether they can fulfil the orders. Although time-consuming, it has enhanced the local character of the hotel (PPT and CTO, 2006). There has also been an increase in some Caribbean islands of focusing on local food purchasing. In Tobago, an 'adopt a farmer' approach was piloted between the Hilton Tobago and Mt St Georges Farmers' Association. After consistent demand was established, farmers were able to sharply increase production. In the first year, seven farmers have been supplying over TT$80,000 worth of local produce (PPT and CTO, 2006). In Jamaica, the Sandals Resort Farmers' Program, initiated and supported by the Sandals Group, also began to source produce from local farmers. The initiative began in 1996 with ten farmers supplying two hotels. By 2004, there were 80 farm-ers supplying hotels across the island. 'As a result of the programme, farmers' sales increased over 55 times in three years, from US$60,000 to $3.3 million. Benefits to hotels include a wider variety of good quality local produce and cost savings. Purchases of watermelon and cantaloupe by one Sandals resort of US$7,200 per month translates into a monthly income of US$100 for 70 families, taking them above the poverty line' (PPT and CTO, 2006: 2). In the isle of Arran in Scotland, an association called 'A Taste of Arran' was set up to bring 11 premier food and drink producers together and act as the single point for sales, marketing and distribution. The island is a gastronomical tourist attraction offering its own whisky, cheese, soap and more (www.taste-of-arran.co.uk). In Canada, Pelee Island in Ontario is known for its viniculture and has paired this with gastronomy to form a niche culinary tourism desti-nation. Salt Spring Island in British Columbia has also followed suit by developing a number of local products that have become an attraction for tourists. Soaps, body products, cheese and agricultural produce have all become popular for tourists to visit and experience Salt Spring culture.

**Figure 9.3** *Fishing and tourism*

## Use of environmental technology

Although islands can face considerable resource challenges due to their size, environmental designs in engineering may be a solution to the problem of scarce resources. The Maho Bay Campground in St John, the US Virgin Islands, has been designed to have minimal impact on the natural environment. The accommodations are built on raised walkways to protect ground cover, and low flush toilets, spring-loaded taps and pull chain cold-water showers ensure energy and water conservation. The new buildings are entirely solar powered and are constructed from recycled products and materials. The accommodations, despite being solar powered, use key cards to conserve energy when the rooms are not in use. Visitors can monitor their energy use on computers and learn new ways to live with low energy use, disconnected from utility companies (Edgell, 2006). In Bonaire, a small-scale desalinization facility powered by solar energy was established. The facility was relatively inexpensive to construct and maintain and is used to provide communities with safe drinking water in an environmentally friendly manner, thus reducing ecological footprint in remote areas (De Koning and Thiesen, 2005). Limnos, Greece has also been using solar, wind, and biomass energy to meet energy demand. The Global Sustainable Energy Islands Initiative (GSEII) has also been working to find ways to make energy use on member SIDS more efficient and more economical. One of their projects has been to perform energy audits in the dominant hotel industry on St Lucia that has reduced energy (www.gseii.org). El Hierro, the smallest island of the Canaries, is also working towards renewable energy. El Hierro's project is an ambitious island project regarding energy self-sufficiency through the use of renewable energies. In a few years, El Hierro will become one of the first islands in the world to

**Figure 9.4** *Water conservation*

meet its energy demand using RESs (renewable energy sources). An important part of the project is devoted to the construction and monitoring of the wind–hydro power station but attention is also being paid to feasibility and economic studies for the development of similar wind–hydro power stations in other islands. Crete and Madeira are already considering this and other islands worldwide that are appropriate for the replication of the system will also be considered. 'On a less technical level, tasks such as the integration and involvement of the island population (acceptance of the system), socio-economic research and knowledge sharing will be implemented' (www.insula. org). The development of island economies might be facilitated through technologies such as solar energy by increasing sustainability and hence market capacity (Pereira, 2009).

## Measurement and evaluation

Sustainability for island tourism must be ultimately linked to continuous improvement that is usually accomplished through measuring or defining boundaries. Tourism is a living industry, often with living communities, and therefore systems are constantly changing. Some management tools for setting limits or managing tourism are assessing carrying capacity, setting limits of acceptable change or developing indicators for tourism optimization. Such techniques that focus on environmental and social protection or environmental impact assessments offer economic benefits at the early stages of project formulation such as the 'improvement in design and siting of plans, savings in capital and operating costs, speedier approval of development approval and avoidance of costly adaptations to the plant once it is established' (Green and

Hunter, 1992: 35). For many islands developing a comprehensive list of indicators or applying complex theoretical applications are not feasible due to their complicated nature; however, they are useful to understand and so will briefly be discussed here. Each resource has a maximum amount of use it can support, termed its carrying capacity. Once a resource is being used near its limit, additional use will degrade its value to its current users. Determining the carrying capacity of island resources to accommodate activity should not be overstepped although operationally carrying capacity presents considerable challenges. As judging capacity is often a process of trial and error and as infrastructure and tourism flows change, often so does capacity (Coccossis, 2002; Johnson and Thomas, 1994). Assessing limits of acceptable change (LAC) attempts to assess stress in both the natural and social and economic environment and to define the maximum degree of change that is tolerable. A composite set of policy criteria including a 'sustainability first' decision rule or a 'safe minimum standard' would seem appropriate. Identifying limits of acceptable change is a management practice developed to 'replace the less realistic "carrying capacity" concept' (McHardy, 2000: 6). In Malta, the concept of carrying capacity has been used to manage tourist attractions. The Hypogeum, one of Malta's oldest archaeological sites, has been restored and entry has been limited based on its carrying capacity. Carrying capacity was also used at St George's Bay to reduce the density of beach users, with a 67:33 ratio of tourists to locals from June to October (Dodds, 2007b). In tourism literature, optimization is now discussed as a management tool (Jongen et al, 2004; Lim and Cooper, 2009; TOMM, 2008). Optimization theory consists of first developing island tourism indicators then identifying levels for the indicators to identify particular stages of tourism development and then understanding the triggers in the tourism system that change the status and level of the destination (Lim and Cooper, 2009: 92). Although an interesting model, optimization is only conceptual in nature. That being said, the use of indicators as a monitoring and evaluation tool of tourism development is useful and should not be undermined.

Indicators that have been used to determine impact assessment include the tourism satellite account (TSA), environmental impact assessments (EIA), environmental auditing (EA) as well as developing a set of standard indicators (Ding and Pigram, 1995; Twining-Ward and Butler, 2002; Warnken and Buckley, 1998; WTO, 2004). In Samao, a set of sustainable tourism indicators (SSTIP) was developed as a management tool and Kangaroo Island used the tourism optimization model known as TOMM (TOMM, 2007).

Although there is a lot of talk about measurement, developing indicators or tools to evaluate development are often complex and confusing. One good achievement has been the recently released Global Sustainable Tourism Criteria. Based on thousands of best practices and existing standards and evaluation tools around the world, a common framework has been put forth to guide evaluation. 'These criteria will be the minimum standard that any tourism business should aspire to reach in order to protect and sustain the world's natural and cultural resources while ensuring tourism meets its potential as a tool for poverty alleviation' (Sustainabletourismcriteria.org).

## Conclusion

Although every destination must shape its own path, success can come from long-term proactive and strategic planning, community participation and multi-stakeholder communication efforts. Diversification beyond solely tourism and limits to growth, as well as implementation of policies which are based on long-term holistic well-being for the community, environment and culture, are necessary. Planning, management, legislative and conservative measures and actively involving all stakeholders are tools needed to move towards making islands more sustainable.

While many island destinations face challenges, even when they attempt positive initiatives, there are lessons to be learned from the forward thinking and attempts at planning in these destinations. The following case studies illustrate innovative initiatives for sustainable tourism. Gili Trawangan in Indonesia showcases how collaborative multi-stakeholder partnerships can solve issues of individualism and apathy. Calviá in Mallorca, Spain, offers insight into the LA21 planning process. Chumbe in Tanzania identified how a success can be achieved when perseverance and working with other stakeholders can benefit all. Moose Factory Island in Canada exemplifies putting community-based tourism and sustainable livelihoods theory into practice and developing a tourism product that involves and benefits the whole community.

# 10
# Gili Trawangan, Indonesia: Collaborative Partnerships

## Introduction

The island of Gili Trawangan, Indonesia, is a primarily a dive and party island that has a large percentage of Western ownership and residents. For many years, Gili Trawangan was primarily underdeveloped; however, in the span of the last six years (from 2004 onwards) the selling of land to Westerners and subsequent rapid development has occurred, putting Gili Trawangan in the growth stage of the life cycle. The community that comprises mostly Westerners and local Indonesians has become increasingly concerned with the state of the environment on the island as development and tourism has led to the degradation of coral reefs, erosion of the beach and a large amount of rubbish littering the island. It is through the leadership of one dive shop that the island has attempted to move the sustainability agenda forward. An eco-trust was developed to deal mostly with illegal fishing around the island; this has quickly led over the years to the attempt to tackle other sustainability issues. This chapter identifies the innovative initiatives employed on Gili Trawangan to deal with overcoming the challenges to sustainability on the island.

## Background

Gili Trawangan is a small island located among the Gili Islands off the coast of Lombok in Indonesia (see Figure 10.1). Gili Trawangan is a sun, sea and sand destination. It is approximately three by two kilometres and low-lying with a small hill to the south, rising to 72 metres above sea level (Hampton, 1998). Gili Trawangan is the most developed of all three Gili Islands (the other two islands being the newly developed Gili Air and the mostly undeveloped Gili Meno). Gili Trawangan has an approximate population of 474 families comprising about 1900 local people (Graci, 2007). There are also several expatriates living and working on the island and this has steadily increased over the last decade. The majority of land use on the island is related to tourism and the remainder is coconut plantation and some small fields of

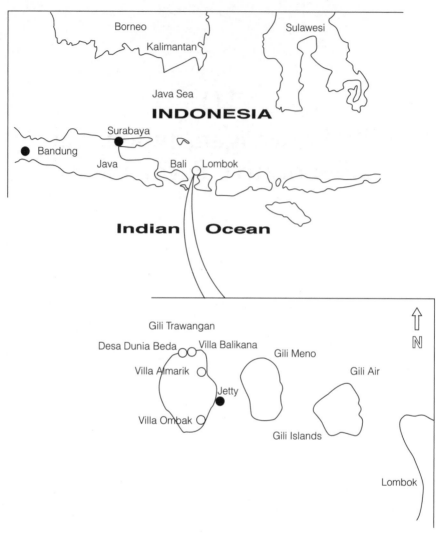

**Figure 10.1** *Map of Gili Trawangan*

agricultural crops and livestock. Tourism is the dominant economic activity on the island and more than 80 per cent of the families on Gili Trawangan are employed by tourism in some form (Graci, 2007). The main tourism season is June–September with smaller peaks in December, January and February (Graci, 2007; Hampton, 1998). Gili Trawangan is not a very developed tourism destination in terms of mass tourism resorts, infrastructure or services. The main tourists on Gili Trawangan are backpackers as there are currently only two high-end resorts and few mid-level accommodations on the island. Island transportation consists of non-motorized sources such as bicycles and cidomos (horse drawn traps) and the roads are unsealed dirt tracks. The island has limited fresh water shipped in barrels from the mainland on a daily basis. Only the high-end resorts, mid-level accommodations and restaurants use the fresh water (Graci, 2007; Hampton, 1998).

The main issues on the island are related to waste management, coral reef degradation, beach erosion, unplanned or unauthorized development, illegal fishing and a divide between the Westerners and the locals. It is also riddled with an unresponsive provincial government that does not provide any contribution to the island. The locals on the island are mainly uneducated and live in poverty. There is a lack of infrastructure such as waste disposal, sewage, roads and fresh water. The electricity is run on generators so there are many blackouts. All possible land on the island has been sold mainly to Westerners in the last three years and this has led to rapid development on the island. Due to these issues, there have been some initiatives implemented in an attempt to increase the sustainability on the island. These initiatives, however, have been faced with slow implementation, and although developed in theory, have not been entirely adopted in practice. One of the initiatives developed by the dive operators on the island is the Gili Trawangan Eco-trust. The purpose of this organization, which is managed collectively by the dive operators, is to manage the collection of a dive tax (US$3 per diver and US$1 per snorkeller). The dive tax has been used to pay the local fishermen to stop detrimental means of fishing such as bombing and using drag nets (Graci, 2007). The Gili Trawangan Eco-trust has tried on numerous occasions to start initiatives such as the collection of waste and beach clean-ups but they have encountered

**Figure 10.2** *Shipping in supplies to Gili Trawangan*

numerous barriers that have halted any action. This has led to frustration on the island as the stakeholders, although motivated, have been faced with a number of challenges that they find difficult to overcome.

## Stage of the life cycle

Gili Trawangan is in the development stage of the life cycle but moving towards consolidation. There is a rapid expansion of more facilities and tourists as most of the land on the island is developed or under development. There is a direct high-speed boat from Bali so accessibility is greatly improved. There is also rising antagonism among the community, as they are entirely dependent on tourism. Gili Trawangan is moving towards consolidation: as with the new developments, it will reach its maximum number of tourists.

## Challenges to sustainable tourism development

Despite the enthusiasm from a number of business owners on the island to clean up the island and focus on preservation and conservation, the sustainable tourism initiatives that are to be implemented continuously face a number of challenges. Despite the numerous ideas for initiatives (e.g. payments to fishermen to stop illegal fishing), without adequate resources many of these plans fail. For example, the Gili Eco-trust attempted to implement a waste management collection system including the building of a landfill with areas to separate and organize recyclables. Due to inadequate resources such as the lack of information, skills, expertise and the reluctance to acquire assistance from outside consultants, the landfill development failed. What resulted was an open dump pit and no real collection system of waste in general, let alone sorted at source. The walls built around the landfill were stolen piece by piece by locals who saw them to be useful for building houses and an open area of hazardous and non-hazardous waste resulted in breeding rodents and leached into the water stream (Graci, 2007). A number of business owners and the current local government identified this as the most prominent issue because without proper systems in place for solid waste, energy and sewage, the environment will degrade even further. The problem remains the ability to implement these systems without the necessary funds and knowledge.

Despite the numerous ideas for how to increase sustainability in Gili Trawangan, and a common belief by a number of business owners that current practices were inadequate, there was a lack of momentum to move forward and implement sustainability initiatives. The lack of momentum was a result of the 'pass the buck' mentality where everyone believed they were too busy to contribute to the development and implementation of initiatives. Despite the concern that the environment on the island was degraded, several business owners did not want to take responsibility for managing the implementation of the initiatives, especially when it involved time and money. It was evident that several of the business owners on the island had numerous complaints about the management of the environment, yet it was difficult to rally support in terms of volunteer time to manage the systems on the island. For example, only one business owner in conjunction with the local government managed the eco-tax funds to pay the fishermen, a practice that was not looked upon favourably as a sustainable solution by many of the business owners; however, no other solutions were put forth. The business owners felt that the fishermen took the payment yet still fished illegally as the one patrol boat was not enough to ensure that fishing did not occur anywhere in the perimeter. It was this one person that managed a number of the complaints on the island because they had a good working relationship with the local people, government and other businesses. However, it is not plausible for one person to organize and maintain the development of initiatives on the island in a voluntary capacity and despite the numerous ideas and enthusiasm from the other business owners, no one was willing to take responsibility and therefore the person who took the lead in moving the ideas forward, lost energy. This was evident with the organization of a beach clean-up team that was funded by the eco-tax collected by the Gili Trawangan Eco-trust. The beach clean-up team was an idea that was supported by all businesses in the Eco-trust; however, without any management of the team it quickly disintegrated. As the beach clean-up team did not receive any direction or motivation on how to proceed with the clean-up on a regular basis, it quickly ceased (Graci, 2007).

In Gili Trawangan, the culture is one where employees and the local community are resistant to change despite the identified benefits associated with sustainable tourism initiatives. Issues have resulted; for example health problems such as asthma from the burning of garbage including plastics and

**Figure 10.3** *Gili Trawangan dock*

hazardous materials and dengue fever from the the open sewage pits that breed mosquitoes (Graci, 2007). It is due to the lack of education regarding the benefits of proper management of waste and sewage that the local people are not willing to participate. This results in unsuccessful attempts at developing initiatives such as a waste management system. This is also evident with illegal fishing as locals have continued to use detrimental bombing practices and drag nets to fish despite the payments to many of the local fisherman. In one instance, a local person caught a nurse shark with the intent to sell to a Chinese customer, despite the informal policy on the island that bans the catching and selling of sharks. The policy is more of a code of conduct between the people on the island to protect the resources that attract tourists. As the majority of the tourists come to Gili Trawangan to dive, it is important that the marine life is protected (Graci, 2007).

Another identified challenge to sustainability was that the provincial and national governments have consistently collected taxes from the island without any investment in infrastructure or development of initiatives or plans to help the island. In addition, the previous local government accepted bribes to build in unauthorized areas (such as beach fronts), and this has caused several environmental and social problems such as erosion of the coastline, sedimentation in the ocean and barring access to a public resource. This is not surprising, however, because the head of the island only earns the equivalent of US$50 a month. Without education about the negative effects of building too close to the high water mark and a low wage – a bribe of $1000 is seen as too good to pass up.

In 1998, the provincial government of Western Nusa Dua developed the Gili Mantra Marine National Park Strategy. In Indonesia, marine park strategies have been highly successful in destinations such as Komodo National Park. The marine park strategy, which was developed as a policy, was never implemented in practice. Locals and Westerners, in addition to the local government, were all unaware of such a strategy. It was the Gili Trawangan Eco-trust that implemented initiatives to curb illegal fishing to protect and generate the coral reefs.

On the local level, corruption has occurred through the random pricing structure that government-appointed businesses charge in terms of waste collection. Expatriate businesses are charged an enormously inflated rate over local businesses despite the success or size of the business. These fees are based on personal relationships so that one expatriate business owner can pay up to triple for the same services as another who has a good relationship with the waste collection agency (Graci, 2007).

The disparity of policies on the island is dependent upon personal relationships, bribes and government corruption. This has led to frustration on the island, especially in terms of volunteering time and money to implement sustainable tourism initiatives. Many initiatives are funded independently and several stakeholders feel powerless to oppose the current structure for fear of making their own lives difficult and negatively affecting their business.

Physical attributes such as infrastructure, or lack thereof, is also an impediment. Gili Trawangan currently ships in barrels of fresh water on a daily basis to the island. Structures such as sewage treatment plants (sewage is currently either disposed of in homemade septic tanks or open pits on the side of the road in the village) cannot be built as salt water will degrade the infrastructure. In addition, technology continues to be a barrier. Even if initiatives such as solar power or a sewage treatment plant were installed it would be difficult to fix or adjust technologies due to the remoteness of the island and lack of skill and cost. In addition, space is an issue on the island as many businesses would like to install composters to dispose of their own organic waste but do not have the room available (Graci, 2007).

Despite the fact that several of the tourists on Gili Trawangan see the need for a sustainability strategy and have no issue contributing to the eco-tax while diving, many tourists are not necessarily aware of the environmental issues nor do they factor this into their motivations for visiting this destination. Tourists on Gili Trawangan are party tourists and divers. The majority of tourists are young (18–24 years old) backpackers and due to the inexpensive nature of their experience on this island do not demand a higher quality of sustainability. Therefore, the tourists will contribute their one-time fee of US$3 if they are diving but will not pay higher premiums for sustainability initiatives nor factor this into their decision when choosing an establishment to eat or stay. They are also satisfied with the status quo and despite attempts at banishing water bottles on the island, still consume water in bottles and contribute to the ever growing waste problem on the island. This is due to the disconnect of the tourist with the rest of the island, as tourists on Gili Trawangan are usually not exposed to the village or are aware of any of the issues.

## Overcoming challenges

Despite the number of challenges this island is facing, they have moved forward and have implemented a number of innovative initiatives. The first innovative initiative on this island was the development of the Gili Trawangan Eco-trust. The Eco-trust, which collects an eco-tax from divers and snorkellers, has funded numerous initiatives such as the patrolling of the ocean for illegal fishing, the development of a sustainable tourism strategy for the island, the implementation of bio rock technology for coral reef regeneration and the hiring of a full time environmental coordinator to implement the sustainability strategy. The sustainable tourism strategy which was conducted in 2005 identified numerous issues on the island and developed a plan to work on reducing these issues. The strategy focused on incorporated alternatives such as composting, employing financial mechanisms such as tourist taxes and developing a multi-stakeholder island committee to oversee the development and implementation of sustainable tourism initiatives. In addition, extensive consultation with the local community and all stakeholders on the island has been and will continue to be conducted to ensure that there is buy-in and motivation to implement the initiatives. The strategy, through the use of an island committee, provides accountability to stakeholders on the island in hope of reducing corruption. Figure 10.4 identifies the main components of the sustainability strategy developed for Gili Trawangan.

**Recommendation 1: Development of a Sustainable Tourism Mission Statement**

**Recommendation 2: Development of an Island Committee**
2.1.  Implement the island committee.
2.2.  Information session and workshops identifying the purpose of the Island Committee, the sustainable tourism strategy, the process that will be undertaken and the projects that will be developed and implemented in the upcoming months. A timetable should be provided along with an identification of the sustainable tourism mission statement.

**Recommendation 3: Waste Management System**
3.1.  Development of a Waste Separation System at Source (for bottles, organic waste, plastic, hazardous waste, paper (including cardboard).
3.2.  Determine markets for the selling of recyclables.
3.3.  Development of a waste collection system (including bins to be used and how the collection system would operate)
3.4.  Development of a fee system for waste collection.
3.5.  Development of a Waste Separation Workshop to educate the community and businesses on how to separate waste properly and what can be included in what section.
3.6.  Hold a Composting Information Session to educate businesses and locals on how to build a backyard composter and what to do with the compost.
3.7.  Development of a properly engineered landfill including industrial composter.
3.8.  Development of a system for the collection and management of hazardous waste.
3.9.  Development and implementation of a beach clean up team.
3.10. Development of a waste exchange for reuse.

**Recommendation 4: Water Conservation**
4.1.  Implement a water conservation policy for the island of Gili Trawangan.
4.2.  Development of a water conservation information session.

**Recommendation 5: Sewage Management**
5.1.  Development of a sewage management strategy including the building of compost toilets for the local village
5.2.  Development of an information session on the benefits and how to use compost toilets.

**Recommendation 6: Pest Management**
6.1.  Information session to be held on how to manage pests.
6.2.  Policy developed on pest management.

**Recommendation 7: Coral Reef Management and Protection**
7.1.  Work with government agencies to implement the Gili Matra Marine Park Proposal.

**Recommendation 8: Eco-Tax**
8.1.  Implement a Gili Trawangan Eco-tax for tourists, dive instructors and dive masters and local businesses to fund initiatives on the island.
8.2.  Work with businesses in Bali and other tourism destinations in Indonesia to sell Gili Trawangan sustainable tourism paraphernalia such as t-shirts and bracelets.

---

**Recommendation 9: Public Education and Awareness**

9.1   Work with tourism publications to market Gili Trawangan as a sustainable tourism destination.

9.2.  Once sustainable tourism strategy is implemented, apply for funding and certification from Project Aware and organizations such as Green Globe.

9.3.  Implement a tourism education strategy on the island to ensure awareness of initiatives such as waste management and where the eco-tax is spent.

9.4.  Implement environmental education in the local school curriculum.

**Recommendation 10: Energy and Solar Power**

10.1. Implement an energy conservation strategy including an information session on how to conserve power.

10.2. Examine the merits of solar energy.

**Recommendation 11: Building Policies**

11.1  Implement a building policy on the island to ensure the sustainable planning and development of the island.

11.2. Have an information session and booklet made to explain the building policy to new investors on Gili Trawangan.

Accommodating green (Graci, 2007: 13)

---

**Figure 10.4** *Sustainability strategy for Gili Trawangan*

The strategy was widely accepted by the local government and businesses and is now in its implementation stage. In three years a permanent environmental coordinator/facilitator was hired and monthly meetings with business owners, local government and the community is the result.

One of the key recommendations of this strategy was to develop a multi-stakeholder partnership for Gili Trawangan to move the sustainability agenda forward. The purpose of the partnership is to begin dialogue among all stakeholders and to create a plan for the island that everyone can adhere to. Each stakeholder involved in the partnership is designated various roles and responsibilities that contribute to the overarching goal of moving the tourism industry towards sustainability. This partnership recommends the development and implementation of several initiatives identified in the sustainable tourism strategy. The purpose of the partnership is to develop a cohesive environmental vision that enables the industry to focus resources, share information, increase environmental action, learn from the leaders and ultimately protect the resources that sustain the destination. The focus of the partnership was and will be stakeholder consultation. The purpose is to bring together joint decision-making from all the stakeholders on the island and to have a collective contribution to decision-making overcoming barriers such as the lack of communication between the Westerners and locals and the lack of momentum to implement initiatives. The partnership includes all stakeholders in Gili Trawangan including representatives of the Western and local tourism

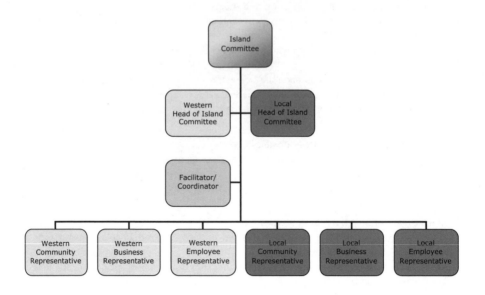

**Figure 10.5** *Model of the multi-stakeholder partnership*

businesses, community and employees (See Figure 10.5 for the model of the multi-stakeholder partnership). The role of the multi-stakeholder partnership is to:

- make decisions and oversee the implementation of the sustainable tourism strategy;
- provide guidance and information to community via community meetings and workshops;
- organize project teams to implement the sustainability initiatives. To create accountability and ownership project teams consisting of one local and one Westerner will be instituted. This team will be responsible for:
  - carrying out the initiative;
  - management of the eco-tax;
  - providing accountability for finances and decisions made;
  - providing a mechanism for complaints on the management of the environment.

The Gili Eco-trust, which now has the participation of numerous stakeholders on the island, has been responsible for working with the local community to monitor the surrounding area to ensure illegal fishing is not occurring; working with the local school to educate children about waste disposal and how to protect the coral reefs; manage the eco-tax; begin dialogue on how to manage waste on the island; start a waste separation programme; organize beach

**Figure 10.6** *Gili Trawangan street scene*

clean-ups; and ensure that the horses that work the cidomo carts have constant access to fresh water and are treated properly. Each dive shop has sponsored its own bio rock in front of their properties. The bio rocks provide low level electrical current to a structure which is placed under water and eventually grows into a coral reef balmy. This balmy attracts fish and leads to the regeneration of the coral reef. Plans for a waste management and green sea turtle strategy in partnership with Masters students from Ryerson University in Canada are currently underway. The environmental coordinator has now been hired full time and is currently learning the local language to negotiate contracts with waste management organizations and the government.

Even if all the initiatives do not get implemented immediately, success is evident through the formation of the partnership that has brought together different stakeholders on the island to create dialogue and build relationships for working together. This partnership will also lead to the sharing of information and best practices, so locals can be educated about Western ideals and Westerners educated about traditional ideals. By including locals in public consultation meetings, the education of locals is being raised and also the Westerners are becoming educated about local values. This has and will lead to new knowledge and overcoming barriers such as the importance of not burning plastics on the island or how to reuse materials to reduce waste. Through the involvement of locals, empowerment has resulted. The locals in 2007 had the first island election and chose to elect a new head of the island. The partnership has led to increased accountability among the government, locals and Westerners. This also led to a cohesive environmental vision and language, where all on the island wanted to protect the resources that sustain the island, not only for the Westerners but also for the locals so they can resume living in a clean environment.

## Conclusion

Despite efforts from a number of local businesses to further sustainability initiatives on the island of Gili Trawangan, barriers to sustainable tourism implementation exist. The purpose of the partnership is to involve all the stakeholders in the tourism industry in Gili Trawangan in order to alleviate the impediments that hinder the increase of sustainability. It also provides a holistic approach to sustainable tourism implementation that includes all stakeholders involved. Barriers to sustainability in this case focus on the inadequacy of resources such as money, access to information and skilled experts to implement the strategy. This case study identifies that innovative initiatives such as conducting an environmental audit and developing a strategy; creating dialogue with stakeholders; implementing an eco-tax to collect money for developing initiatives; and the creation of multi-stakeholder partnerships and collaboration can be implemented in an island destination with success. As indicated, the momentum is there; however, with the development of a partnership and a full time coordinator employed to lead the initiatives, successful movement towards sustainability can result. As the numerous barriers have been identified in this island, it has also resulted in a high level of awareness of the environmental and social issues on the island. As indicated, however, without responsibility to overcome these initiatives, hiring outside expertise to develop a sustainable tourism strategy, and leadership to work with all stakeholders to implement the strategy, barriers cannot be overcome. This case study illustrates that with stakeholder consultation to identify barriers, a cohesive and inclusive strategy can be developed to move a tourist destination towards sustainability.

# 11

# Calviá, Mallorca, Spain: Implementing a Multi-stakeholder Policy

## Introduction

Since the 1960s, many parts of Southern Europe have developed into a mass pleasure tourism periphery for Northern Europe. The Mediterranean is the biggest tourism region in the world, accounting for approximately one-third of all international arrivals in Spain with approximately 220 million visitors per year (Yunis, 2000). Spain is the second most popular tourist destination in the world and attracted 55.7 million international visitors in 2002 (7.4 per cent of total international arrivals) and US$33.6 billion in tourist receipts (WTO, 2003 in Dodds, 2007a). Of this number of visitors to Spain, Calviá located on the southwest tip of the island of Mallorca attracts approximately 3 per cent (1.6 million) of the country's total arrivals. While many islands do not have specific sustainability measures in their development or management policies (if such policies even exist), Calviá, which includes the resort area of Magaluf and Palma Nova, is one example of an island municipality that has developed, implemented and monitored a sustainability policy using a multi-stakeholder inclusive planning process.

## Background

The island of Mallorca is part of the Balearic Islands and is located in the Mediterranean Sea off the west coast of Spain (see Figure 11.1). Mallorca is an island covering 3640km², 40 per cent of which is a national park. The island has 554km of coastline and an average annual temperature of 18.7 degrees Celsius. Calviá is a municipality on Mallorca and has a high degree of investment in the tourism industry, which is built upon strong infrastructure, encouraged by its relatively close proximity to major European cities and frequent ferry service to mainland Spain. Calviá has a resident population of 42,000 (approximately 6 per cent of the island's total) and embraces six

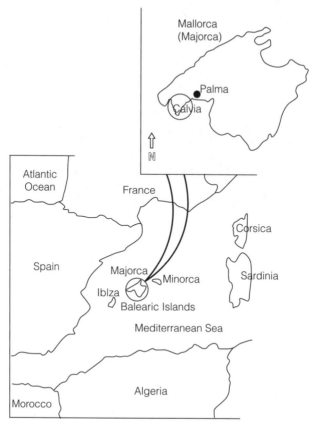

**Figure 11.1** *Map of Calviá located in Mallorca, Balearic Islands*

tourist zones encompassing 10 per cent of the island's coastline, 27 beaches and 120,000 tourist units (Govern de les Illes Balears, 2003). Calviá also attracts 20 per cent of the island's total tourists. As one of the most popular Mediterranean summer resorts, approximately 1.6 million tourists visit Calviá annually, mainly between May and September. This equates to approximately 20 per cent of the annual visitors to the island of Mallorca where Calviá is located (6.2 million visitors).

The region of Calviá can be seen as archetypal example of package-holiday mass tourism, and like many Mediterranean second-generation resorts it has experienced over-development, environmental damage, over-dependence on the tour operator and marketing dependence on pricing. The island receives a high economic contribution from tourism and has faced economic decline in the recent past through a decrease in tourism numbers due to increased competition and from environmental and social degradation. Calviá has also been tour-operator-dependent, with its two main markets being the UK and Germany and the majority of visitors coming for the three 'sun, sea and sand' experience.

## Stage of the life cycle

Calviá can be considered in the rejuvenation stage of the life cycle. After developing rapidly through the 1970s and 1980s, the island destination faced decline. This chapter outlines how through a multi-stakeholder policy approach, the island set to rejuvenate its tourism industry through addressing social, economic and environmental decline.

## Challenges to sustainable tourism development

Calviá's largest industry is tourism and approximately 95 per cent of jobs in the municipality are directly or indirectly related to tourism. In the 1960s, Calviá had a population of 3000 residents, 6800 tourism units and 112 tourist establishments. By 1997, there were 35,000 registered residents and approximately 50,000 de facto residents, 120,000 tourist beds and 256 tourist establishments (Dodds, 2007a: 300). Calviá, as many other island resorts, was developed heavily on an ad hoc basis during the 1960s and 1970s and this resulted in unplanned tourism resorts and environmental and social degradation. In the early 1990s, tourism reached a maturity level and started to decline. In the main tourist season of July and August, there are five times as many tourists as permanent residents. The island destination also felt the rise of income but at a cost of education. In the 1950s Calviá was relatively poor, but today Calviá is Spain's richest municipality and one of the richest in Europe. Although Calviá is now considered wealthy, it has the lowest level of education in Spain, which itself has the lowest in Europe (Dodds, 2007a, 2008a).

**Figure 11.2** *Crowded beaches in Calviá, Magaluf*

There have been immense social and environmental pressures that have arisen as a result of uncontrolled tourism growth. In 1995 Calviá undertook a baseline study to determine the impact of tourism. Figures from studies showed that there was a scarcity of rainfall ($65hm^3$/year) that was subject to heavy pressures by tourist consumption. Along with the scarce rainfall, 30 per cent of the water used in Calviá comes from local underground water, which was currently being overdrawn. Only 2 per cent of energy used in Calviá was renewable, and the average energy consumption was 2.14kWh per tourist per night's stay in a hotel. Fifty-eight per cent of carbon dioxide came from transporting tourists and this was a major cause of traffic congestion, which was heightened by a lack of public transportation. There was also a high amount of waste being generated on the island, and the options for disposal were limited. Land use was also an issue and there was continuous land occupation from urbanization. Because of this, 57 per cent of heritage sites were at high risk of deterioration (Ajuntament de Calviá, 1997; Dodds, 2007a) (see Table 11.1).

Calviá also suffered from increased competition from other tourism destinations (Canaries, Turkey, Greece and Tunisia), and saw a decline in tourism numbers. The overall image of Mallorca was declining and it was seen as

**Table 11.1** *Calviá's environmental and social pressures documented in 1995*

| | |
|---|---|
| Water: | • There was a scarcity of rainfall (65 hm³/year) which was subject to heavy pressures by tourist consumption. The annual water consumption amounted to 10hm³ (130 litres per day by resident and 160 litres per day by tourist – 1995 statistic). |
| | • 30% of the water used in Calviá comes from local underground water which is being overdrawn. |
| Energy: | • Annual consumption of primary energy in Calviá amount to 72,000TEP/year, of which only 2% is renewable. |
| | • Consumption was 6.47kWh per res/day and 2.14kWh per tourist per one night stay in a hotel. |
| Transport: | • Emissions of carbon dioxide equalled 1,400,000 tonnes (58% due to transporting tourists). |
| | • There were 70 million journeys per year (1995 statistic) and tourists account for 50 million of these journeys and are a major cause of traffic congestion. |
| | • Lack of public transport (bus in only used for 18% of journeys). Residents use cars for 95% of journeys. |
| Urban waste: | • In 1995 Calviá produced 41,000 tonnes of urban waste (and 190,000 tonnes of debris and inert material – approximately 1.25kg per resident/day and 1kg per tourist per day). Options for disposal were limited. |
| Land Use: | • Over 60% of Calviá's territory was affected by soil erosion. |
| | • There was continuous land occupation by urbanization and development of new infrastructure damage done by quarries and waste dumps and devastation by forest fire. |
| | • 57% of archaeological heritage sites were at high risk of deterioration. |
| Social: | • There has been high immigration and low social integration. |
| | • Lowest education standard in Spain. |
| | • Lack of trained skilled professionals (majority of employment are waiters and house cleaners). |

*Source:* Ayuntament de Calviá, (1997, p. 16–22) in Dodds, (2007a)

overdeveloped with reduced perceived attractiveness due to mass marketing of resorts.

## Overcoming challenges

The decrease of tourism numbers in Calviá and in the Balearic Islands as a whole prompted regulations and efforts to move towards addressing the problems of the degradation of the island environment, deterioration of social systems and facilities, and the threat of further tourism decline. In 1995 a decision by Calvia's town council, in collaboration with a wide range of working groups, was made to promote an overall long-term strategy through the preparation of LA21, according to the guidelines of the Earth Summit in Rio in 1992 and the fifth programme of the EU (1992). Calviá decided to approve new urban plans and adopt a model for sustainable development using the Local Agenda 21 approach. The LA21 approach was a long-term strategy set out to reshape the destination's approach to tourism development. The LA21 for Calviá defined the programme as the 'Complete Rehabilitation Setting' and targeted natural heritage conservation, modernization of the tourist sector and restoration of existing heritage (Ayuntament de Calviá, 1997: 2). The LA21 curative aim was to tackle the problem of uncontrolled growth and to 'restore the resort and surrounding landscape, to limit the increase in the number of beds, to demolish unsuitable facilities, to improve the quality of amenities and to develop appropriate products' (UNEP/ICLEI, 2003: 13). Some of the principles of Calviá's LA21 were to consult and inform the wider community, engage the customer (tour operator and visitor) and encourage initiatives from others in addition to the local authority. It also aimed to ensure sustainability was integrated into the overall policies and actions of an area.

The first initiative in this process was for the Town Council to draw up an 'Initial Document' that was circulated and discussed with local groups and representatives. This Document was largely developed because it became apparent that sectoral objectives and actions had limitations and that strategies needed to be medium- to long-term and integrated into wider economic, social, territorial and environmental actions. Environmental factors emerged as the key aspects for the area's sustainable development (Ajuntament de Calviá, 1997), as can be seen in Table 11.1.

In May 1998, a proposal of 40 actions and 15 key points was published, which became part of a Citizens' forum. A new structure (not just an environmental department) was created to support the structure. The methodology used was the method of alternative settings which analysed the *initial situation*, the *perspective situation* (if no action were taken and present trends and development continued) and the *completely restored setting* (one that would be reached if building and population growth were to be controlled).

The criteria outlined in the Plan were:

- an integrated conceptual approach to local development;
- (and the need to adapt to new tourist demands carrying capacity and defining limits of acceptable change);

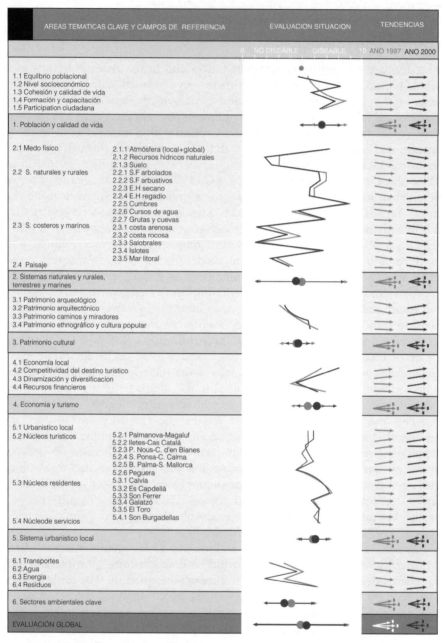

*Source:* Ajuntament de Calviá, 2001

**Figure 11.3** *Indicators used in Calviá for evaluation 1997–2000*

- consideration of time and seasonality and the analysis of Calviá's evolution;
- an overall analysis of local and island space;
- participatory and open working methods (using experts, citizens' forum and information to the general public);
- specific lines of action, initiatives and working programmes (Ayuntament de Calviá, 1997).

The priorities were defined by a citizens' forum using a voting system (for the ten strategic lines of action and 40 initiatives). Social participation was one of the fundamental aims of the LA21 approach and comprised the following:

- Management Committee of the Council (Chaired by the Mayor).
- Group of Experts (Special Commission of Academics, Scientists and others – provided methodologies and scientific rigour).
- Citizens' Forum (was an open consultation council with participation from 150 citizens who met, debated opinions and provided references for local interest).
- Thematic Commission – an average of 30 participants evaluated theme-based questions with different spatial effects on the municipality.
- People consultation, which begun in 1997 under the slogan 'Mission Possible' (an evaluation survey of the 10 Lines of Action and 40 Initiatives of the Action Plan). The household opinion survey was conducted after the consultation period then the final document was drawn up. There was an involvement by 30 per cent of the adult population (Ayuntament de Calviá, 2001: 6).

The strategy was integrated into wider sectors and the Balearic Autonomous Community at large. A new Balearic law for Calviá was set out in 1998 to limit accommodation growth, restore existing hotels and to protect 40 per cent of the natural areas. The objectives of the LA21 plan consisted of 10 strategic lines of action and 40 initiatives.

The 10 lines of action set in motion were:

1  to contain the human pressure, to limit the growth and favour the comprehensive restoration of the territory and its littoral;
2  to favour the integration, cohabitation and the quality of life of the resident population;
3  to maintain the land and sea natural heritage and promote the creation of a tourist and regional eco-tax with environmental purpose;
4  to recover the historical, cultural and natural heritage;
5  to promote the comprehensive restoration of the residential and tourist population centres;
6  to improve Calviá as a tourist destination: substitute growth by sustainable quality, to find out the increase of expenses per visitor and try to balance the tourist season;

7   to improve the public transport and favour the services for passers-by and cyclists between and inside the population centres;
8   to introduce a sustainable management in the key environmental sectors: water, energy and waste products;
9   to invest in human and knowledge resources, to invigorate and diversify the economic system;
10  to innovate the local government and to extend the capacity of state assisted public–private investment (Ayuntament de Calviá, 1997).

This was one of the first examples of a policy document that was not only based on a baseline and had specific objectives, it was also measurable. There were originally 27 fields of reference and 750 indicators in order to allow study and evaluation; however, this was then modified to a more manageable 40 indicators with a 1–10 indicator value.

## Successes in sustainable tourism

Looking at all the strategic action items and the 40 initiatives laid out in the 1997 LA21 Action Plan, it can be concluded that many of the initiatives were successful and there has been a general movement toward sustainability in Calviá. Some of the ways Calviá achieved success was through a multi-stakeholder participation and inclusion, autonomy, communication and measurement. As Calviá's government is fairly autonomous, it was able to adopt and implement many initiatives without the need for collaboration from higher governing bodies. In addition, the basic structure for Calviá's development plan came from well-established committees who did a complete diagnostic of the situation from an economic, social and environmental perspective (there was a general consensus that the LA21 approach was beneficial).

A number of projects were initiated in a wide range of areas, including land declassification, ecological urban planning, waste management and recycling, training for workers in the tourism industry, public education campaigns and public transit initiatives. Seasonality was significantly reduced, with 15 per cent more tourists in the winter season in 1997 than in summer. Although not all initiatives were implemented and many key objectives were long term in nature, there were many tangible achievements. A declassification law created to change land zoned for urbanization allowed for 647 hectares to be preserved. There was also a zero increase in the number of hotels and apartments – in fact, 200 tourist beds have disappeared since the declassification law came into effect. Tourist areas were upgraded by creating pedestrian zones and planting trees, improving the overall quality of the area. A management plan for the national resources and heritage sites was also formed. There were also new regulations for mooring and anchoring-in-place and proposals for floating moorings (removable in winter) pending in order to limit anchor damage and harbour congestion caused by boats. In addition, sea dredging, a practice used to regenerate beaches, was terminated and more environmentally friendly measures put in place to minimize erosion. A recycling and urban waste reduction plan was implemented to ensure that 70 per cent of all urban waste is separated at origin, facilitating and reducing the cost of recycling effort and minimizing landfill use.

LA21 was implemented in Calviá, in order to strengthen major European community environmental policies in the tourism sector (Integrated Coastal Zone Management, Urban regeneration, public participation, Ecolabel, Tourism Agenda 21). Results included the improvement of the private operator's environmental performance, such as developing guidelines for green purchasing in hotels, guidelines for EU Ecolabel in hotels and guidelines for hotel-simplified environmental management. One hundred and fifty hotels, the Hotel Owners' Associations and other key organizations were involved in the design, testing phase, final draft and guidelines. Tourist environmental education packages were also developed to increase tourist awareness (available at information points, in the hotels and through media campaign). Today, Calviá is part of the Network for Cities for Sustainable Tourism.

Some of the principles of Calviá's LA21 which helped to make it successful included consultation with and informing the wider community, engagement of the customer (tour operator and visitor) and encouraging initiatives from others in addition to the local authority. It also aimed to ensure sustainability was integrated into the overall policies and actions of the area.

There was also effective dissemination of information about the situation in Calviá that illustrated the need for change, hence the original adoption of and support for the policy from the wider community. For example, 10,000 copies of the 1995 diagnostic plan were distributed in Calviá and surrounding areas. Documents were practical and solution-oriented, as they were aimed at addressing overcapacity and limiting growth while improving the quality of life within Calviá. The social commitment of stakeholders was achieved through the communication effort and in 1998 the municipality collected 6500 signatures to support the action plan and identified the priorities for action (total 30,000 population in 1997). This was equivalent to 50 per cent of the population who voted the following year (total 12,500 votes) to support this political party.

There was also a long-term and holistic view included with the plan. In addition, there was good, positive communication in the early stages between the municipality and the private sector. The general level of consciousness of sustainability had increased in Calviá since the adoption of the policy. Part of the success of this initiative was leadership. Mayoress Margarta Najera's initial effort to change public consciousness through her leadership led to the involvement and engagement of different stakeholders.

One key element for planning and development is measurement and accountability. In 1997 the municipality produced a technical instrument – Calviá 2000 (a municipal corporation for water and waste management) and in 2001 a 'Revision of the Observatory and the Plan' was undertaken to benchmark performance. Table 11.2 illustrates some of the indicators measured.

The reason for the increase in growth that jeopardized the performance of the Action Plan was attributed to a good economic climate and performance of the tourist sector in the Balearics. As Table 11.2 points out, $CO_2$ emissions

**Table 11.2** *Evaluation of human pressures and environmental factors*

| Human Pressure | 1995 | 2000 | % |
|---|---|---|---|
| Resident population | 43,310 | 52,630 | 24 |
| Maximum tourist/day | 112,930 | 122,963 | 9 |
| Maximum pop/day | 155,240 | 175,593 | 16 |
| | | | |
| Environmental Key Factors | 1997 | 2000 | % |
| Water - mill n1/year | 9.35 | 11.38 | 19 |
| Waste - mill kg/year | 42.50 | 50.40 | 19 |
| Energy - mill TEP/year | 31.00 | 36.60 | 16 |
| Trips – mill/year | 70 (1995) | 83 | 18 |
| $CO_2$ emissions – Access and mobility | 608,000 (1995) | 708,000 | 16 |

*Source*: Ajuntament de Calviá (2001: 12)

increased by 15–20 per cent and populations of both residents and tourists increased by 25 per cent and 9 per cent respectively. Of the 46 indicators developed, the overall balance in 2000 showed that 17 indicators (37 per cent) improved, 13 (28 per cent) did not change and 16 (35 per cent) continued to worsen (Ayuntament de Calviá, 2001: 14) in relation to the situation in 1997. There were significant improvements to the Paseo de Calviá, towards integrating the community, and the recovery of heritage was seen to be substantial with regard to the Archaeological Park on the Puig de sa Morisca.

## Conclusion

The Calviá local Agenda 21 won the 'European Prize for Sustainable Cities' in 1997, and was designated 'Best Practice' in localizing Agenda 21 by the UN-Habitat in 1998. Calviá is often quoted as the most successful example of a mass tourism destination that has implemented a sustainable tourism policy (UNEP/ICLEI, 2003; Yunis, 2000). The municipality has received many awards for its sustainability initiatives including the European Union's 1997 Sustainable Town Prize; the Green Globe award (in 1998); the prize for the Ecological Commune in Spain in 1999 and the UNEP Sustainable Summit Business Award for Sustainable Development Partnerships in 2002.

Overall, although Calvià has been successful in implementing much of its Action Plan, there is still significant progress to be made for it to be a sustainable destination (Dodds, 2005). Reviewing the policy formulation and implementation process since 1995, a number of lessons can be learned from Calvià's approach that could be useful for other destinations that are attempting to implement sustainability policies/measures. First, an adaptive and flexible management approach was successful in raising the awareness of sustainability issues and engaging the support of a wide group of stakeholders in the policy process. It is imperative, however, to engage the wider local population on an ongoing basis and to make stakeholders more accountable for the implementation and not just the formulation of sustainable tourism measures. Second, a preliminary diagnostic was extremely useful in determining evaluation and measurement (Dodds, 2006, 2008b).

**Figure 11.4** *Promotion of renewable energy*

Tourism policy, to be successful, needs to be an integral and central value within the governing policy of a municipality, i.e. tourism as the central focus with social, transportation, planning and other factors all supporting as they are all interdependent. Policy needs to be adaptable to change and be able to react quickly. Economic success of a destination ultimately depends on the social and environmental welfare of the destination; however, in the case of Calviá this was not recognized until the economic situation deteriorated. Calviá moved towards integrating a multi-stakeholder policy through political will, and thus has become an example for other tourist destinations that strive towards sustainability.

# 12
# Chumbe Island, Tanzania: Strong Leadership and Partnership Overcomes Great Obstacles

## Introduction

Chumbe Island is one of the islands located in the Indian Ocean channel off the coast of the semi-autonomous region of Zanzibar in Tanzania. A relatively small island, it is Tanzania's first managed Marine Park. As Tanzania and Zanzibar had little interest in marine conservation and were, in the early 1990s, rather focused on attracting investments in tourism, the idea of Chumbe as a privately established and managed Marine Park was originally presented to the government of Zanzibar as a tourist development. After struggles with bureaucracy and fundraising, Chumbe is now recognized as a world-class eco-tourism destination that is funding a nature reserve and has used collaborative partnerships, education and long-term park management and tourism planning to achieve sustainable tourism.

The sustainable management of nature reserves as island tourism destinations has proven difficult in many countries due to the nature of traditional tourism development and institutional weakness (Levine, 2002; Riedmiller, 1998). Many developing countries as well as islands in tropical areas have relied on tourism to generate additional income and this is also the case for many sub-Saharan African countries (Kweka, Morrissey, and Blake, 2003). In many islands as well as coastal destinations around the world, tourism has had negative consequences for the sustainable use of the resources that in turn has had an effect on ecosystem integrity (Gössling, 2001). In particular, coral reefs globally are under serious threat from acidification caused by climate change, dynamite fishing and overexploitation, pollution and sedimentation from coastal development (McClanahan et al, 1999; Riedmiller, 1998; Svensson et al, 2009). While many coastal communities in Tanzania survive on fishing, there is little evidence of traditional reef management to protect the resource. Even government-managed parks invest only a small fraction of their tourism proceeds into reserve management or related services, and nature reserves thus

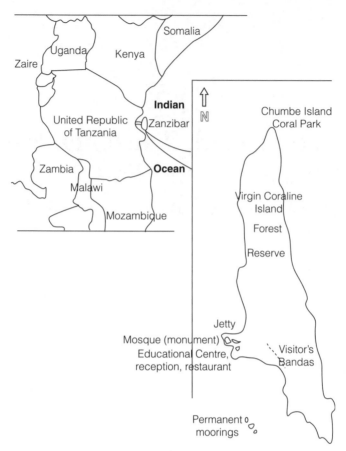

**Figure 12.1** *Map of Chumbe*

suffer from 'conflicting interests between different user groups, particularly traditional users and tourism' (Riedmiller, 1998: 222). As Charnley (2005) and Goldstein (2005) outline, for communities to benefit from tourism, they need secure land tenure over the area in which it takes place, as well as the ability to make land use decisions for that area. Dieke (2003) also outlines that for sustainable tourism to succeed in Africa, there is a need for regional cooperation and control with clear tourism development objectives that involve and benefit locals.

## Background

To promote awareness for marine conservation and sustainable tourism management, Chumbe Island Coral Park Ltd (CHICOP) turned uninhabited Chumbe Island into a fully managed, internationally recognized tourism destination and marine park. CHICOP is a private nature reserve that was developed from 1991 for the conservation and sustainable management of uninhabited Chumbe Island. Recognized by the Zanzibar government from

1994 and UNEP–WCMC from 1995, the park includes a 30-hectare marine reef sanctuary and coral-rag forest covering most of the island's 22 hectares. After several years of campaigning, the fringing reef west of Chumbe Island in October 1992 was officially closed. As Chumbe is located upstream of the most important fishing grounds opposite Zanzibar's capital, Stonetown, the Chumbe marine park was expected to become a breeding ground for fish, corals and other species, which would then spread out to recolonize nearby overfished and degraded areas. On 24 December 1994 the Zanzibar Government officially gazetted the reef as the 'Chumbe Reef Sanctuary' and with this Chumbe had become the first marine park in Tanzania (www.chumbeisland.com) and the first private marine park in the world. Following this, Chumbe became registered as a UN recognized Protected Area.

The island is approximately 6km from Zanzibar and about 30km from Tanzania mainland. One of the last relatively pristine coral islands in the region, the marine park includes a fully protected coral reef sanctuary and forest reserve that harbour rare and endangered animals (the park is home to 400 species of fish and 200 species of coral), a visitor centre, small eco-lodge, nature trails and historical ruins. Chumbe Island offers high-end simple luxury tourism. The island has seven bungalows for overnight tourists and offers limited day trips for visitors from Zanzibar to snorkel and learn about the coral reef. Only staff for the marine park and eco-lodge live on the island and there is no other population.

The concept for tourism development as a source of funding for marine conservation was a long-term strategy put forth by a passionate leader – Sibylle Riedmiller. Offering a combination of simple luxury and education, all buildings and operations are based on state-of-the-art eco-technology aiming at zero impact on the environment. The company objectives are

*Source:* © Hal Thompson

**Figure 12.2** *Chumbe Island*

non-commercial, while operations follow commercial principles. The aim of CHICOP is to establish a model of financially and ecologically sustainable park management, where eco-tourism can maintain and support conservation, research and environmental education programmes and other benefits for local people (Riedmiller, 1998). Leadership by individuals such as Sibylle Riedmiller, founder and owner, have served to negotiate with seven Zanzibar government departments to allow the park, find financing and coordinate and motivate volunteers and employees to create a sustainably run successful park and island tourism destination.

## Stage of the life cycle

Chumbe, when examining Butler's (1980) life cycle, can be seen as a destination which from a mass tourism perspective would be in the growth stage; however, due to the planning and long-term vision for Chumbe, this island is already in the maturity stage. It has set a carrying capacity for few bungalows and has reached high occupancy levels. Its strategy has focused on conservation and unlike other destinations is happy with the tourism numbers and has in fact capped the total allowed to visit the island per year.

## Challenges to sustainable tourism development

Although decades of experience exist in terrestrial nature conservation, in Tanzania, marine conservation policies are fairly recent and law enforcement is weak. Illegal and destructive fishing is commonplace, corruption is often rife and there is a lack of transparency in park management. There are also many environmental and social issues arising from tourism development in the region. According to Gössling (2001), the region is water poor, relying on fresh water derived from seasonal rains and stored in inefficient aquifers. There has been rapid tourism growth in the area, especially in Zanzibar, and this development is expected to put additional pressure on the fresh water resources of the east coast, which already show signs of over-use. These determine the living conditions in coastal areas and affect the well-being of both the local population and the tourism industry.

Chumbe is one of the islands close to Zanzibar and is accessible by local boat from Zanzibar. For foreign citizens and organizations such as CHICOP, land tenure in Tanzania (including Zanzibar) is generally only available for approved investment purposes through leasehold. Recently several small islands around Zanzibar have been developed for conventional tourism. There are also disincentives for private investment in conservation that need more years of operations than conventional tourism investments until generating profits. Furthermore the policy, legal and institutional framework in many areas of Tanzania is not supportive for a number of reasons:

- Investment security is limited by the fact that land tenure is only available on leasehold, while land leases can be revoked by the State with relative ease, thus further weakening long-term security of tenure.

- There is no tax or other incentives for investing into environmental conservation.
- The investment climate presents challenges as there are multiple and cumbersome bureaucratic requirements and wide discretionary powers for government officials, often leading to corruption and seriously delayed operations.
- Generous donor aid for nature conservation tolerates high overheads of state run institutions and is not sustainable. Private investor conservation initiatives are also not always welcome and at times not supported or even sabotaged.

Zanzibar, the nearby larger island, is facing huge rubbish and pollution problems. There is a need for education about littering and conservation as well as about sustainability in general. In the national language Kiswahili corals are referred to as 'rocks and stones' and marine conservation is hardly taught about in schools.

The legal structure in this semi-autonomous region as well as in mainland Tanzania is also complex and not always conducive for nature conservation. In Tanzania, the government owns all wildlife, even on community land and conservation is a state monopoly. Although 'poverty eradication' is now the declared aim of most donor aid in Africa, substantial support goes to state institutions that have associated problems of transparency and accountability, rather than into genuine community-driven or private sector led conservation initiatives that benefit local resource users.

Tourism also faces challenges. Tourism in Zanzibar is increasingly developing into mass tourism with a short-term focus on sand, sun and sea tourism that has a high degree of foreign ownership, therefore resulting in leakage.

## Overcoming challenges

Since 2000, Chumbe Island Coral Park is financially sustainable. After ten years of commercial operations, occupancy levels have increased from 13 per cent in 1998 to approximately 85 per cent in 2008 and the annual turnover has reached US$550,000.

Approximately US$1.2 million were invested in development from 1991 to 1998. The project initiator put up half, a quarter were small donor grants for non-commercial project components while another quarter was professional work contributed by over 50 volunteers over many years (Riedmiller, 1991, 1995). From an economic standpoint, the island is also doing well. An occupancy rate of 40 per cent is sufficient to finance park operations. With 43 full-time local staff, two expatriates and several part-time workers during the yearly renovations, CHICOP employs three times more staff than the international average of ecolodges. Through successful management, Chumbe Island now boasts a number of achievements.

In order to turn Chumbe Island into a marine park, CHICOP sought a multi-stakeholder partnership with local communities through village meetings before and during project development. Partnerships were also formed with government, universities and village representatives. Chumbe also recognized that a long-term vision and plan was needed to ensure that the business case for a marine park would be recognized. A 1995–2005 Management Plan for the reserve was developed with wide stakeholder participation and extended and updated for 2006–16. Constant monitoring and evaluation have also helped report progress. To set an example for transparency, CHICOP issues quarterly and yearly progress reports and actively reports on park management and business operations to all respective sectoral government departments. Chumbe is also actively engaged in monitoring of the marine park. To establish the conservation value and document the terrestrial and marine resources of Chumbe Island species lists, reports and studies have been produced on fishes, corals, amphibians and reptiles, birds, bats, butterflies and vascular plants. Research is jointly conducted with the Institute of Marine Sciences of the University of Dar es Salaam and the Departments of Environment, Forestry and Fisheries respectively. Studies are regularly conducted by visiting researchers from both national and international institutions and both graduate and PhD studies have used Chumbe as a base.

Another innovation is Environmental Education offered by CHICOP. Employment and training of former fishermen as park rangers was done and marine rescue services to local fishermen in distress served to gain respect from fishermen (as there was no such service in Tanzania). Guests also see Chumbe as an educational experience as they learn about and enjoy a unique experience of conservation, the guidance by rangers, the exhibits in the Visitors' Centre and meeting local people. Visitors are actively discouraged from buying corals and shells in local markets.

*Source:* © Chumbeisland.com

**Figure 12.3** *Lamu and Misali exchange visits.* © *Chumbeisland.com*

Chumbe maintains a strong connection to neighbouring communities through the education programme where park rangers act as community educators. The park is an attraction not only for tourists but also for local schools. As one of Chumbe's visions was to promote coral reef and marine conservation, they established a comprehensive Environmental Education program. As school education in Zanzibar has little relationship to the outside world and does not yet provide environmental education on marine issues, this program aims at building environmental awareness in Zanzibar. As extra-curricular activities, such as field excursions, are rarely organized, very few children have a chance to visit coral reefs and coral-rag forests. This is also partly due to the fact that school children, and particularly girls, normally do not learn how to swim or snorkel (Riedmiller, 1991, 2003). The Chumbe Environmental Education Program sponsors local schools to visit the island, prepared through in-service teacher training workshops and the development of teaching aids. Up to end 2009, over 4500 school children and 750 teachers have visited Chumbe Island. Revenue from tourism supports park management and the education programs. In 2001, the Chumbe Environmental Education Program developed a module on 'The Coral Reef', which was recognized by the Ministry of Education as an official teaching aid (www.chumbeisland.com). The program was expanded to encompass teacher training workshops and evaluation seminars, where teachers were trained to link field learning experiences with the science syllabus in particular, something that was rarely done before (www.chumbeisland.com).

Working with the Ministry, CHICOP is now developing further teaching modules for subjects ranging from 'Eco-tourism' to 'Biodiversity', 'Eco-technology' and 'Conservation'. These modules are being developed to form a teaching resource for all secondary school teachers in Zanzibar, to advise and provide information about field-based education, with the ultimate aim to produce a course manual of exemplary teaching modules. The vision is that 'this will give teachers and students a concrete model on how to make classroom teaching more relevant to the environment, and create awareness on coral reefs and coral island ecology that is badly needed in Zanzibar (www. chumbeisland.com). The Chumbe Education Programme is now leading the way for environmental education in Zanzibar. The teacher training college incorporates classes on Chumbe for all trainee teachers in Zanzibar each year, and representatives from the Ministry of Education are encouraging teachers to introduce environmental education through fieldwork. This educational effort is also a good example of working in collaboration with multiple stakeholders. Start-up phases received support from the Marine Education, Awareness and Biodiversity Program (MEAB-WWF, the Wildlife and Environment Society of South Africa (WESSA), the US-National Fish and Wildlife Foundation (NFWF), the International Coral Reef Action Network (ICRAN) and the South African Development Cooperation–Reef Environmental Education Program (SADC–REEP) (Chumbe Island, 2009).

Biodiversity in the park has also increased. The Reef Sanctuary has become one of the most pristine coral reefs in the region with approximately 420 fish species and 200 species of hard coral – 90 per cent of all recorded in

**Figure 12.4** *Teacher training for alternative livelihoods*

East Africa (Fiebig, 1995; Riedmiller, 2003). The Forest Reserve is one of the last undisturbed semi-arid coral rag forests in Zanzibar and now gives sanctuary to highly endangered endemic Aders' duikers (*Cephalophus adersi*) threatened by poaching and habitat destruction on Zanzibar, and also has the world's largest known population of rare coconut crabs (*Birgus latro*). Since September 2006, Chumbe has been participating in a global sea grass monitoring program called SeagrassNet (Chumbe Island, 2009). A specific coral reef monitoring system was set up in 2006 and has since been implemented by island based park rangers since then. Forest and marine trails were developed with information materials in English and Kiswahili.

Many jobs and new sources of income for local people were also created by CHICOP. Often when no-take marine parks are created, local fishermen lose their fishing grounds and thus livelihood. To support nature conservation, local people must understand why it is a good thing and also benefit from it. Chumbe recruited former fishermen from adjacent villages to be employed and trained as park rangers. These fishermen were the key people in early outreach programmes to raise awareness among the local community on marine ecology and sustainable management of natural resources. These rangers now manage the protection of the reserve and keep records of any incidents and observations on the reef sanctuary and the forest reserve. Two of them have also learned scuba-diving and were the first East Africans to witness the coral spawning (coral reproduction) observed in 1994.

The rangers are also involved in numerous research projects conducted on the island and have been trained to guide visitors, for snorkeling in the reef sanctuary and over forest nature trails. Additionally a key role of these rangers is to lead the school excursions of the Chumbe Education Program mentioned (Chumbe Island, 2009). Biological reference literature and laminated fish guides for underwater use are available, and numerous reports have been commissioned and produced regarding the island's fauna and flora, both marine and forest. 'Floating underwater information modules' (FIMs) have been developed to aid visitors to the park, accompanied by laminated information cards and identification guides depicting fishes, invertebrates and molluscs found in the reef. Nature trails and educational material are open to schoolchildren, eco-tourists and local people alike (Chumbe Island, 2009).

Almost all the staff on Chumbe are local Zanzibaris from neighbouring fishing communities, trained as 'marine rangers', who spend two weeks on the island and then one week back in their villages. As a result of no-take zone, catches, which have been steadily declining in Zanzibar over the past few years due to overfishing, are reported to be increasing in adjacent reefs around Chumbe.

The island also is a good example of eco-architecture. On Chumbe, the local building technologies, materials and spatial design maximize natural ventilation. Seven visitor bungalows were constructed according to state-of-the-art eco-architecture (rainwater catchment, grey water filtration, composting toilets, photovoltaic power generation) in order to minimize environmental impact. As occupancy increased, the grey water filtration system could not cope with the nutrient-rich kitchen water, and wood ash of the staff kitchen reached a saturation point (Lindstroem, 2007). In order to adapt, ashes are now removed from the island since 2008, and a new grey water vegetative filtration plantbed was constructed for the restaurant kitchen, which absorbs phosphates and nitrates before the water enters the ecosystem.

All shower water comes from rainwater collection, and there is no sewage as all toilets are composting toilets, where no flush water is used. The resulting compost is recycled in plant beds. All electricity is supplied by solar panels.

Chumbe also demonstrated innovation in marketing. Like most small sustainability projects CHICOP did not have a large marketing budget and thus chose to go for renowned international awards and recognition from the international conservation community, for effective niche marketing. Chumbe Island has won the 1999 British Airways Tourism for Tomorrow Global award; the 2000 UNEP Global 500 Roll of Honour; Worldwide Project and Golden Award of the 2000 Expo in Hanover, Germany; the 2001 Green Hotel of the Year award of the International Hotel and Restaurant Association (IH&RA); the 2001 Eco-tourism Destination Award from CondeNast Traveller Magazine (Riedmiller, 2003, 2000) and many more awards.

## Conclusion

In many coastal areas including islands, a number of new models of collaborative marine resource management have been established within the last decade and central to the success of these programs have been international conservation NGOs and private sector tourist operations (Levine, 2002). Conservation of biodiversity in marine protected areas will only succeed if they are linked up with broader strategies for sustainable development and local communities and other key stakeholders are involved in their establishment and management (Francis et al, 2002). The Chumbe Island experience suggests that private management of ecologically sensitive protected areas that are surrounded by local communities can become successful sustainable tourism destinations. The achievements of CHICOP have been widely acknowledged by international conservation organizations, among them the International Union for Conservation of Nature (IUCN), the World Wide Fund for Nature (WWF), UNESCO-Directorate for Environment and Development in Coastal Regions and Small Islands (CSI) and the United Nations Environment Programme (UNEP).

While Tanzania's system of designating terrestrial parks and protected areas has been historically exclusionary, recent conservation initiatives such as those demonstrated by Chumbe Island have acknowledged the need to involve local people and provide benefits to resource-dependent island communities (Levine, 2002). Although costs increased from the original feasibility study, management was still able to generate enough profit to ensure that financial sustainability could prevail, therefore ensuring local benefits both socially and environmentally. Training local fishermen as park rangers by volunteers proved to be not only cost-effective but also crucial to the success of the marine park and facilitated direct partnerships with local stakeholders (Riedmiller, 2003). Leadership, perseverance, long-term planning and monitoring as well as many examples of multi-stakeholder collaborative partnerships have turned a once ideal hope into a sustainable, profitable island tourism destination. Sustainable tourism development in islands cannot operate in isolation: communication and cooperation with other stakeholder groups ensures that good practice is shared and strong leadership is vital to perseverance.

### *Acknowledgement*

A special thank you to Chumbe Island and especially Sibylle Riedmiller for her help with this case study.

# 13
# Moose Factory Island, Ontario: Putting Community-Based Tourism into Practice

## Introduction

The Cree Village eco-lodge, on Moose Factory Island in Northern Ontario, Canada, is an example of community-based tourism that has worked to create sustainable livelihoods through capacity and skills development in the community. The MoCreebec Aboriginal tribe decided to invest community funds and open the Cree Village eco-lodge in the year 2000. The eco-lodge has served as a means of bringing tourists to the community, which has created a tourism-based economy on an otherwise economically weak island. It has also led to the employment of several Cree peoples and serves as a place for social gatherings on the island. In addition, a community that had been poor and lost much of its culture in the past, has, through tourism, revisited its ideologies regarding land and Aboriginal culture and has integrated these values, shifting from an otherwise culturally and economically impoverished community to a success story.

## Background

Moose Factory is a small island in the Cochrane District of Northern Ontario, Canada (see Figure 13.1). The island is located at the southern end of James Bay, which is an area of the sub-Arctic. The overall population of Moose Factory Island is approximately 2700 people. It is a small island that is only three miles in length by two miles wide. The majority of the island's population are Cree Indian. The island is typical of the sub-Arctic regions and is abundant in forest and wildlife. Pods of beluga whales and seals are regular occurrences on the island. There is very little commercial development; however, it is the location of the only full service hospital in the area. There is also a provincial park and Cree native reserve on the island. The island is also home to the Cree Village eco-lodge, which has been

**Figure 13.1** *Map of Moose Factory Island*

referred to as Canada's most environmentally friendly lodge (Stewart, 2006).

On the nearby mainland as well as on the island of Moose Factory, there is very little in terms of tourist accommodation. There is also very little recreational tourism; however, due to diamond mining and other resource extraction in Northern Ontario there is a lot of business travel. In Moosonee, however, due to the Polar Bear Express and the fact that the Hudson's Bay Company opened its first post in this area, it has been marketed as one of Canada's 'Last Frontiers'. However, as 80 per cent of tourism in Ontario occurs in the southern part of the province, there is room for tourism to develop in the North. The product is unique and currently there is not an over-saturation of an indigenous tourism product in the area. Therefore, the MoCreebec tribe decided that there was a potential for a 20 room lodge and invested in the economic development on the island. The MoCreebec tribe has approximately 500 members and is led by Chief Randy Kapashesit. The lodge, which was built in 2000, is managed by a committee of tribe members. The eco-lodge was initially going to be a hotel/motel; however, due to the philosophy and culture of this tribe, an environmentally and socially sustainable lodge seemed most in line with the tribe's values. In order to design and construct this lodge, they consulted with the community to ensure that the MoCreebec values were reflected.

The lodge is run as a not-for-profit organization with all proceeds either invested back into the lodge or re-invested in the community. At present, the lodge has only managed to break even and reinvest in the lodge; however, once the lodge is able to make a profit, this will be invested in the local community. The lodge retains an occupancy rate of 60 per cent; however, the months of January, February and May to August are at capacity. The clientele that travel to the island in the summer months are mainly from Canada's largest city, Toronto, as well as the surrounding areas in Ontario and internationally. The visitor base shifts in the winter months when island accommodation serves the business population as the surrounding communities are lacking in decent accommodation. Tourists come to participate in traditional winter and summer activities of the Canadian North such as kayaking, fishing, paddling, cross-country skiing, snow-shoeing, camping and snowmobiling. The lodge is surrounded by nature and boasts untouched forest, beluga whales and seals and the MoCreebec's philosophy of living lightly on the land is entrenched in all operations. The facility was designed by the local MoCreebec people as a means of seeking local development in a way that meshes with their identities and beliefs. The lodge was designed to incorporate various environmental features and this philosophy is reflected in every decision in the lodge from flooring to food. The lodge uses materials that have a minimal environmental impact (low maintenance finishes, no off gassing and required low embodied energy); uses low maintenance appliances and mechanical systems and is a gathering place for the community.

Environmentally benign products are used throughout the lodge and include carpeting made from wool, organic mattresses, pure wool blankets and bedding from organic cotton. Furniture is purchased from companies that use only sustainably harvested wood and the walls are made from cedar, which is native to the area. Dispensers supply organic soaps and shampoos in the bathrooms and biodegradable cleaning supplies are used throughout the lodge. All the window blinds are of slatted birch and the lampshades of recycled steel. Natural materials like local stone and cedar have been used in the lodge's construction. The lodge installed composting toilets; however, due to the flooding in 2008 the toilets are too damaged to remain in use. Within three years the Cree Village will develop sufficient solar and wind energy to bring itself almost entirely off the electrical grid. If this is successful, additional solar and wind projects will begin within the local MoCreebec communities. The

**Figure 13.2** *Cree Village eco-lodge, sustainably designed to reflect cultural elements*

food served in the lodge consists mainly of traditional foods prepared in traditional ways such as caribou and trout and wild rice hand-picked by First Nation communities. The philosophy on food is to have a menu that reflects the MoCreebec's original values and high fat foods are discouraged. Future plans include planting native plants and local flowers around the lodge and expanding the vegetable garden. The lodge employs local people, most of whom are Aboriginal. The lodge also serves an important social function as it is now the meeting place for social activities on the island. It was designed to include a Shabatwon or Great Hall to reflect the culture of the tribe. The lodge also serves as the main means to preserving, sharing and inspiring the traditions of the MoCreebec culture. It has led to economic development in the community as the lodge works with the local community to provide tourism products and services to the tourists. For example, if tourists wish to participate in a sweat lodge ceremony or go winter camping or experience the traditional way of hunting or fishing, the local community works with the lodge to provide these services. The lodge also uses supplies where possible from the local community and involves the community through education and training to raise the standard of living in the tribe. In the future, the lodge hopes to work more closely in providing skills and education to the community. The lodge, which is built at the edge of the sub-Arctic, has become one of northern Canada's foremost tourist destinations. It was built in an area that is lacking in tourism facilities and used the cultural component of the community's lifestyle to build an environmentally, socially and economically sound product to create tourism on this island.

## Stage in the life cycle

When examining Butler's (1980) life cycle, Moose Factory Island can be seen as a destination which would be in the exploration stage and currently entering the growth stage of development. The MoCreebec is not planning expansion of the lodge, nor are any other Cree tribes on the island looking to develop but it has not been ruled out as a future endeavour. On the mainland, two new eco-lodges are being built by the Moose Cree First Nations.

## Challenges to sustainable tourism development in cold water climates

Tourism development in Northern Ontario is not very developed and has been created in a fashion that serves the bare minimum of purpose for usually the business traveller or VFR (people visiting friends and relatives). The remoteness of Moose Factory Island has led to several challenges in the development of tourism, not only from a sustainability perspective. The Island is located a far distance from the province's main urban centres of Toronto and Ottawa (approximately 849km from Toronto) and transportation is a challenge. To get to Moose Factory Island from Toronto, one would have to take the train (called the Polar Bear Express) and then either in the winter take the ice road from Moosonee, which is located on the shore, or in the summer take the barge. In the ice break months of November and April, it is difficult to arrive in Moose Factory Island as the ice road is melting and the barge cannot get through the breaking ice. The infrastructure to travel to Northern Ontario is nonexistent as it is mainly by car. The train is often expensive and not reliable and takes over 12–15 hours to reach the destination of Cochrane (the biggest town in the region) and then approximately three more hours to Moose Factory Island. It is often not easy for tourists who fly into Toronto or Ottawa to travel great distances if they have time constraints. It is also very expensive to fly to Northern Ontario, sometimes costing more than a flight from Europe to Toronto. From a sustainability perspective, the long distances required for travel to Moose Factory Island create issues in relation to greenhouse gas production, something that the islanders are very conscious of.

The location of Moose Factory Island also resulted in challenges to building. Due to weather restrictions, timing and scheduling of material deliveries had to be precise. Design and construction had to be consistent with building codes in the Province Ontario and also needed to incorporate considerations for harsh winters. The composting toilets in the Cree Village eco-lodge are an excellent idea; however, due to the quickly melting ice in the spring of 2008, flooding on the island occurred, damaging the composting toilets beyond repair. Increasingly, the island is in danger of flooding due to higher temperature because of climate change and this flood also damaged the lodge to the point that it had to be closed for repair for an entire year. Being on an island, the community is vulnerable to climate change impacts such as flooding and as water levels in the area continue to rise, emergency planning by the community must take place to be prepared for increasing flash floods and other climate-related island issues.

Another challenge the island faces is that the Aboriginal tourism product is not promoted in Ontario. Many international tourists come to Toronto and visit Niagara Falls, then travel to British Columbia to experience the Canadian Aboriginal tourism experience. In Ontario, this potential has not been realized and despite the fact that the Cree Village eco-lodge has been promoted in the Canadian Tourism Commission's Significant 28 Aboriginal Tourism products, without the required transportation infrastructure or promotion about this island tourism product, many tourists within and outside of Ontario are unaware of this lodge and with a limited marketing budget, occupancy is a challenge.

Another major challenge to tourism development on the island is the numerous social issues. The MoCreebec have traditionally been a nomadic people and have moved from place to place depending on the seasons and by needs. Many of the MoCreebec have traditionally been living in substandard living conditions such as tents and in the last few decades have moved into more permanent dwellings. As Aboriginal communities in Ontario (and many other countries) have not been treated fairly in the past and were often put on reserves and had their livelihoods restricted, this has resulted in a community riddled with drug, alcohol and sexual abuse and loss of cultural traditions. The Cree tribe on Moose Factory Island were placed in Christian schools in the last century, which resulted in sexual abuse by the people who ran the schools and a loss of cultural traditions that define the livelihoods of the Aboriginal people. As many of the community have not retained or lost many of their traditions, to develop a tourism product based on these traditions has been difficult. Many of the employees do not know how to answer some visitor questions regarding community culture, traditions or stories because they were told so often not to tell their stories or practise their traditions that they are too afraid to answer people's questions (Kapashesit, 2010). In addition, the motivations of the community to become engaged to provide other services on the island (such as spin-offs from tourism development through

**Figure 13.3** *Moose Factory Island, Ontario, Canada*

souvenirs, entertainment, banking services, etc.) has not yet been developed due to lack of skills of the islanders. It has also been difficult to hire only local people from the area as many of them are not educated in hospitality nor have the skills necessary for this position. When the tribal islanders do get trained, there is often a high turnover rate as they may migrate to work in the Cree Village eco-lodge on the mainland or other such endeavours. In addition, many of the current employees leave for months at a time as they live on the land through traditional hunting and fishing.

Many of the community on Moose Factory Island are also not open to tourists visiting their island. There has been a case of reverse racism where the community has not wanted outside visitors to visit. There has been a lot of resistance to working in a position to serve the tourists. There has been an effort to educate the community about the benefits that tourism brings, not only economically but socially and culturally as well. In addition, this had also led to the native community opening up and accepting outsiders as potential friends that respect their culture versus the past vision of the 'white man'.

## Overcoming challenges

Before the Cree Village eco-lodge was built, visitors to Moose Factory Island were limited to a quick tour as part of a day trip. Now they can stay at an eco-lodge that reflects the historical values of the James Bay Cree, who have traditionally lived in harmony with nature. They can also enjoy unique and varied outdoor and cultural experiences that include the community giving guests the opportunity to meet the Cree elders and local families. The Moose Factory Island eco-lodge has embraced tourism on Cree terms and has

Source: © Cree Village Ecolodge

**Figure 13.4** *Experiencing local culture and practices*

provided a source of economic stability to the community. It has also instilled a new respect for Cree values in the community and is a role model for tourism development locally and in other northern communities (TIAC, 2005).

The MoCreebec people have identified in their constitutional framework that the guiding principle of the MoCreebec is to renew the social contract of Sharing, Kindness, Strength and Honesty, which was the basis for the first meeting of Aboriginal and European peoples (MoCreebec, 2005). The MoCreebec decided to take the social, environmental and economic issues facing their peoples into their own hands and to build and invest in Cree businesses. They decided that in order to break the poverty cycle that was riddling their community, it was best to invest in a Cree economy and promote individual and collective business opportunities that support the values of Cree people. The purpose was to create a sustainable form of economic livelihood to help the community be self-sufficient and create jobs for the current and future members of the community. The primary goal was to initiate community economic development projects that build assets for the organization, contribute to the economy and provide employment to the local labour force. The MoCreebec also sought to address ongoing basic needs such as education and health care. In order to do this, the MoCreebec Council identified that an indigenous owned eco-lodge in Northern Canada that promotes environment and culture will benefit the community on the island as a whole by stimulating the economy.

It was decided by the MoCreebec Council that in order to overcome challenges to sustainable tourism development in Canada's North as well as challenges of social discourse and economic development, it was pertinent to invest in community capacity-building. Funded by government loans, the

MoCreebec designed a lodge that reflects community values as well as integrates the community into the operations. The lodge provides a very important social space to the community as there are currently not many places on Moose Factory Island where the community can congregate. The architects consulted and worked with all members of the community to ensure authentic design and construction that combined Cree values with a building that worked well in the sub-arctic. This has led to a space that is welcomed by the community. Despite the fact that some members of the community are still not comfortable with the presence of tourists, it has enabled the sharing of their culture and the remembering of traditions that were long since buried. This resulted in the Shabatwon, a 21st century version of the Cree gathering place. The working together of local people and having a community designed, owned, and run tourism establishment on the island has led to positive effects for the community. This created ownership among the community and has created capacity through the community becoming involved not only through consultation but through micro-enterprise. The Cree on Moose Factory Island are slowly becoming involved in tourism either as employees in the lodge (or other lodges on the mainland) or through providing other services or products to supplement the visitor experience on the island. Prior to this the jobs on the island were either unionized positions in the hospital or low paying retail. This also allows the community the opportunity to develop their own forms of economic prosperity that enriches and protects their culture and the land around them. The indigenous people are still able to practise their traditional livelihoods such as hunting and living a nomadic lifestyle off the land but are able to retain a community-based profit-sharing lodge that provides a sustainable livelihood to the community.

In addition, education is occurring and spreading throughout the Island. Education about conservation of energy and water and recycling programmes are being introduced community wide. Garbage clean-up on the island has also been implemented. Because of the environmental and social consciousness of tourism development on the island, there is a push in the community towards becoming aware of their environmental impact. The indigenous people are beginning once again to become connected to the land, which has led to understanding their consumption patterns and how this affects the greater global system. The lodge also provides a safe space for the community and is available for families in crisis. The lodge provides support through such activities as providing meals to families during a funeral, and space for meetings or events that are needed by the community.

It also provides a means to manage the land and integrate sustainability practices into the community. Emergency planning to reflect the impending vulnerabilities to climate change and the subsequent flooding and energy conservation initiatives such as solar and wind energy are being integrated. Moose Factory Island is an excellent example to other Northern communities, Aboriginal or otherwise, that are facing an economic downturn and developing a tourism product that reflects the community in a viable way to rejuvenate an island destination that has limited resources other than its nature and culture.

## Conclusion

The Cree Village eco-lodge has recently been listed as one of the Top Ten Eco-Destinations in North America by Natural Home Magazine. In 2005, the Cree Village eco-lodge was the recipient of the Air Canada Business of the Year Award by the Tourism Industry Association of Canada. This project was successful as it was led by the indigenous community representatives and was the result of a collective vision and leadership from the MoCreebec Steering Committee. This chapter identifies that community capacity development must be integral to communities in island destinations when developing tourism products, infrastructure and values that reflect the culture of the community. It also demonstrates that active leadership and involvement are needed to develop sustainable forms of tourism that also provide sustainable livelihoods. The Moose Factory Island is in a remote location in Northern Ontario, with little transportation infrastructure and very little tourism development in the area. This case portrays that successful initiatives can be developed in the absence of such infrastructure and identifies that one tourism project can lead to the long-term sustainability of a community.

### Acknowledgement

A special thank you to Chief Randy Kapashesit of the MoCreebec Council of the Cree Nation for the information that contributed to this case study.

# PART IV

# SYNTHESIS

# 14
# Innovative Initiatives to Sustainable Tourism Development

## Introduction

In order to overcome the challenges to managing island destinations in a sustainable manner, innovative initiatives can help identify practical ways to move forward. Innovative initiatives can consist of varying forms, and in several destinations have enabled the progression of sustainability through the principles of long-term planning, collaboration, education, the creation of dialogue and creating a cohesive vision for the destination. To move towards sustainability, island destinations require the participation of the local people, the definition of long-term strategies; a carefully designed tourism plan, intensive capacity-building and training of both national public officials and management in the destination and infrastructure support (Fennell, 2003; Hashimoto, 2004). This chapter provides details about innovative initiatives undertaken in various island destinations that were outlined in the previous good-practice case studies. Gili Trawangan, Indonesia, showcased the use of multi-stakeholder partnerships, leadership and education and awareness. Chumbe showcased leadership and education and awareness in addition to continuously evaluating and approving operations. Calviá, Spain, was the first tourism example of Local Agenda 21 and successfully executed the process from multiple stakeholder collaboration into the development and monitoring of a policy. Moose Factory Island illustrates community capacity-building and leadership through an integrated community-based tourism strategy. Gili Trawangan and Calviá also implemented an eco-tax, which although facing challenges in Calviá later in its life cycle, is a showcase for good governance because it identifies that funds to improve a destination can come from those who use it.

## Innovation one: Multi-stakeholder partnerships

Collaboration is seen as key to moving the tourist accommodation industry towards sustainability. Throughout the literature, cross-sector partnerships are recommended for their likelihood to result in sustainable development outcomes (Bramwell and Alletorp, 2001; Bramwell and Lane, 1993; Selin, 1999). A central role for sustainable destination management involves bringing together different organizations in order to establish common goals and create a framework for joint action (Berresford, 2004). The UNWTO revealed that public–private partnerships are the key principle for successful destination management (Foggin and Munster, 2003). Participants that have traditionally acted in isolation from each other need to learn how to cooperate (Halme, 2001). As no one organization does or can deliver tourism development a collaborative multi-stakeholder approach is necessary.

Collaboration through partnerships is described as a loosely coupled system of organizations and individuals that belong to various public and private sectors that come together in order to reach certain goals unattainable by the partners individually (Fadeeva, 2004; Selin, 1999). Partnership development involves starting dialogue and creating relationships between stakeholders to tackle a common issue. Each stakeholder individually has strengths to bring to the table such as knowledge, expertise and capital, and is more effective as a joint effort rather than an individual one. By working together, stakeholders can exchange information, learn from each other, develop innovative policies, adapt successfully to a changing environment and channel energy towards a collective good (Carr et al, 1998; Kernel, 2005).

> *A true partnership between the producer (the environment, the local culture and the people), the supplier (the tourism industry) and the consumer (the tourist) is critical for integrating community needs with the sustainable use of the environment while at the same time providing substantial profits to both foreign investors and local people (Carbone, 2005: 563).*

An inclusive collaborative approach has the ability to create social capital and thus contributes to the development of more sustainable forms of tourism (Kernel, 2005). It is through partnerships that organizations, government and communities are able to collectively address concerns and determine mutually agreed upon objectives that will benefit all stakeholders involved, thus embarking on a more sustainable approach to tourism development. The purpose of a partnership is to eventually produce consensus, harmony that will lead to new opportunities and innovative solutions. Partnerships must include the views of all stakeholders in a destination and identify various roles and responsibilities for each stakeholder so that they can contribute to the overarching goal of moving an island destination towards sustainable tourism. The key element of a partnership is that all:

- stakeholders are interdependent;
- solutions emerge by dealing constructively with differences;
- joint ownership of decisions are involved;
- stakeholders assume collective responsibility for the future direction of the domain; and

- partnerships remain a dynamic, emergent process (Gray, 1989: 11 in Selin, 1999: 262).

These key elements are the underlying principles for a multi-stakeholder partnership that provides a cohesive environmental vision that enables the island destination to focus resources, share information, increase environmental and social action in the destination, learn from the leaders and ultimately protect the resources that sustain the destination. The partnership must identify the initiatives that must be developed and implemented in addition to the roles and responsibilities of each stakeholder.

As adapted from Gray (1989), there are three phases to developing and implementing a partnership. These phases – which consist of identifying the problem setting; defining the problem; and implementing the problem – are necessary in order for a successful partnership to be implemented. In Gili Trawangan, the first two phases were implemented; however, there has been a gap in implementation. Implementation is the most difficult phase, as it requires the doing; however, with stakeholder dialogue, initiatives can be implemented.

### Phase one: Problem setting

1. Identify the common definition of the problem with all stakeholders.
2. Stakeholders must commit to collaboration and require shared values to be identified.
3. An inclusive process with all stakeholders must be implemented.
4. Identify the legitimacy, power and urgency of each stakeholder.
5. Identify an unbiased leader to facilitate the partnership development.
6. Identify key resources such as funding to support the partnership and information on best practices on how to move the sustainability agenda forward.

### Phase two: Direction setting

1. Identify the roles and responsibilities of each stakeholder in the partnership. Then identify accountability mechanisms such as reporting and monthly meetings relating to expertise and power.
2. Collaborate to identify a common, cohesive vision and create dialogue to work towards identifying key objectives and priorities.
3. Organize smaller working groups to determine ways to achieve the objectives.
4. Explore options and alternatives to achieving the stated objectives.
5. Consistently attempt to reach agreements on how issues will be dealt with and how objectives will be achieved.

### Phase three: Implementation

1. Consult with constituents to discuss the key objectives identified and how these will be achieved. Create dialogue to ensure constituents understand the trade-offs and support the agreement.
2. Build external support with the broader group of stakeholders to ensure compliance and implementation of initiatives.

3  Solidify a formal structure for decision-making within the community. The island committee may become formal to deal with issues or it may result in another organization developed to manage the initiatives in place.
4  Monitor the agreement and ensure continuous improvement results. (Adapted from Gray (1996: 61–64)

On the island of Gili Trawangan, Indonesia, a multi-stakeholder partnership was developed to deal with the issues relating to sustainability on the island. The partnership, which included both the local community and local businesses in addition to the foreign community and businesses and led by the local government, was perceived to be a vehicle for the development of a collective vision. The purpose of the partnership was to provide accountability and transparency to the operations of the Gili Eco-Trust and its revenue and to identify roles, responsibilities and accountability for the stakeholders on the island. In order to move past stakeholders not taking accountability for their actions or to push the accountability onto solely the local government, a multi-stakeholder partnership created dialogue between all stakeholders on the island on what the priorities on the island are (coral reef protection and regeneration and waste management were the two immediate concerns identified). The partnership, which is managed by an unbiased environmental coordinator/facilitator, has enabled the stakeholders to voice their concerns but also become involved in how to solve the major issues on the island. Stakeholders such as the businesses on the island have contributed time and capital to implementing environmental initiatives such as bio rock installations to regenerate coral, education programmes for conservation and recycling in the local schools, and waste collection bins for the island. This also contributed to a monthly meeting where all stakeholders can discuss issues to move the sustainability agenda forward.

In Moose Factory Island, multiple stakeholders were included in the development, design and management and operations of the eco-lodge to ensure that the community gained from the benefits. Running the lodge as a non-profit organization and putting the community needs at the forefront ensured that a meeting place for community members was provided and that local tribe members benefitted. Moose Factory Island is a unique example of how all three phases were achieved from the recognition of the challenges that the island community was facing as well as direction setting and implementation. Although the lodge is only at a break-even point, economic profitability has not been the only focus for this venture. Education and lifting community members out of poverty have also been achieved in addition to a renewed sense of pride and empowerment.

Managing relationships with primary stakeholders can result in more than just continued participation. By developing long-term relationships with primary stakeholders, a set of value-creating exchanges happen that are relational rather than transactional since 'transactional interactions can be easily duplicated and thus offer little potential for competitive advantage' (Hillman and Keim, 2001: 127). Collaboration and mutual trust leads to better cooperation and long-term viability; however, this will only be successful if the process is open, consultative and aims to set objectives where each stakeholder will benefit. Effective stakeholder management will build trust and give stakeholders a sense of empowerment and ownership in the development process.

## Innovation two: Policy development with implementation

Policies must promote development and management of a diverse tourism base that is integrated with other local economic activities, thereby reducing leakages from the destination and building linkages within (Hashimoto, 2004; ODI, 2007; Telfer, 2004).

It is well documented that policy is needed for sustainable tourism development and that policy is not static but is a progressive, adaptive, dynamic process that must be integrated and emphasizes the benefits of the local community (Aynsley, 1997; Crosby, 1996; Briassoulis, 2002; Dodds and Butler, 2010; Eber, 1992; Hall, 1994; Inskeep, 1991; Jackson and Morpeth, 1999; Krippendorf, 1982; Lickorish, 1992; Vera and Rippin, 1996). Policy players must also be accountable and although local involvement is fundamental to the planning and management of destinations (Coccossis, 1996; Meethan, 1998; Middleton and Hawkins, 1998; Ryan, 2002), actualization of empowerment by the community is needed.

The development of well designed effective policies are the building blocks for sustainable development; however, it must be implemented to be truly effective. Policy development plays a critical role in the potential sustainability of tourism destinations as it can provide a written document outlining future direction. Policy also needs to be proactive rather than reactive. According to the WTO (1998) there are many benefits to implementing a policy process. These are:

- logical staging and promotion of development projects;
- effective organization of public and private sectors;
- appropriate legislation for tourism including land use and environmental protection;
- regulation and tourist facility standards;
- use of critical path analysis techniques;
- securing of financing from both private and public sector tourist projects;
- strategy for financing tourist development should be secured;
- involvement of communities;
- human resource development for tourism given priority in order to offer quality expected by tourism markets (i.e. systematic approach of development personnel needs and determining training);
- effective marketing through objectives and strategies and coordination between various levels of government and between tourism office and private sector (WTO, 1998: 97–98).

One of the most well known forms of policy is the Local Agenda 21 (LA21) concept that was provided to local governments after being adopted at the

1992 Earth Summit in Rio de Janeiro. Although 6500 municipalities have participated in the LA21 process worldwide since 1992, there are few examples of this concept being applied in tourism, let alone islands. The LA21 approach aims to allow each community to set its own path towards sustainable development that is participatory and involves multiple stakeholders. LA21 can play a key role in ensuring the involvement of all stakeholders, taking into account such elements as ecosystems, planning, urbanization, transportation, agri- and aqua-culture. The LA21 approaches promote discussion and widespread public dissemination of projects and processes. The process itself has been criticized as being too high level and bureaucratic; however, the principles of this approach are innovative because it enables long-term visioning and stakeholder participation in setting the policy context of the destination. Allowing a local community to set its own development path and ensuring that all stakeholders have buy-in and accountability into this development plan is the benefit of a process like Local Agenda 21. In order for the policy development process to be successful in an island, the following initiatives must be implemented by an accountable, governing body that has the authority to make decisions. The process consists of the following steps:

1   Determine the current situation, impacts, issues and opportunities for tourism development (through the use of a multi-stakeholder approach).
2   Develop baseline indicators and benchmarks and outline options for development (e.g. no limits put in place, moderate limits, restrictions or other options).
3   Communicate this assessment to all stakeholders to gain input and feedback.
4   Using feedback and baseline indications, develop a policy that is holistic and adaptable and has measurable, actionable, time-specific objectives.
5   Implement the policy providing different stakeholders with key actions as well as accountability measures for their actions.
6   Continue to evaluate and monitor implementation and revise and adapt policy as necessary.

For successful policy and its implementation to take place, the authority that is in charge of developing and implementing the policy must be able to take a long-term view, involve all relevant stakeholders and have the responsibility and power to influence tourism development where necessary. A top-down as well as bottom-up approach is necessary. The results of LA21 initiatives frequently emphasize the value of creating communities in which people feel involved and committed (Wild and Marshall, 1999).

Calviá in Mallorca, Spain, is an example of an island destination that used this innovative method for policy development. Calviá actually conducted, implemented and evaluated the LA21 process. It utilized a comprehensive approach to decision-making that focused on long-term planning, integrating stakeholders to determine a cohesive vision for the destination and determined a means to diversify their tourism base and move from mass tourism to varying forms of eco-based tourism. This destination was able to innovate their tourism industry through the use of a comprehensive approach to inclusive decision-making.

## Innovation three: Community capacity-building

In order to achieve sustainable tourism there is a need to examine how empowerment through tourism can be fostered. If communities are able to participate in decision-making about tourism development they need first to understand tourism development processes, tourist needs and wants and the variety of development options. Access to relevant information is essential. The early stages of empowerment can then be transformed into the ability to determine their own development (Cole, 2006: 633).

It is vital for the local community to be incorporated in the tourism industry as they indicate the values and needs of society, speak for culture of the destination and reveal the attitude of the community towards tourism development (Lewis, 2005). Local people should contribute more as entrepreneurs and decision-makers in tourism and not only as employees. Locally owned, small-scale tourism is considered the most fitting means to achieve this, given that the benefits flow directly to the local populations; however, empowerment can happen at all levels and as much tourism development in islands is already developed as mass tourism, community capacity-building must be considered at all stages.

In relation to this, building community capacity is integral in the implementation of sustainability in island destinations. It has been identified that several of the challenges in islands are related to the lack of integration of the community in tourism planning and development. Developing local enterprises often requires appropriate support and mentoring together with training opportunities. Communities with a commitment to cultural and natural heritage protection through tourism have a higher degree of dependency upon the local natural environment (Fotiou et al, 2002). Capacity-building ensures the benefit of tourism to the local community by creating mechanisms whereby local people can be involved not only through consultation but through developing skills and entrepreneurial spirit to become part of the tourism industry and reduce the effects of leakage. Community capacity development places at the forefront local community needs, participatory approaches to decision-making, access to resources, equitable distribution of economic benefits, local entrepreneurship and economic diversity. Involvement of the local community includes ownership of the decision-making process and public participation in the positive economic benefits of tourism, typically by way of small-scale businesses whose incomes stay primarily within the local economy (Al-Oun and Al-Homoud, 2008). Local involvement creates a sense of ownership in the community, which translates into a willingness to participate in creating linkages with others in the destination and pride in ensuring its long-term viability (Swarbrooke, 1999).

Community capacity development is created through:

- consulting community members and identifying if and how they would like to participate in tourism development;
- providing training and education to community members on the potential for how they could participate in tourism development;
- encouraging the development of partnerships within the community and with other stakeholders such as industry to create support, foster trust and share best practices;
- developing funding mechanisms such as low-interest loans and revolving funds to support any entrepreneurial activities that the community or members thereof wish to focus on;
- providing skills development training for local community members;
- identifying mechanisms for feedback and measurement of success;
- determining if there is further guidance that can be provided to establish or maintain community-based tourism initiatives;
- establishing an appropriate policy framework to support this development.

In some islands, communities may not wish to be involved; however, they should be given the opportunity to participate and contribute to tourism development and their voice needs to be heard. As discussed in the previous chapter on Chumbe in Tanzania, community capacity was developed through the leadership of the private tourism business that pushed for multiple stakeholder collaboration, including the community, to be involved in conservation and tourism development. The local community was prompted to participate in sustainable tourism development by increasing their education and working as guides, thereby creating alternative sources of livelihood apart from solely fishing. In addition, many community members have gained increased knowledge and therefore are empowered to share this knowledge in their own villages.

In the case of Moose Factory Island, the island has and is facing a number of current challenges such as flooding and water level rise from climate change threats as well as poverty and loss of cultural identity. The Chief and his people collaboratively developed an eco-lodge as an attempt to provide a source of livelihood from an economic but also social and cultural position. The sustainable livelihoods approach, as discussed in Chapter 2, focuses on people rather than resources and it adopts an approach that looks at the vulnerability of assets of people. It was using this approach in order to build community capacity that the eco-lodge was built. The eco-lodge served as a means of bringing tourists to the community and has created a tourism-based economy on an otherwise economically weak island. It has also led to the employment of several Cree peoples and serves as a place for social gatherings on the island.

## Innovation four: Leadership

Each individual can make a difference and collectively people can empower and motivate others to move mountains. As demonstrated in Chumbe, it was one woman's vision, dedication and leadership that changed the island from an unknown island into a top eco-tourism lodge and an excellent example of how to foster alternative and sustainable livelihoods. Leadership by the Chief and the MoCreebec Steering Commitment on Moose Factory Island helped lead the community to embrace tourism on Cree terms and has provided a source of economic stability to the community. It has also instilled a new respect for Cree values in the community and is a role model for tourism development locally and in other northern communities. For sustainable tourism practices and policies to commence, leadership is required. Commitment to conservation and tourism development in islands is one of the most important factors for operational success. Since the natural environment is the primary attraction on islands it is imperative that the public, private and NGOs cooperate in managing these resources and enforcing an agreed-upon framework for its management. Individuals can be leaders for change; however, governments in developing and developed countries should provide political commitment to the sustainability of tourism in order to maintain the long-term viability of their destination (Fennel and Malloy, 1999; Robertson, 1989).

As discussed, governments can create challenges for sustainable tourism development; however, they can also be the catalysts for change. As identified in Calviá, the presence of a strong and visionary mayor led to the implementation of LA21, which started the change of the destination to adapt and implement measures for more sustainable tourism. Governments need to be strong leaders in order to move the agenda forward in terms of sustainable tourism and can do so by employing different economic or legislative instruments to impose a certain course on development. Options open to the government include supply side economics that involves the pursuit of policies aimed not at increasing demand but at increasing control. Once governments realize that tourism development is not just about increasing tourism numbers but instead increasing the well-being of the community and providing a long-term viable economy for businesses, they will plan and manage that destination differently. Instruments which could help to control land use such methods as taxation or regulation by law for land, building regulations, tax structures, financial and investment options, decreases in capital cost and operating costs (Font and Ahjem, 1999).

Incentive-driven non-regulatory approaches such as revolving fund mechanisms, tax breaks and regulatory relief for industry leaders are innovative initiatives that can be implemented to increase sustainability in islands. Fotiou et al (2002) identifies a strong need for fiscal and financial incentives and support for the private sector to implement environmental measures, especially for small and medium enterprises. These initiatives should be backed by policies and regulatory measures. The disproportionate degradation in environmental quality occurs when the pricing of tourist services is too low, as these prices do not consider public infrastructure and the environmental effects related to the development of the tourist industry (Palmer and Riera, 2003). These costs are produced, as the social and environmental costs of tourism are greater than the income generated. Tourism services are then undervalued by the tourists and in order to offset the very low costs associated with travel a tax can be levied. However, at the time of writing, there were not any positive examples of this being implemented in relation to tourism development in islands. An eco-tax, however, has been implemented in island destinations to fund sustainability initiatives in tourism and if properly implemented and managed, can be a successful tool.

## Eco-tax

One innovative initiative that can be implemented to fund sustainability projects in island destinations is an eco-tax. This can achieve an optimum social solution as the divergence between private and social costs may be eliminated so that the maximum social benefit from tourism is obtained. A tax is not necessarily a controlling measure, but more a source of additional revenue for the government or body to fund sustainability practices. It can be used as a tool in shifting the direction of tourism in the islands towards sustainability and quality. Examples of projects supported could include the purchase and improvement of a natural coastal area for public use, removal of unsightly or degraded buildings, financial assistance to farmers, technology initiatives, etc.

Establishing a price, tax or levy for tourist activities in order to internalize the external costs can be a useful mechanism (Palmer and Riera, 2003). As the consumer is becoming increasingly conscious about the environment in which they travel, in some instances they are willing to pay a tax to offset the environmental and social impacts caused by their actions (Dodds, Graci and Holmes, 2010). There are increasing examples demonstrating that the visitor is willing to pay for conservation measures in a destination (Becken, 2007; Dodds, Graci and Holmes, 2010; Lindsey and Holmes, 2002; Manaktola and Jauhari, 2007; Scott et al, 2003). Manaktola and Jauhari (2007) determined that the consumer is conscious about environmentally friendly practices and would prefer to use tourism products that have adapted these practices. They found that financial gains appear less prevalent than the more arcane 'feel-good' factor and that amplified awareness, conservation and partnerships need to take precedence over financial considerations when a voluntary payment made by visitors towards conservation is undertaken (Scott, Christie and Tench, 2003). In Gili Trawangan and Koh Phi Phi, the study from Dodds, Graci and Holmes (2010) indicated that the majority of tourists (75 per cent in Koh Phi Phi and 95 per cent in Gili Trawangan) were willing to pay an eco-tax of up to US$10 to protect and help conserve the islands' social and environmental aspects.

In Gili Trawangan, Indonesia, the development of an eco-tax was implemented by the dive shop owners to initially fund the fishermen to stop detrimental fishing practices. US$3 was charged per diver and US$1 per snorkeller. The funds from the eco-tax were initially used to fund the fishermen to stop fishing and to hire a coast guard to patrol illegal fishing. The money levied from the eco-tax, however, grew very quickly and is now being used to pay the salary of an environmental coordinator, install bio rocks for coral reef regeneration and deal with waste management issues on the island.

In the Balearic Islands, where Calviá is located, an eco-tax was implemented to develop a means to finance activities focused on improving the environment and level of basic infrastructure. The tax involved a flat rate charge averaging around one euro per night per adult tourist, collected by hoteliers. In the first year approximately 45m euros were raised. The tax is simply an instrument designed to generate revenue to assist in developing initiatives more in line with needs generated as a result of the pressure of tourism (Palmer and Riera, 2003). For a successful eco-tax, proper collection and transparency of monies must be communicated or it may result in a backlash from the tourism and local community (as turned out to be the case in Calviá) (Dodds, 2007a). Although many tourists and local residents were in favour of the tax, hoteliers and tour operators were very opposed to it. It was considered to be unfairly applied (it did not reach the many tourists staying in self-catering or unregistered accommodation), and was assumed to be one reason for a downturn in demand for the Balearics in the year it was introduced.

## Conclusion

The creation and implementation of multi-stakeholder partnerships, planning and policy principles being implemented into action, building local community capacity and developing financial mechanisms to support sustainability are practices that could be implemented in all destinations to help achieve sustainable tourism.

Some authors have criticized sustainable tourism, saying that it is not achievable in practice; however, this may be because they do not approach it in a holistic way. In order for tourism to be developed sustainably, many traditional development models do not provide the necessary adaptation and dynamic elements which are required to meet the needs of all stakeholders. This chapter sought to identify how practical-based solutions to sustainable tourism development could be implemented. These innovative initiatives are designed to overcome the specific challenges that face sustainable tourism development in island destinations. As tourism is a major focus of island destinations, the way forward must be determined in order to preserve the resources that economic growth and sustenance are based upon.

# 15
# Conclusion and The Way Forward

## Introduction

Due to their size and isolation, marginalization and resource limitations, islands can face significant challenges for the sustainable development of tourism. These same characteristics, however, also offer good examples of how islands can utilize innovative coping mechanisms. The resourcefulness of people on islands displays the ability of these communities to be resilient. This is shown in the promotion of their social capital (Baldacchino, 2005; Scheyvens and Momsen, 2008), which includes leadership, forward planning and long-term vision, successful partnership development and adaptability.

Although there is no single tool that addresses all social, environmental and economic issues at all levels, there are a number of basic principles that can aid in future sustainable tourism development. Achieving sustainable tourism, however, is not without its challenges and islands must adapt to ensure that they continuously monitor progress and realize that a dynamic and adaptive approach is considered.

## Ethical considerations in achieving sustainable tourism

While this book has outlined challenges to developing sustainable tourism and mentioned a number of issues that tourism faces to become more sustainable, it is also important to consider that sustainable tourism needs to be considered in an ethical context, especially when considering conflicting livelihoods. For example, tourism livelihoods sometimes conflict with fishing-based livelihoods, leading to violent protests and clashes (as occurred in the Galápagos Islands in September 2004, the Philippines, Honduras, etc). An ethical question arises in the decision to support one livelihood over another as well as who should have control over these management decisions for the well-being of islanders' livelihoods. With the pressure for advancement into the global market and need for jobs and economic income, some islands have welcomed foreign investors' money to build grand scale hotels on their beachfront, often cutting off access for locals (e.g. in Jamaica). Valuing money over the long-term implications of social well-being and environmental conservation is hardly ethical and should be actively opposed; yet few legal mechanisms exist that would enable such opposition against sovereign states, island or non-island, which choose to harm their natural heritage for profit (Kelman, 2007a). An ethical dilemma also appears in that once harm is realized, those in the know try to halt development or take bribes to stay quiet. This ethical issue is also the case for procurement. Since the small population of islands does not always supply the legal, technical and management expertise for large-scale tourism development, resources are essential yet outside assistance is often obtained, using government funds which could be seen as asking locals to accept payment for this development. As was demonstrated in St Kitts, a port was built to accommodate large cruise ships without regard to economic benefits that were not proportional to the level of visitations that resulted and the local population did not necessarily see the benefit. In addition, there were plans to build a new golf course and coastal hotel development that may provide short-term return but may not be sustainable because of impacts on the environment that supports them. In Malta, the development of a golf course on the water-scarce island of Gozo went ahead due to politics and power plays even though developers and government knew the impacts this would have. Such projects in islands may indeed extend competitiveness as a tourism destination and defer its decline in the life cycle, but cannot be regarded as an alternative to long-term planning and the decisions made could be questionable in regard to their ethics.

## Achieving sustainable tourism

No one ever said that achieving sustainable tourism would be easy and in almost every case, as demonstrated in this book, even the good case studies have identified that challenges exist. Sustainability is a global rather than local ideal and tourism can never be fully sustainable but it can move towards achieving it. The execution of sustainability initiatives proves difficult and many goals are not reached despite the impacts of existing forms of tourism being clear. One can argue, therefore, that the problem with achieving sustainability lies in implementation rather than definition (Dodds and Butler, 2010). It may be that one believes that achieving sustainable tourism development requires little more than a shift away from the traditional mode of tourism; however, a more holistic view must be considered. In order to ensure more sustainable tourism in the future, tourism must not operate in isolation from other industries and must take into consideration social, economic, environmental and political considerations. The idea that tourism must ensure that the local community is empowered and local interests are protected is often strongly challenged by an investor-based philosophy that stresses that community-based tourism and local empowerment are throwbacks to a discredited communist theory of governance – whereby everyone owns everything and the beneficiary profile becomes unclear, muddled and confused (Sinclair and Jayawardena, 2003). Issues with achieving sustainable tourism can also be related to a rampant sense of individualism that often takes priority over the common good. Tourism cannot survive if it continues to adapt to a traditional

**Figure 15.1** *Will we be here for future generations?*

ad hoc approach with static goals because the future environment, ecosystem, political, social and economic changes are unpredictable.

The following eight principles to achieve sustainable tourism concluded here cannot operate in isolation from each other and are not exhaustive in nature. Tourism is a dynamic industry and consumer and market forces are always shifting. Adapting to these forces while considering the long-term well-being of tourism as an industry as well as all stakeholders' interests is critical and values and interests of each player in the tourism development process should be carefully weighed. Focusing on the social capital or assets that people have and need and are affected by is a more holistic view than solely considering the resources which islands possess. As each island and each tourism development situation have different characteristics, each island must therefore consider their unique concerns and adapt accordingly. This book aimed to discuss the varying challenges which island tourism faces and offer some insight, through real-life case studies of innovations and successes that other island communities may benefit from.

## Multi-stakeholder partnerships and collaboration

Increasing levels of local involvement and considering the views of all stake-holders are pertinent in achieving sustainable tourism measures as they bring a wider group of stakeholders with common interests together (Farrell, 1994; Fasari et al, 2003; Middleton and Hawkins, 1998; Puppim de Oliviera, 2003; Tosun, 2001). Further, residents are regarded as the rightful custodians of an area and their needs should not be overridden by outside interests (Din, 1993; Ruhanen, 2009). Each stakeholder has a different view and in order to achieve more sustainable tourism, multiple stakeholders working together in collaboration to achieve goals which benefit the greater good is important. Collaboration and participation are needed to address the overall concept of the public good as well as environmental and social concerns in the context of development rather than solely market interests. It also must be mindful of the many other sectors – taxation, transportation, housing, social development, environmental conservation and protection and resource management. As these different industries all affect tourism, it cannot operate in isolation and for successful island sustainable tourism to result it must benefit more than just the business owners.

Chumbe Island demonstrated this through a collaborative effort in education. Training and education programmes about marine recreation were built through collaboration with the local island fishermen, schools as well as Chumbe staff and external environmental associations (MEAB, WWF, WESSA and NFWF). Not only does this programme benefit Chumbe, it also benefits school children, teachers, the guests who visit the island and local islanders who have been provided additional sources of livelihood. Gili Trawangan also showcases how the challenges of environmental and social issues can be overcome by developing a multi-stakeholder partnership. Involving foreigners, local islanders and their businesses, Gili Trawangan set up the eco-Trust as an avenue to work collaboratively with stakeholders to address identified issues. Additionally, one of the successes of Calviá's policy implementation was that multiple stakeholders collaborated to determine the baseline issues in tourism and worked together to develop indicators and policy for the rejuvenation of the area. This was an inclusive process, rather than relying on formal authority and hierarchal steering.

## Policy

Policy essentially sets out what a governing body should or should not do. Establishing an agreed-upon set of principles or objectives can help provide a vision for long-term development that considers multiple parties to help manage a destination. Governments need to establish an effective policy environment and play a stronger regulatory role if sustainable, equity-enhancing tourism is to emerge (Hall, 1999; Hall, 2000; Hall and Jenkins, 1995; Hunter-Jones, Hughes et al, 1995 and 2002; Scheyvens and Momsen, 2008; Stabler and Goodall, 1996). Effective policy formulation mechanisms need to be open and to encourage active participation from all stakeholders in order to engage their support and see through the implementation of policy objectives. It has to be dynamic, manage the continual tension between tourism development and sustainable development and involve a focus on communication, cooperation and the exchange of information and research, all with the objective of avoiding or solving conflict and gaining support for sustainable development (Elliot, 1997). Policy can provide positive incentives and promote conservation, ensure equality and guard against external forces – however, *only* if implemented. Policy implementation in tourism has various complexities such as the conflicting and different definitions, uncertain tourism growth predictions and the short-term view of operations within the tourism industry. Often challenges exist such as what type of government is in power, external market forces or who is implementing it. Often policy objectives are vague and there is no clear delineation of who should be responsible for its implementation. As Bianchi (2004) suggests, many problems of tourism development are associated with 'poor implementation of existing planning frameworks rather than being linked to the power struggles embedded in the changing political and economic landscapes of tourism development' (p. 497).

Calviá's LA21 initiative set forth a policy with specific indicators and measurement to limit growth. Calviá is one of the few island tourism destinations that actually set and then implemented a policy that was clear, concise and measurable. Through an inclusive process and led by a local government and strong leader, Calviá demonstrates how an island destination, even in its deterioration stage of the life cycle, can develop a policy which focuses on sustainable tourism. Although there have been challenges, Calviá has been used as an example worldwide for destinations moving towards sustainability policy. Although Hall and Jenkins (1995) declare that local participation to date may be more a form of accommodation rather than giving power to communities to make their own decisions, consultation and involvement in Calviá is an example of the policy process being more than just lip service. Calviá illustrates that with public participation in planning activities and gaining buy-in from stakeholders, shared decision-making and consensus building can help move ideas into actionable and measurable policies.

## Community capacity-building

The role of the community in island tourism development is important to the well-being of the host and to ensure fair and equitable benefits. Community capacity-building is not just empowering the local community to make informed decisions but also recognizing that each island community must acknowledge that fostering tourism's future on its unique assets may help differentiate itself to remain competitive and viable. By focusing on culture and the notion of social capital one can gain insight into how some islands have managed to enhance their position. Sibylle Riedmiller at Chumbe Island recognized that the local community must benefit from tourism and since its inception, local training has resulted in increased prosperity of people to enter other forms of livelihood. In order to break the poverty cycle that was riddling their community, it was decided by the MoCreebec Council on Moose Factory Island that it was best to invest in a Cree economy and promote individual and collective business opportunities that support the values of Cree people. The community overcame challenges to sustainable tourism development in Canada's North as well as challenges of social discourse and economic development by investing in community capacity-building. When residents feel like they had control over tourism, they are less likely to experience what others may see as negative cultural or social impacts (Berno, 2003). Milne (1993) suggests that where there are high levels of local ownership of business and strong economic linkages between tourism and other industries, benefits can be great. Building community capacity also is linked to good planning. The planning process could be enhanced by listening to and including stronger local participation (Boxill, 2004; Scheyvens and Momsen, 2008).

As described above, there must be adequate policy and management as well as local control and ownership. Building community capacity can lead to empowerment and local control and ownership and these principles ensure that conserving natural heritage for mainly tourism reasons does not lead to issues such as less interest in natural heritage without tourism (Kelman, 2007). Additionally islanders need to maintain control of their own livelihoods as often tourists bring their 'conservation concerns to islands leading at times to a colonialist mentality that superior outsiders must explain to inferior islanders how to manage their land and its resources' (p. 105).

In Calviá, the area has moved from solely mass tourism to developing agro-tourism and other forms of local tourism, and this is providing more income to local farmers helping sustain the agriculture industry in Mallorca and providing more control to local groups in deciding what types of tourism they want to develop. As communities gain control and make their own money they in turn become more self-sufficient and gain a sense of pride and self-dignity.

## Long-term planning

Long-term planning, although obvious to some, is limited in its approach in tourism development. Historically, there has been a mentality in tourism of 'if we build it, they will come'. This lack of planning to manage or optimize growth is very difficult to curtail after development has occurred (Dodds, 2007a). Destination management processes need to be based on a holistic framework for long-term planning and development that ensures that the benefits of tourism are equally distributed. A more collective and vision-oriented approach to tourism planning is needed to address broader and more pervasive environmental and sustainability challenges (Williams and Ponsford, 2009).

Illustrated in the case studies of Koh Phi Phi and St Kitts, as well as the other case studies, lack of planning has led these islands to develop with little consideration for the long-term well-being of the island. In Koh Phi Phi, the type of tourism developed was decided by few landowners who saw tourism as a quick way to make an economic return and the lack of long-term planning has resulted in a 'sun, sea and sand' tourism for the masses with little thought to water, sewage and other resource management and social consequences. Unsustainable construction from a lack of infrastructure planning was devastating when the 2004 Tsunami hit and lack of planning for infrastructure as well as increased growth has resulted in issues such as open sewage and waste problems in Koh Phi Phi and Hainan. In St Kitts, the island has not thought about a long-term development strategy for the island and has instead copied other destinations efforts, which has led to loss of competitive advantage and reliance on foreign air connections and hotels.

**Figure 15.2** *What will be her livelihood?*

Planning must not be a stand-alone practice and integration of planning efforts is needed. Wilkinson (1989) claims that government involvement in integrating tourism into national and regional planning is much needed as multinational hotels, tours and airline companies often have their own agendas and are not sensitive to local issues. Calviá ensured that when formulating their LA21 approach, multiple stakeholders were involved and that a long-term vision was developed. As Bianchi (2004) and Dodds (2007a,b) outline, a 20–30 year time frame for resource management and longevity of the industry should be considered. Stakeholders must be consulted, especially the local population, and buy-in to a long-term vision is imperative. As illustrated in Chumbe, a management plan was developed with extensive stakeholder participation and input. The island first developed a ten-year plan and has recently updated a 2006–16 plan. Much of Chumbe's success has been due to long-term planning and adequate management and a holistic vision for conservation and tourism.

## Leadership

Strong leaders who identify key agents/champions for change towards sustainable tourism or guide this process are another key element in achieving sustainable tourism. Leadership is a key characteristic for sustainable tourism. As outlined in the definition for sustainable tourism by the UNWTO (2005), 'Sustainable tourism development requires the informed participation of all relevant stakeholders, as well as strong political leadership to ensure wide participation and consensus building.'

In tourism strong leadership recognizes that tourism must be for quality than for growth. In Calviá, Margarita Najera Aranzabal, the mayoress, was a strong advocate of sustainable principles and it was under her leadership until

2003 when policy initiatives were mainly achieved. On Moose Factory Island, the project was successful as it was led by the indigenous community representatives and was the result of a collective vision and leadership from the MoCreebec Steering Committee. Leadership in sustainable tourism requires finding a balance between social, environmental and economic issues; however, there is no perfect solution and therefore compromise and balance must be felt.

Leadership, however, should not be considered solely in a governance context. One person can facilitate change as is evident in companies where one person creates and leads a green team or one person can champion an idea. Without having someone to get others excited about and understand why sustainability matters, often even the most well-intentioned plans and policies fail. In Chumbe, the vision and leadership of Sibylle Riedmiller enabled Chumbe to succeed but years of dealing with bureaucratic agencies and finding funding were part of her challenge. In Gili Trawangan, the leadership of Anna Walker, owner of the Big Bubble Dive Shop, led to the collection of the dive tax and subsequent implementation of the Gili Trawangan eco-trust. Often leaders face enormous challenges, as it requires passion, perseverance and patience for change to take place.

## Continuous improvement and evaluation

As sustainable tourism development issues are not exactly the same from place to place an evaluation procedure is necessary. As many authors have outlined, the formulation and evaluation of indicators or other forms of evaluation and measurement are needed (Lim and Cooper, 2009; Miller, 2006; Ruhahen, 2008; Tsaur, Wang et al, 1997). The use of indicators for monitoring progress towards sustainability has been advocated and discussed by many tourism researchers and tourism organizations (Ceron and Dubois, 2003; Choi and Sirakaya, 2006; Lim and Cooper, 2009; Miller, 2001; Miller and Twining-Ward, 2005; WTO, 2004). Indicators are good for measuring progress and also educating and promoting overall understanding of sustainability goals within the community. In order for sustainable tourism to be achieved, one must measure what they manage. In Calviá, there were originally 27 fields of reference and 750 indicators in order to allow study and evaluation; however, this was then modified to a more manageable 40 indicators with a 1–10 indicator value. Sustainability initiatives were also measured and evaluated. In 2001 figures were evaluated to show specific measurable improvements and issues. Of the 46 indicators developed, the overall balance in 2000 showed that 17 indicators (37 per cent) improved, 13 (28 per cent) did not change and 16 (35 per cent) continued to worsen (Ajuntament de Calviá 2001: 14).

In Chumbe, evaluation is an ongoing process and island management is continuously improving. CHICOP posts evaluation reports on its website and to its partners to update as well as provide wider education about both its successes as well as challenges. Improvements in tourism must start with evaluation. Sustainability must be defined in each island setting with clear, measurable objectives set in order for continuous improvement to be achieved.

## Education and awareness

Education is a key element needed in achieving more sustainable tourism; however, one must also add awareness to this as the widespread lack of adoption of the relatively few sustainability policies could be linked to company complacency, perceived cost or general lack of knowledge (Stabler and Goodall, 1997). As all stakeholders do not have equal power and influence over the decision-making process (Bianchi, 2004; Dodds, 2007a,b; Dodds and

Figure 15.3 *Education*

Butler, 2009; Hall, 2008), education and awareness building is necessary to ensure that all stakeholders understand tourism development and also the impacts and issues that it may cause. As in the case study of Sanya, China, although there was an idea of an eco-province, the elements of eco did not get implemented, as the concept was not understood. Despite the fact that policies about sustainability were in place, there was not only a lack of implementation; there was also little if any understanding about what sustainability is. In Sanya, many workers are migrant workers and most businesses are small and medium sized, operating on a short-term boom–bust cycle and education about long-term planning for sustainability was lacking. In Koh Phi Phi, the level of environmental awareness on the part of local developers as well as the government is evident in the failure to hold land encroachment in check. In many other islands lack of awareness or education has also resulted in failure to manage overdevelopment, reluctance to establish a marine or protected area and absence of controls over the dumping of wastes (Dodds and McElroy, 2007).

For sustainable tourism to be achieved, an understanding about what sustainability is as well as its benefits is needed. In Calviá the lack of awareness about the need for sustainability had resulted in mass tourism overdevelopment. It was only when information about the impacts of tourism were shared during the LA21 process that the need for change was illustrated. The adaptation of the LA21 policy in Calviá was only successful because the wider community was made aware of it. Calviá then undertook education programmes and campaigns that provided a cultural shift towards sustainability. Over 6000 citizens, almost 30 per cent of the adult population in Calviá, signed the document supporting the change model that LA21 represented. Calviá also undertook a number of educational programmes to facilitate change. For example, businesses were made aware that they could save money by recycling and reducing waste. Through this process, businesses increased recycling efforts by up to 70 per cent.

In Gili Trawangan, education of the tourists in the dive shops and hotels to refill their water bottles resulted in reducing waste. They also successfully educated the children about the importance of the reef and not littering, which in turn brought this information back to the home as the children were educating their parents. In both Gili Trawangan and Chumbe, it was through education about the importance of the reef that stopped fishermen using dynamite.

## Good governance and accountability

Good governance or governing for the benefit of all rather than the few is needed to ensure sustainable tourism development. For good governance to take place, it is often linked to leadership, as the political will of a dynamic, charismatic leader is needed to influence various stakeholders to participate and support sustainability initiatives and to raise awareness of the benefits of environmental and social integration into policy issues. As Trousade (1999) states, 'Better governance should clearly delineate local, regional and national roles and incorporate community input to mitigate against the adverse effects of tourism development while maximizing benefits' (p. 840). Good governance is also about transparency and accountability.

In Calviá, indicators for measuring were not only developed, they were reported on. Public reports and status of achievements as well as candid explanations of those that were not was part of the strength of the LA21 approach. Good governance also means enlightened government and this requires finding a balance between social, environmental and economic issues and in order to achieve this compromise, balance must be considered. New governance structures must ensure that open and informed debate occurs over community development issues without threats or fear of violent reprisals to outspoken individuals. Governance, sustainability or, for that matter, tourism development, cannot be discussed without considering the context of power. Power struggles arise from many different elements and have impeded policy implementation in all facets of government and industry and across many sectors, not just tourism (Dodds, 2007a,b; Hall, 1994). From the case studies illustrated in this book as well as a number of the examples from other authors, the quest for power rears its ugly head in many instances. Back-handed bribes have enticed government bureaucrats to overturn planning regulations and landowners' quests for economic returns have resulted in overdevelopment of accommodation infrastructure. Politicians, wishing for more votes, have often approved developments such as golf courses in water-scarce areas or casinos that end up causing social issues in the local population rather than generating money from tourists. It is difficult for those benefiting from tourism to make changes, as tourists do not vote. Different stakeholders often have different agendas and there is often a disconnect between ideal policy or development goals and achievable outcomes. Often the power of one does not necessarily translate into the well-being of all. 'Rampant individualism' is where individuals are free to act on what they believe to be their own immediate self-interest – essentially a mismatch between what is good for society or the community and what individual people think is good for them personally (Portney, 2003). Good governance means that the commons must be managed as a collective resource rather than benefiting the individual.

## Conclusion

This book has considered sustainable tourism in islands and has drawn attention to the challenges and successes that islands can face in tourism development. Chapter 1 first introduced the book by outlining the growth of tourism and its impacts. Definitions of sustainability have been historically vague and sustainable development, not to mention sustainable tourism, has faced increased issues because no one definition is agreed upon. The need for sustainability, however, is not contested and this chapter outlined specific impacts to showcase why movement towards sustainability practices is required. Chapter 2 then set the stage by discussing stakeholders in island destinations as well as the infamous tourism life cycle which is a useful tool to illustrate a destination's place along a development cycle. Stakeholder theory and an identification of key stakeholders as well as sustainable livelihoods were explained to give context to the discussions that would follow. Chapter 3 examined challenges and successes specific to islands as well as providing a definition of islands. Although there are thousands of different islands in the world, many share similar characteristics no matter if they are in warm or cold water or if they are large or small, independent or part of a larger nation. The purpose of this book was to demonstrate practical case studies surrounding sustainable tourism through challenges as well as successes. Parts II and III provide an overview of challenges and successes and three case studies to further illustrate these points. Six case study chapters illustrate these challenges and innovations and this book's aim was to provide a systematic approach to addressing sustainable tourism of islands through the illustration of useful and practical examples.

No manager or tourism developer, however, has all the answers, nor can they extrapolate information without guidance. Therefore Part IV of this book sought to illustrate some examples and provide eight guiding principles for moving forward.

Developing sustainable tourism development brings about many challenges that islands and their populations must face. Often islands, while labelled as tiny, vulnerable or fragile, can develop more sustainable forms of tourism successfully and it is hoped that, with the information provided in this book, managers, investors, planners and others will gain insight into both impediments and innovations for achieving sustainable tourism. As it becomes more obvious that for the future of tourism, ecosystems and biodiversity need to be preserved, growth is not always beneficial and the quality of life of the community is needed. Therefore, it is important to learn from other destinations and share both good and bad practices.

## Key management implications

When examining islands and tourism development options available, it is first useful to identify at what stage of Butler's tourist area life cycle islands are as well as understand the broad economic, social and environmental forces that affect them.

An emerging issue from this book as well as other studies of tourism is that tourism is dynamic and changing and is influenced by a complex number of factors. Such factors include the level of competition, the political environment, globalization, economic forces and infrastructure to identify a few.

Tourism faces constant changes due to market forces, environmental threats as well as society's expectations. In order to manage island destinations for a long-term viable future, it is important to share lessons learned. Chapters on Hainan, Koh Phi Phi, St Kitts and Cayos Cochinos illustrate that islands can be very different and face unique challenges from the development of tourism. They also illustrate that destinations may follow several different development paths.

Understanding the different views, beliefs and concerns of all stakeholders is one way to manage a destination. As illustrated in Chapters 2 and 4, stakeholder inclusion is necessary in tourism development and exclusion can even impede development in some cases. In addition, the livelihoods of these stakeholders, especially at the community level, need to be considered if sustainability can be truly achieved.

The difficulty of managing growth is an issue that has occurred in both Hainan and Koh Phi Phi and policy and governance is illustrated as a challenge in both. The race for economic returns has affected the attractiveness of both destinations and their attractiveness is at risk because of environmental pressures. In Honduras the opposite was seen. Conservation must not come at a cost to sustainable livelihoods for those living in the area and if it prevails, this can lead to alienation and feuding between stakeholders. Social issues in the Cayos Cochinos were more evident than environmental ones; however, as an island destination it is also at the beginning of its life cycle and could learn from others further along the development path. Unfortunately examining impacts for tourism and planning for growth is difficult as most studies examine consequences after they have occurred and moving forward can be difficult once infrastructure and damage has already been done. For islands earlier in their life cycle, these case studies provide three different examples of challenges faced. As Chapter 4 illustrates, there are a number of issues to consider and almost every island will be able to identify with the barriers to achieving sustainability.

While one must learn from mistakes, positive examples provide useful tools for managers. In Chapters 9–13, positive and practical examples of management, planning and stakeholder inclusion through the form of partnerships and collaboration are put forward. Due to their size and unique location, islands can benefit from tourism without losing their appeal. Chumbe and Moose Factory Island illustrate that the local community must benefit but gains are not instantaneous. As an island destination, growth has been capped and the pristine environment that attracts tourism is preserved and coveted. Although it has been a long process, Chumbe now has high occupancy and tourism income pays for conservation and education efforts. Moose Factory Island is providing alternative and sustainable livelihood contribution to the whole community, and this has helped restore empowerment and connection to traditional values. Calviá in Mallorca showcases that policy, when formed with an inclusive approach, can see benefits but leadership and communication are necessary. Although this example is from the early 2000s and leadership has changed and some negative issues have arisen, many benefits were felt and overall the island has shifted gears in tourism management and has a much longer-term vision. Gili Trawangan outlines that collaboration can solve apathy and make substantial change which benefits both foreign and local business owners and residents. These case studies, although unique, offer ideas of how tourism can be done more sustainably.

Although there is a wealth of literature about sustainable tourism as well as islands, successes tend to be one offs and not always applicable across broader contexts. This book has tried to illustrate case studies that could be applied to other islands even though governance and other specific characteristics may differ. The authors of this book tried to specify details of the nature of tourism development as well as the settings in which tourism took place.

Costs and benefits have been highlighted in each case study with specific details of tourism numbers, social and environmental impacts outlined. Stakeholders in the case studies were outlined and an understanding of the consequences, both positive and negative, were explained so that the reader could define what elements were responsible for change.

## Future issues and research

### Transportation and climate change

This book's purpose was to discuss sustainable tourism in islands; however, a critical issue that must be considered for the future viability of tourism to islands is transport. How one gets to the destination is continuing to be a contested issue in tourism as the impacts of climate change increase. Should the UK or Europe, top outbound travelling markets, start to limit flights or should aviation become more expensive with the increased scarcity of fuel are key issues that need to be considered in the sustainability of islands. Future research is needed to examine the impacts and potential solutions to transport and what options are available to islands.

### Competitiveness and adaptation

Competitiveness is also an issue that requires further investigation. The challenge to remain competitive is not about implementing new services or infrastructure, it is also about adaptation and survival and this too links to impeding threats of climate change in islands – many of which are the most low lying land masses. As Cooper (2006: 58) states, 'it addresses the critical issues of organizational adaptation, survival and competitiveness in the face of increasing discontinuous environmental change'.

Many island destinations have now developed 'sun, sea and sand' tourism and the product faces competition from not only other islands but coastal mainland areas as well. Rejuvenation has been the focus of some literature (Dodds, 2008b; Bianchi, 2004 and others) and further studies about how islands can grapple with areas that have already been developed should be illustrated.

Good management is about understanding issues and opportunities as well as using this knowledge to share information, create linkages and adapt to new realities. Competitiveness is about optimizing knowledge management and applying the knowledge assets available to destinations in order to create competitive advantage (Cooper, 2005: 59). This book has briefly touched on adaptive management; however, further studies are needed to look at tourism's linkages to other sectors.

### Innovation

Although this book has discussed some successes of islanders having sustainable livelihoods and new technologies benefiting long-term sustainability through resource management, further research into innovations specifically for islands would be useful. Are there other industries or sectors that have demonstrated innovations that could be applied to tourism? As tourism is an industry made of many different sectors, different disciplines could be examined to see what advances could be applied to island tourism.

## The way forward

To achieve sustainability, island tourism must look at existing major problems in the industry rather than just concentrating on minor new developments (Butler, 1998; Wheeler, 1993) and must be holistic and integrated in its approach. For many tourism destinations, especially islands, there is high competition and low differentiating factors and the product has become commoditized. As tourism has been put forth as the key driver for economic growth and sustainability within the island, long-term strategies need to be put in place to adapt to changing trends and markets.

Experience from the life cycle literature suggests that sustainable destinations must constantly innovate to maintain and grow their position in a

**Figure 15.4** *Fishing boats or tourist boats?*

changing global marketplace. Tourism communities have the opportunity to reinvent themselves as sustainable destinations – using sustainability as a marketable quality. In today's changing marketplace, the consumer is increasingly becoming aware of the impacts of tourism. The eight principles which were illustrated by the case studies presented hope to offer a framework for moving sustainable tourism forward to become the norm, rather than the exception in tourism development.

This book has attempted to address a gap in the current literature by providing a synthesized, practical look at challenges and successes in achieving sustainable tourism in islands. Rather than collecting a number of different chapters, the authors wrote this book from first-hand knowledge of good and bad elements of tourism development that they have witnessed in islands. Worldwide case studies and examples of islands have examined stakeholder issues, planning challenges and long-term management strategies. In particular this book has incorporated a detailed analysis of socio-cultural, environmental, political and economic issues that islands have experienced in different stages of development. Given the plethora of island studies that have been undertaken worldwide, this book has advanced the conceptual understanding of island tourism development as it relates to sustainable tourism.

# References

Agarwal, S. (1997) 'The resort cycle and seaside tourism: an assessment of its applicability and validity', *Tourism Management*, 18(2): 65–73

Agarwal, S. (2002) 'Restructuring seaside tourism: the resort lifecycle', *Annals of Tourism Research*, 29(1): 25–55

Agrawal, A. (2001) 'Common property institutions and sustainable governance of resources', *World Development*, 29(10): 1649–72

Aguilo, P.M., Alegre, J. and Riera, A. (2001) 'Determinants of the price of German packages on the island of Mallorca', *Tourism Economics*, 7(1): 59–74

Altinay, L., Var, T., Hines, S. and Hussain, K. (2007) 'Barriers to sustainable tourism development in Jamaica', *Tourism Analysis*, 12(1–2): 1–13

Alvarez Gil, M. J., Burgos Jimenez J., et al (2001) 'An analysis of environmental management, organizational context and performance of Spanish hotels', *Omega. The International Journal of Management Science*, 29: 457–71

Andriotis, K. (2001) 'Tourism planning and development in Crete: recent tourism policies and their efficacy', *Journal of Sustainable Tourism*, 9(4): 298–316

Anguera, N., Ayuso, S. et al (2000) Implementation of EMS's in seasonal hotels. In: R. Hillary, *Assuring Sustainability. ISO 14000 Case Studies and Practical Experiences*. Sheffield: Greenleaf Publishing: 162–71

Aragon-Correa, J. A. and Sharma, S. (2003) 'A contingent resource-based view of proactive corporate environmental strategies', *Academy of Management Review*, 28(1): 71–88

Ashley, C. and Carney, D. (1999) *Sustainable Livelihoods: Lessons from Early Experience*. London: DFID

Aynsley, K. (1997) 'Problems in international environmental governance or a policy analysis look at the world', *Australian Journal of Public Administration*, 56(2): 54–66

Ayuntament de Calvia (1997) Calvia Local Agenda 21 Plan of Action. Calvia, Spain

Ayuntament de Calvia (2001) Calvia Local Agenda 21: Observatory on sustainability and quality of life: 1997–2000. Calvia, Spain

Baldacchino, G. (2005) 'The contribution of 'social capital' to economic growth: lessons from island jurisdictions', *The Round Table*, 94(1): 31–46

Baldacchino, G. (2007) *A World of Islands: An Island Studies Reader*. Agenda Academic and Institute of Island Studies, Malta and Canada

Baldacchino, G. and Milne, D. (eds) (2009) *The Case for Non-Sovereignty: Lessons from Sub-National Island Jurisdictions*. London: Taylor and Francis

Bansal, P. and Roth, K. (2000) 'Why companies go green: a model of ecological responsiveness', *Academy of Management Journal*, 43(4): 717–36

Bardolet, E. and Sheldon, P. (2008) 'Tourism in archipelagos: Hawaii and the Balearics', *Annals of Tourism Research*, 35(4): 900–23

Barrowclough, D. (2007) 'Foreign investment in tourism and small island developing states', *Tourism Economics*, 13(4): 615–38

Baum, T. (1997) The fascination of islands: a tourist perspective. In: D. Lockhart and D. Drakakis-Smith (eds) *Island Tourism: Problems and Perspectives*. London: Mansell: pp 21–35

Baum, T. (1999) 'Themes and issues in comparative destination research: cases from the North Atlantic', *Tourism Management*, 20(3): 627–33

Becherel, L. and Vellas, F. (1999) The marketing concept and international tourism marketing. In: F. Vellas and L. Becherel (eds), *The International Marketing of Travel and Tourism: A Strategic Approach*. Gosport: Palgrave

Becken, S. (2007) 'Tourists' perception of international air travel's impact on the global climate and potential climate change policies', *Journal of Sustainable Tourism*, 15(7): 351–368

Beenntje, H.J. (1990) *A Reconnaissance Survey of Zanzibar Forests and Coastal Thicket*. Zanzibar: Finnida-Cole

Berman, S. L., Wicks, A.C. et al (1999) 'Does stakeholder orientation matter? The relationship between stakeholder management models and firm financial performance', *Academy of Management Journal*, 42(5): 488–508

Berno, T. (2003) Local control and the sustainability of tourism in the Pacific. In: D. Harrison (ed), *Pacific Island Tourism*. London: Cognizant Publications (pp 94–109)

Berresford, J. (2004) *Tourism in the Region. Regional Review Hearing*, pp 1–11

Berry, M.A. and Rondinelli, D.A. (1998) 'Proactive corporate environmental management: a new industrial revolution', *Academy of Management*, 12(2): 38–50

Bianchi, R.V. (2004) 'Tourism restructuring and the politics of sustainability: a critical view from the European periphery (The Canary Islands)', *Journal of Sustainable Tourism*, 12(6): 495–529

Black, A. (1996) Negotiating the tourist gaze: the example of Malta. In: J. Boissevain (ed), *Coping with Tourists: European Reactions to Mass Tourism*. USA: Bergham Books

Bohdanowicz, P. (2005) 'European hoteliers' environmental attitudes: Greening the business', *Cornell Hotel and Restaurant Administration Quarterly*, 46(2): 188–204

Boissevain, J. and Theuma, N. (1998) Contested space. Planners, tourists, developers and environmentalists in Malta. In: S. Abram et al (eds), *Anthropological Perspectives on Local Development*. London: Routledge, pp 96–119

Boxill, I. (2004) 'Towards an alternative tourism for Jamaica', *International Journal of Contemporary Hospitality Management*, 16(4): 269–72

Bramwell, B. and Lane, B. (1993) 'Sustainable tourism: an evolving global approach', *Journal of Sustainable Tourism*, 1(1): 1–4

Bramwell, B. and Alletorp, L. (2001) 'Attitudes in the Danish tourism industry to the roles of business and government in sustainable tourism', *International Journal of Tourism Research*, 3: 91–103

Bressers, H.T.A. and Rosenbaum, W.A. (2000) 'Innovation, learning, and environmental policy: overcoming 'a plague of uncertainties'', *Policy Studies Journal*, 28(3): 523–539

Brewer, J. and Hunter, A. (1989) *Multimethod Research. A Synthesis of Styles*. Newbury Park: Sage Publications

Briassoulis, H. (2002) 'Sustainable tourism and the question of the commons', *Annals of Tourism Research*, 29(4): 1065–85

Briguglio, L. and Briguglio, M. (1995) Sustainable tourism in the Maltese Islands. In: Briguglio et al (eds) (1996) *Sustainable Tourism in Islands and Small States: Case Studies*. London: Pinter, pp 162–79

Brondo, K. (2005) *Cayos Cochinos Social Science Season 2005 Report*. Michigan State University, East Lansing, MI

Brondo, K.V. and Woods, L. (2007) 'Garifuna land rights and ecotourism as economic development in Honduras' Cayos Cochinos marine protected area', *Ecological and Environmental Anthropology*, 3(1): 2–18

Bruce, D. and Cantallops, A.S. (1996) The walled town of Alcudia as a focus for an alternative tourism in Mallorca. In: L. Briguglio, R. Butler, D. Harrison, and W.L. Filho (eds), *Sustainable Tourism in Island and Small States: Case Studies*. London: Pinter, pp 241–61

Bruner, A., Rosenfeld, A. et al (1999) *The Green Host Effect: An Integrated Approach to Sustainable Tourism and Resort Development*. Washington, DC: Conservation International

Brunkhorst, D.J. and Coop, P. (2003) 'Tibuster commons: synergies of theory and action in new agricultural commons on private land', *Ecological Management and Restoration*, 4(1): 13–22

Budeanu, A. (1999) A tour to sustainability. A discussion on tour operators possibilities for promoting sustainable tourism. *International Institute for Industrial Environmental Economics*. Lund, Sweden: Lund University, p 84

Buhalis, D. (1999) 'Relationship in the distribution channel of tourism: Conflicts between hoteliers and tour operators in the Mediterranean region', *International Journal of Hospitality and Tourism Administration*, 1(1): 113–39

Butler, R.W. (1980) 'The concept of a tourist area cycle of evolutions: implications for management of resources', *Canadian Geographer*, 24(1): 5–12

Butler, R.W. (1990) 'Alternative tourism: pious hope or Trojan horse?', *Journal of Travel Research*, 28(3): 40–5

Butler, R.W. (1993) Tourism – an evolutionary perspective. In: J.G. Nelson, R. Butler and G. Wall (eds) *Tourism and Sustainable Development: Monitoring, Planning and Managing*, Department of Geography Publication Series No. 37. Waterloo: University of Waterloo

Butler, R.W. (1998) 'Sustainable tourism – looking backwards in order to progress?' In: C.M. Hall and A. Lew (eds), *Sustainable Tourism: A Geographical Perspective*. Harlow: Longman, pp 25–34

Butler, R.W. (1999) 'Sustainable tourism: a state-of-the-art review', *Tourism Geographies*, 1(1): 7–25

Carbone, M. (2005) 'Sustainable tourism in developing countries: poverty alleviation, participatory planning and ethical issues', *The European Journal of Development Research* 17: 59–565

Carney, D. (n.d.) *Sustainable Livelihoods Approach: Progress and Possibilities for Change*. London: DFID

Carr, D.S., Selin, S.W. and Schuett, M.A. (1998) 'Managing public forests: understanding the role of collaborative planning', *Environmental Management*, 22(5): 767–76

Carroll, A.B. (2000) The four faces of corporate citizenship. In: J.E. Richardson (ed) *Business Ethics*, Vol 1. Guildford, CT: Dushkin/McGraw-Hill, pp 187–91

Carter T.R. (1991) *The Hatch Index of Climatic Favourability*. Helsinki: Finnish Meteorological Institute, 18pp

Cass, C. (2006) The economic value of tourism to the communities within the marine protected area of the Cayos Cochinos and how this value can be enhanced. Retrieved

on 6 May 2008 from http://www.opwall.com/Library/Honduras/Honduras%20
Marine/Socioeconomic/2005%20Claire%20Cass%20dissertation.pdf

Central Intelligence Agency (2007) Saint Kitts and Nevis, *The World Factbook*
online at: https://www/cia/gov/library/publications/the-world-factbook/geos/sc.html
(accessed Nov 2007)

Ceron, J.P. and Dubois, G. (2003) 'Tourism and sustainable development indicators.
The gap between theoretical demands and practical achievements', *Current Issues in
Tourism*, 6(1): 54–73

Cespedes Lorente, J.J., Burgos Jimenez, J. et al (2003) 'Stakeholders' environmental
influence: an empirical analysis in the Spanish hotel industry', *Scandinavian Journal
of Management*, 19: 333–58

Chambers, R. and Conway, G.R. (1992) *Sustainable Rural Livelihoods: Practical
Concepts for the 21st Century*, Discussion Paper 296. Brighton: University of
Sussex, Institute of Development Studies

Charnley, S. (2005) 'From nature tourism to ecotourism? The case of the Ngoro Ngoro
conservation area, Tanzania', *Human Organization*, 64(1): 75–88

Cheyne, J. and Barnett, S. (2001) 'The greening of accommodation. Stakeholder perspectives of environmental programmes in New Zealand hotels and luxury lodges',
*Journal of Corporate Citizenship*, Spring

Child, J. and Tse, D.K. (2001) 'China's transition and its implications for international
business', *Journal of International Business Studies*, 32(1): 5–29

China, N. T. A. o. t. P. s. R. o. (2002) *The Yearbook of China Tourism Statistics.*
Beijing: National Tourism Administration of the People's Republic of China

Choi, S., Lehto, X.Y. and O'Leary, J.T. (2007) 'What does the consumer want from a
DMO website? A study of US and Canadian tourists' perspectives', *International
Journal of Tourism Research*, 9(2): 59–72

Choi, H.C. and Sirakaya, E. (2006) 'Sustainability indicators for managing community
tourism', *Tourism Management*, 27(6): 1274–89

Choy, Dexter, J.L. (1992) 'Life cycle models for Pacific Island destinations', *Journal of
Travel Research*, 30(3): 26–31

Chumbe Island Coral Park (2009) *The Chumbe Island Coral Park Project in
Zanzibar/Tanzania: Saving a Pristine Coral Island for Future Generations.* Chumbe
Island, Tanzania. Retrieved from www.chumbeisland.com

Clarke, H. (1997) 'Australian tourism industry policy: a new view', *Tourism
Economics*, 3(4): 361–77

Clarkson, M. (1995) 'A stakeholder framework for analyzing and evaluating corporate
social performance', *Academy of Management Review*, 20(1): 92–117

Clifton, J. and Benson, A. (2006) 'Planning for sustainable ecotourism: the case for
research ecotourism in developing country destinations', *Journal of Sustainable
Tourism*, 14: 238–54

Cloin, J. (2006) *Overview of Pacific Regional Biofuel Activities*, Suva, Fiji: SOPAC
(Pacific Islands Applied Geoscience Commission)

Coccossis, H. (1996) Tourism and sustainability: perspectives and implementation. In:
G.K. Priestley, J.A. Edwards and H. Coccossis (eds) *Sustainable Tourism: European
Perspectives*. UK: CAB Internationa

Coccossis, H. (2002) Island tourism development and carrying capacity. In D.J. Gayle,
Y. Apostologpoulos (eds) *Island Tourism and Sustainable Development: Caribbean,
Pacific and Mediterranean Experiences*. Westport, CT: Praeger, pp 131–44

Cole, S. (2006) 'Information and empowerment: the keys to achieving sustainable
tourism. *Journal of Sustainable Tourism*', 14(6): 629–44

Collins, A. (1999) 'Tourism development and natural capital', *Annals of Tourism
Research*, 26(1): 98–109

Conlin, M. (1995) Rejuvenation planning for island tourism: the Bermuda example. In: M. Conlin and T. Baum (eds), *Island Tourism: Management Principles and Practice*. UK: Wiley, pp 181–202

Colin, M.V. (1996) Revitalizing Bermuda: tourism policy planning in a mature island destination. In: L. Harrison and W. Husbands (eds), *Practicing Responsible Tourism*. Canada: Wiley, pp 80–101

Conlin, M.V. and Baum, T. (1994) Comprehensive human resource planning: an essential key to sustainable tourism in island settings. In: C.P. Cooper and A. Lockwood (eds), *Progress in Tourism and Hospitality Management*. London: Wiley, pp 259–70

Conlin, M.V. and Baum, T. (1995) *Island Tourism: Management Principles and Practice*. Chichester, UK: Wiley

Connell, J. (2007) 'Islands, idylls, and the detours of development', *Singapore Journal of Tropical Geography*, 28(2): 116–35

Cooper, C. (2006) 'Knowledge management', *Annals of Tourism Research*, 22(1): 47–64

Cooper, C., Fletcher, J. Gilbert, D. and Wanhill, S. (1998) *Tourism: Principals and Practice*, 2nd edn. London: Pearson

Cooper C. and Lim, C. (2009) 'Beyond sustainability: optimising island tourism development', *International Journal of Tourism Research*, 11(1): 89–101

Cree Village Ecolodge (2010) http://www.creevillage.com/. Last accessed March 19, 2010

Crosby, B. (1996) 'Policy implementation: the organizational challenge', *World Development*, 24(9): 1403–15

Cushman, C.A., Arry, B., Field, C., Aniel, D., Ass, L. and Stevens, T.H. (2004) 'External costs from increased island visitation: results from the southern Thai islands', *Tourism Economics*, 10(2): 207–19

Dalrymple, K., Wallace, J. and Williamson, I. (2004) 'Innovations in rural land policy and tenure in southeast Asia', *Mekong Update and Dialogue*, 9(2): 2–4

De Albuquerque, K. and McElroy, J.L. (1992) 'Caribbean small-island tourism styles and sustainable strategies', *Environmental Management*, 16(6): 619–32

De Koning, J. and Thiesen, S. (2005) 'Aqua Solaris – an optimized small scale desalination system with 40 litres output per square metre based upon solar-thermal distillation', *Desalination*, 182: 503–9

Denscombe, M. (1998) *The Good Research Guide for Small Scale Social Research Projects*. Buckingham: Open University Press

Dieke, P.U.C. (2003) 'Tourism in Africa's economic development: Policy implications', *Management Decision*, 41(3): 287

Din, K. (1993) Dialogue with hosts: an educational strategy towards sustainable tourism. In: M. Hitchcock, V. King, and M. Parnwell (eds), *Tourism in South-East Asia*. London, New York: Routledge, p 328

Dodds, R. (2003) Is sustainable tourism policy a viable option for rejuvenating traditional destinations, *Developing New Markets for Traditional Destinations*. TTRA – Canada Conference, Saint John, NB, October 2–5

Dodds, R. (2005) *Calvia, Spain: Local Agenda 21 and Resort Rejuvenation in Making Tourism More Sustainable*. UNEP/WTO, pp 167–71

Dodds, R. (2006) *Caribbean Regional Sustainable Tourism Development Programme Report for Soft Adventure Study*, Barbados: CTO/EU, Barbados

Dodds, R. (2007a) 'Sustainable tourism and policy implementation: lessons from the case of Calviá, Spain', *Current Issues in Tourism*, 10(1): 296–322

Dodds, R. (2007b) 'Malta's tourism policy: standing still or advancing towards sustainability?', *Island Studies Journal*, 2(1): 47–66

Dodds, R. (2008a) *Power and Politics: Sustainability in Islands? Determining Barriers and Successes to Implementing Sustainable Tourism Policy in Two Mediterranean Islands: Calvia, Spain and Malta.* Saarbrücken, Germany: VDM Verlag

Dodds, R (2008b) 'Sustainable tourism – rejuvenation or critical strategic initiative?', *Anatolia,* 18(2): 277–98

Dodds, R. and Basu. S. (2008) *Is Change a Constant? An Assessment of Stakeholders Participation in Sustainable Tourism Practices in Tofino, BC.* TTRA Canada Conference, Victoria, BC, 15–17 October 2008

Dodds, R. and Butler, R.W. (2009) Inaction more than action: barriers to the implementation of sustainable tourism policies. In: S. Gössling, M. Hall and D.B. Weaver (eds) *Sustainable Tourism Futures.* New York: Routledge

Dodds, R. and Butler, R.W. (2010) 'Barriers to implementing sustainable tourism policy in mass tourism destinations', *Tourismos: An International Journal of Tourism* (in press)

Dodds, R., and Graci, S. (2009) 'Canada's tourism industry – mitigating the effects of climate change: a lot of concern but little action', *Tourism and Hospitality: Planning and Development,* 6(1): 39–51

Dodds, R. and Kelman, I. (2008) 'How climate change is considered in sustainable tourism policies: a case of the Mediterranean islands of Malta and Mallorca', *Tourism Review International,* 12(1): 57–70

Dodds, R. and McElroy, J. (2008) 'St Kitts at a crossroads', *ARA Journal of Travel Research,* 1(2): 1–10

Dodds, R., Graci, S. and Holmes, M. (2010) 'Does the tourist care? A comparison of visitors to Koh Phi Phi, Thailand and Gili Trawangan, Indonesia', *Journal of Sustainable Tourism,* 19(2): 207–22

Domroes, M. (2001) 'Conceptualizing state-controlled resort islands for an environmentally friendly development of tourism: the Maldivian experience', *Journal of Tropical Geography,* 22(2): 122–37

Donaldson, T. and Preston, L.E. (1995) 'The stakeholder theory of the corporation: concepts and evidence', *Academy of Management Review,* 20(1): 65–86

Douglas, C.H. (2006) 'Small island states and territories: sustainable development issues and strategies – challenges for islands in a changing world', *Sustainable Development,* 14: 75–80

Dredge, D. (2006) 'Policy networks and the local organization of tourism', *Tourism Management,* April: 269–80

Duffy, R. (2000) 'Shadow players: ecotourism development, corruption and state politics in Belize', *Third World Quarterly,* 21(3): 549–65

Easterly, W. and Kraay, A. (2000) 'Small states, small problems? Income, growth, and volatility in small states', *World Development,* 28(11), 2013–27

Eber, S. (1992) *Beyond the green horizon: a discussion paper on principals for sustainable tourism,* Goldalming, Surrey: Tourism Concern/WWF

EcoPlanet.net (1995) *Sustainable Tourism Policies and Guidelines.* Nassau: Out Islands of the Bahamas, Ministry of Tourism

Edgell, D. (1995) 'A barrier-free future for tourism?', *Tourism Management,* 16(2): 107–10

Edgell, D.L. (1999) *Tourism Policy: The Next Millennium.* USA: Sagamore Publishing

Edgell, D. (2006) *Managing Sustainable Tourism: A Legacy for the Future.* London: Haworth Hospitality Press

Edgell, D.L, DelMastro Allen M., Smith, G. and Swanson, J.R. (2008) *Tourism Policy and Planning. Yesterday, Today and Tomorrow.* London: Butterworth-Heinemann

Elliot, J. (1997) *Tourism: Politics and Public Sector Management.* USA: Routledge

English People's Daily Online (17 Feb 2006) Tourism plans called off for Phi Phi island in Thailand. Retrieved 6 Nov 2007 from http://english.people.com.cn/200602/17/eng20060217_243634.html

Fadeeva, Z. (2004) 'Translation of sustainability ideas in tourism networks: some roles of cross-sectoral networks in change towards sustainable development', *Journal of Cleaner Production*, 13(2): 175–89

Farrell, B. (1994) Tourism as an element in sustainable development: Hong, Maui. In: Smith et al (eds), *Tourism Alternatives*. UK: Wiley, pp 115–32

Fayos-Sola, E. (1996) 'Tourism policy: a midsummer night's dream', *Tourism Management*, 17(6): 405–12

Fennel, D.A. and Malloy, D.C. (1999) 'Measuring the ethical nature of tourism operators', *Annals of Tourism Research*, 26: 928–44

Fennell, D. (2003) *Ecotourism*, 2nd edn. London: Routledge

Fiebig, S. (1995) *Fish Species List and Management Report on the Chumbe Reef Sanctuary*

Filho, W. L. (1996) Putting principles into practices: sustainable tourism in small island states. In L. Brigugulio and M. Briguglio (eds) *Sustainable Tourism in Islands and Small States: Issues and Policies*. New York: Pinter, pp 61–8

First-Ever Global Sustainable Tourism Criteria (6 Oct 2008). US Fed News Service, Including US State News. Retrieved 27 Aug 2009, from Research Library (Document ID: 1578879731)

Flagestad, A. (2001) *Strategic Success and Organizational Structure in Winter Sport Destinations. A Multiple Stakeholder Approach to Measuring Organizational Performance in Scandinavian and Swiss Case Studie*s. Bradford: Bradford University

Foggin, T., Munster, D.O. (2003) 'Finding the middle ground between communities and tourism', *Africa Insight* 33(1/2): 18–22

Font, X. and Ahjem, T.E. (1999) 'Searching for a balance in tourism development strategies', *International Journal of Contemporary Hospitality Management*, 11 (2/3): 73–7

Fotiou, S., Buhalis, D. and Vereczi, G. (2002) 'Sustainable development of ecotourism in small island developing states (SIDS) and other small islands', *Tourism and Hospitality Research*, 4(1): 79–88

Francis, J., Nilsson, A., and Waruings, D. (2002) 'Marine protected areas in the Eastern African region: how successful are they?', *Ambio: Royal Swedish Academy of Sciences*, 31(7–8): 503–11

Frangialli, F. (1999) *Sustainable Tourism*. Madrid: WTO

Freeman, R. E. (1984) *Strategic Management: A Stakeholder Approach*. Marshfield: Pitman

Getz, D. (1992) 'Tourism planning and destination life cycle', *Annals of Tourism Research*, 19: 752–70

Ghina, F. (2003) 'Sustainable development in small island developing states: The case of the Maldives', *Environment, Development and Sustainability*, 5(1): 139–65

Ghobadian, A., Viney, H. et al (1998) 'Extending linear approaches to mapping environmental behaviour', *Business Strategy and the Environment*, 7(13): 13–23

Giannoni, S. and Maupertuis, M.A. (2007) 'Environmental quality and optimal investment in tourism infrastructures: a small island perspective', *Tourism Economies*, 13(4): 499–513

Global Sustainable Energy Islands Initiative. Accessed 15 January 2010 from www.gseii.org

Godfrey, K. (1996) Towards sustainability: tourism in the Republic of Cyprus. In: L. Harrison and W. Husbands (eds), *Practicing Responsible Tourism*. Canada: Wiley, pp 58–78

Godfrey, K.B. (1998) 'Attitudes towards "sustainable tourism" in the UK: a view from local government', *Tourism Management*, 3: 213–24

Goldstein, G. (2005) 'The legal system and wildlife conservation: History and the law's effect on indigenous people and community conservation in Tanzania', *Georgetown International Environmental Law Review*, 17(3): 481–515

Gonzalez-Benito, J. and Gonzalez-Benito, O. (2005) 'Environmental proactivity and business performance: an empirical analysis', *Omega*, 33(1): 1–15

Gossling, S. (2001) 'The consequences of tourism for sustainable water use on a tropical island: Zanzibar, Tanzania', *Journal of Environmental Management*, 61(2): 179–91

Gössling, S., Bredberg, M., Randow, A., Svensson, P. and Swedlin, E. (2006) 'Tourist perceptions of climate change', *Current Issues in Tourism*, 9 (4,5): 419–35

Gössling, S. and Wall, G. (2007) Island tourism. In: G. Baldacchino (ed) *A World of Islands: An Island Studies Reader, Malta and Canada*, Agenda Academic and Institute of Island Studies, pp 427–41

Govern de les Illes Balears (2003) *Resum del flux turistic arribat a les Illes Balears*. Mallorca: Consellean de Turisme, No. 129

Graci, S. (2007) Accommodating green: Examining barriers to sustainable tourism development. TTRA Canada Conference, Montebello, Quebec

Graci, S. (2009) *Can Hotels Accommodate Green? Examining What Influences Environmental Commitment in the Hotel Industry*. Verlag: Germany

Graci, S. (2010) 'Examining the factors that impede sustainability in China's tourism accommodation industry: a case study of Sanya, Hainan, China', *Journal of Hospitality Marketing and Management*, 19(1): 38–55

Graci, S. and Dodds, R. (2009) 'Why go green? The business case for environmental commitment in the Canadian hotel industry', *Anatolia: An International Journal of Tourism and Hospitality Research*, 19(2): 250–70

Gray, B. (1989) *Collaborating*. San Francisco: Jossey-Bass

Gray, B. (1996) Cross-sectoral partners: collaborative alliances among business, government and communities. In: C. Huxham (ed), *Creating Collaborative Advantage*. London: Sage

Green, H. and Hunter, C. (1992) The environmental impact assessment of tourism development. In: P. Johnson, and B. Thomas (eds), *Perspectives on Tourism Policy*. London: Mansell

Greenhotelier (2003) *Integration*. London: International Hotel Environmental Initiative, p 72

Guide, S. B. (2003) *Sanya Business Guide*. Sanya, China: Sanya Business Bureau

Gunn, C.A. (1994) *Tourism Planning: Basic Concept Cases*, 3rd edn. USA: Taylor and Francis

Hall, C.M. (1994) *Tourism and Politics: Policy, Power and Place*. UK: Wiley

Hall, C.M. (1999) 'Rethinking collaboration and partnership: a public policy perspective', *Journal of Sustainable Tourism*, 7(3,4): 274–89

Hall, C.M. (2000) Tourism Planning: Policies, Processes and Relationships, Singapore: Pearson Education

Hall, C.M (2008) *Tourism Planning: Policies, Processes and Relationships*, 2nd edn. USA: Routledge

Hall, C.M. and Jenkins, J. (1995) *Tourism and Public Policy*. USA: Routledge

Hampton, M.P. (1998) 'Backpacker tourism and economic development', *Annals of Tourism Research*, 25: 639–60

Hansen, B. (2006) 'Wastewater treatment plant to resemble butterfly, flower', *Civil Engineering* pp 26–27

Hardin, G. (1968) 'The tragedy of the commons', *Science*, 162: 1243–8

Harrison, J. (2003) *Being a Tourist: Finding Meaning in Pleasure Travel*. Victoria: UBC Press

Hart, S.L. (1995) 'A natural-resource based view of the Firm', *Academy of Management Review*, 20(4): 986–1014

Hartley, K and Hooper, N. (1992) Tourism policy: market failure and public choice. In: P. Johnson and B. Thomas (eds), *Perspectives on Tourism Policy*. London: Mansell

Harvey, B. and Schaefer. A. (2001) 'Managing relationships with environmental stake-holders: a study of UK water and electricity utilities', *Journal of Business Ethics*, 30 (3): 243–60

Hashimoto, A. (2004) Tourism and sociocultural development issues. In: R. Sharley and D.J. Telfer (eds) *Tourism and Development: Concepts and Issues*. Clevedon: Channel View Publications, pp 202–30

Healy, R.G. (1994) 'The 'common pool' problem in tourism landscapes', *Annals of Tourism Research*, 21(3): 596–611

Henderson, J.C. (2007) 'Corporate social responsibility and tourism: hotel companies in Phuket, Thailand, after the Indian Ocean tsunami', *International Journal of Hospitality Management*, 26: 228–39

Henriques, I. and Sadorsky, P. (1999) 'The relationship between environmental com-mitment and managerial perceptions of stakeholder importance', *The Academy of Management Journal*, 42(1): 87–99

Hillman, A.J. and Keim, G.D. (2001) 'Shareholder value, stakeholder management, and social issues: what's the bottom line?', *Strategic Management Journal*, 22: 125–39

Honduran Coral Reef Fund (2005) Location. Honduran Coral Reef Fund: Conserving and Protecting the Natural Resources of Cayos Cochinos (online). HCRF: La Ceiba, Atlántida, Honduras, CA. Available from: http://www.cayoscochinos.org/index.php?page=location&lang=eng> (accessed 14 February 2006)

Howie, F. (2005) *Managing the Tourist Destination*. London: Cengage Learning

Hunter, C.J. (1995) 'On the need to re-conceptualize sustainable tourism development', *Journal of Sustainable Tourism*, 3(3):155–65

Hunter, C. (2002) 'Sustainable tourism and the touristic ecological footprint', *Environment, Development and Sustainability*, 4: 7–20

Hunter-Jones, P.A., Hughes, H.L., Eastwood, I.W. and Morrison, A.A. (1997) Practical approaches to sustainability: a Spanish perspective: In: M.J. Stabler (ed), *Tourism and Sustainability: Principles to Practice*. UK: CAB International, pp 263–74

IFAD (n.d.) http://www.ifad.org/sla/index.htm

Inskeep, E. (1994) *National and Regional Tourism Planning*. London: Routledge

Intergovernmental Panel on Climate Change (IPCC) (2001) *Third Assessment Report*. Geneva, Switzerland: IPCC

Ioannides, D. (1996) 'A flawed implementation of sustainable tourism: The experience of Akamas, Cyprus', *Tourism Management*, 16(8): 583–92

Ioannides, D. (2001) Sustainable development and shifting attitudes of tourism stake-holders: toward a dynamic framework. In: S. F. McCool and R. N. Moisey (eds), *Tourism, Recreation and Sustainability: Linking Culture and the Environment*. Oxon, UK: CABI Publishing

Ioannides, D. and Holcomb, B. (2001) Raising the stakes: implications of up market tourism policies in Cyprus and Malta. In: D. Ioannides et al (eds), *Mediterranean Islands and Sustainable Tourism Development: Practices, Management and Policies*. London: Continuum, pp 234–58

Ives, A. (2007) Cayos Cochinos, Honduras and the areas of influence. Report sponsored by The Nature Conservancy, New York

Jackson, G. and Morpeth, N. (1999) 'Local Agenda 21 and Community Participation in Tourism Policy and Planning: Future or Fallacy', *Current Issues In Tourism*, 2(1): 1–45

Jie Wen, J. and Tisdell, C.A. (2001) *Tourism and China's Development. Policies, Regional Economic Growth and Ecotourism*. Singapore: World Scientific Publishing Co.

Johnson, S.D. (1998) 'Application of the balanced scorecard approach', *Corporate Environmental Strategy*, 5(4): 35–41

Johnson, P. and Thomas, B. (1994) The notion of capacity in tourism: a review of issues. In: C. Cooper and A. Lockwood (eds) *Tourism, Recreation and Hospitality Management*. Chichester: Wiley, pp 279–308

Johnston, R.J. and Tyrell, T.J. (2005) 'A dynamic model of sustainable tourism', *Journal of Travel Research*, 2(44): 124–34

Jongen, H.T., Meer, K. and Triesch, E. (2004) *Optimization Theory*. Boston: Kluwer

Kaewkuntee, D. (2006) 'Land tenure, land conflicts and post tsunami relocation in Thailand', *Mekong Update and Dialogue*, 9(2): 2–4

Kapashesit, R. (2010) Personal Interview held on 6 March 2010. Toronto, Ontario, Canada

Kazmin, A. (2005) 'After the wave, a fight for Phi Phi', *Financial Times*, London, 7 May 2005, p 17

Kelley, P. (1991) 'Factors that influence the development of trade information in political behaviour', *Research in Corporate Social Performance and Policy*, 12: 93–142

Kelman, I. (2007a) 'The island advantage', *ID21 Insights*, pp 1–2

Kelman, I. (2007b) 'Sustainable livelihoods from natural heritage on islands', *Island Studies Journal*, 2(1): 101–14

Kelman, I. (2009) 'Overcoming island vulnerability', *Emergencies Bulletin*, January–April 2009, No. 1

Kelman, I. and Lewis, J. (2005) 'Ecology and vulnerability: islands and sustainable risk management', *International Journal of Island Affairs*, 14(2): 4–12

Kernel, P. (2005) 'Creating and implementing a model for sustainable development in tourism enterprises', *Journal of Cleaner Production*, 13: 151–64

Kerr, S.A. (2005) 'What is small island sustainable development about?', *Ocean and Coastal Management*, 48: 503–24

King, R. (1999) Islands and migration. In E. Biagine and B. Hoyle (eds) *Insularity and Development International Perspectives on Islands*. London: Pinter, pp 93–115

Kirk, D. (1995) 'Environmental management in hotels', *International Journal of Contemporary Hospitality Management*, 7(6): 3–8

Kirkland, L. and Thompson, D. (1999) 'Challenges in designing, implementing and operating an environmental management system', *Business Strategy and the Environment*, 8: 128–41

Kirstges, T. (2002) 'Basic questions of 'sustainable tourism': Does ecological and socially acceptable tourism have a chance?', *Current Issues in Tourism*, 5(3,4): 173–92

Klak, T. (1998) *Globalization and Neoliberalism. The Caribbean Context*. Lanham: Rowman and Littlefield

Krippendorf, J. (1982) 'Towards new tourism policies', *Tourism Management*, 3(3): 135–48

Krippendorf, J. (1987) *The Holiday Makers: Understanding the Impact of Leisure and Travel*, London: Heinemann

Krozer, K. and Christensen-Redzepovic, E. (2006) 'Sustainable innovations at tourist destinations', *Tourism Review International*, 10(1): 113–24

Kweka J., Morrissey O. and Blake A. (2003) 'The economic potential of tourism in Tanzania', *Journal of International Development*, 15: 335–51

Lansing P. and De Vries, P. (2007) 'Sustainable tourism: ethical alternative or marketing ploy?', *Journal of Business Ethics*, 72: 77–85

Lantos, G.P. (2001) 'The boundaries of strategic corporate social responsibility', *Journal of Consumer Marketing*, 18(7): 595–630

Laverack, G. and Thangphet, S. (2007) 'Building community capacity for locally managed ecotourism in Northern Thailand', *Community Development Journal*, 44: 172–85

Levine, A. (2002) Global Partnerships in Tanzania's Marine Resource Management: NGOs, The Private Sector and Local Communities. University of California, Berkeley

Lewis, J. (1999) *Development in Disaster-prone Places: Studies of Vulnerability.* London: Intermediate Technology Publications

Lewis, J. (2005) Sustainable alpine tourism: the British ski industry's role in developing sustainability in the French alps. Master's thesis. London: Imperial College, University of London

Lickorish, L.J. (1991) 'Developing a single European tourism policy', *Tourism Management*, 178–84

Lim, C.C. and Cooper, C. (2009) 'Beyond sustainability: optimising island tourism development', *International Journal of Tourism Research*, 11(1): 89–103

Lindsey, G. and Holmes, A. (2002) 'Tourist support for marine protection in Nha Trang, Vietnam', *Journal of Environmental Planning and Management*, 45(4): 461–80

Lindstroem, B. (2007) Phosphorus Budget for the Eco-tourist Resort of Chumbe Island Coral Park, Zanzibar. Master's thesis. Swedish University of Agricultural Sciences

Lippmann, S. (1999) 'Supply chain environmental management: elements for success', *Corporate Environmental Strategy* 6(3): 175–81

Liu, Z. (2003) 'Sustainable tourism development: a critique', *Journal of Sustainable Tourism*, 11(6): 459–75

Lockhart, D.G. (1997) Islands and tourism: an overview. In: D.G. Lockhart and D. Drakakis-Smith (eds) *Island Tourism – Trends and Perspectives*. London: Pinter: pp 3–21

Lopez, D.E.P. and Baum, T. (2004) An Analysis of Supply-Side Relationships in Small Island Destinations: The Role of Tour Operators, Travel Agencies and Tourism Transport in the Canary Islands

Malvarez, G., Pollard, J. and Rodriguez, R.D. (2003) 'The planning and practice of coastal zone management in southern Spain', *Journal of Sustainable Tourism*, 11(2,3): 204–23

Manaktola, K. and Jauhari, V. (2007) 'Exploring consumer attitude and behaviour towards green practices in the lodging industry in India', *International Journal of Contemporary Hospitality Management*, 19(5): 364–77

Mastny, L. (2002) Redirecting international tourism. In: L. Starke, *State of the World 2002*. New York: Norton, pp 101–26

Mathieson, A. and Wall, G. (1982) *Tourism: Economic, Physical and Social Impacts.* Harlow: Longman

Mauser, A. (2001) *The Greening of Business. Environmental Management and Performance Evaluation: An Empirical Study in the Dutch Dairy Industry.* Delft: Eburon

May, V. (1991) 'Tourism, environment and development', *Tourism Management*, 112–118

Mbaiwa, J.E. (2005) 'Enclave tourism and its socio-economic impacts in the Okavango Delta, Botswana', *Tourism Management*, 26: 157–72

McClanahan, T.R., Muthiga, N.A., Kamukuru, A.T., Machano, H. and Kiambo, R.W. (1999) 'The effects of marine parks and fishing on coral reefs of northern Tanzania', *Biological Conservation*, 89(2): 161–82

McElroy, J.L. (2002a) Tourism development in small islands across the world. In: *Islands of the World VII: New Horizons in Island Studies* (conference proceedings). Cape Breton: New Horizons for Island Studies, North Atlantic Forum

McElroy, J.L. (2002b) Sustainable Tourism Coastal Development: Some Policy Suggestions, Conference: Workshop of Coastal Tourism Policy, British Columbia: Simon Fraser University

McElroy, J.L. (2006) 'Small island tourist economies across the life cycle', *Asia Pacific Viewpoint*, 47: 61–77

McElroy, J.L. and De Albuquerque, K. (1998) 'Tourism penetration index in small Caribbean islands', *Annals of Tourism Research*, 25(1): 145–68

McElroy, J. and Dodds, R. (2007) 'What does sustainable tourism mean for islands?, *ID21 Island Insights*, p 3. Special issue invited contribution

McNamara, K and Gibson, C. (2008) 'Environmental sustainability in practice? A macro-scale profile of tourist accommodation facilities in Australia's coastal zone', *Journal of Sustainable Tourism*, 16(1): 85–100

McNutt, P. and Oreja-Rodriguez, J.R. (1996) Economic strategies for sustainable tourism in islands: the case of Teneriffe. In: Bruguglio et al (eds), *Sustainable Tourism in Island and Small States*. London: Pinter, pp 261–80

McHardy, P. (2000) *Regional Sustainable Tourism Policy Framework: Promoting Environmentally Sustainable Tourism in the Caribbean*. Barbados: Caribbean Tourism Organization and US Agency for International Development

Meethan, K. (1998) 'New tourism for old? Policy developments in Cornwall and Devon', *Tourism Management*, 19(6): 583–93

Mekong Update and Dialogue (2006) Retrieved June 2008 from: http://www.mekong.es.usyd.edu.au/publications/mekong_updates/update9.3.pdf

Middleton, V.T.C. (1998) *Sustainable Tourism: A Marketing Perspective*. New York: Longman

Middleton, V. and Hawkins, R. (1998) *Sustainable Tourism: A Marketing Perspective*, Oxford: Butterworth-Heinemann

Miller, G. (2001) 'The development of indicators for sustainable tourism: Results of a Delphi survey of tourism researchers', *Tourism Management*, 22(4): 351–62

Milne, S. (1997) Tourism, dependency and South Pacific microstates: beyond the vicious cycle? In: D.G. Lockhart and D. Drakakis-Smith (eds) *Island Tourism: Trends and Prospects*. New York: Palgrave Macmillan

Milne, S.S. (1993) Tourism and sustainable development: exploring the global – local nexus. In: C.M. Hall and A.A. Lew (eds), *Sustainable Tourism: A Geographical Perspective*. New York: Addison Wesley Longman, pp 35–48

Mitchell, J. (1996) Presenting the past: cultural tour-guides and the sustaining of European identity in Malta. In: Bruguglio et al (eds), *Sustainable Tourism in Islands and Small States: Case Studies*. London: Pinter, pp 199–219

Mitchell, R.K. et al (1997) 'Toward a theory of stakeholder identification and salience: Defining the principle of who and what really counts', *The Academy of Management Review*, 22(4): 853–87

Mo'Cree Bec Council of the Cree Nations (2005) 25th Year Commemorative Report. www.mocreebec.com last Accessed 19 March 2010

MTA (2002) *Malta Tourist Authority Strategic Plan 2002–2004*, Valletta: Malta Tourism Authority

Murphy, P. (1994) Tourism and sustainable development. In: W. Theobald (ed), *Global Tourism: The Next Decade*. Oxford: Butterworth-Heinemann, pp 274–90

Mycoo, M. (2006) 'Sustainable tourism using regulations, market mechanisms and green certification: a case study of Barbados', *Journal of Sustainable Tourism*, 14(5): 489–511

Narayanan, V.K. and Nath, R. (1993) Organization Theory: A Strategic Approach. Homewood, Ill, Richard D. Irwin Inc.

Nowak, J.J. and Sahli, M. (2007) 'Coastal tourism and Dutch elm disease in a small island economy', *Tourism Economics*, 13(1): 49–65

Ouyang, H.T. (1999) Resort morphology and local economic development example from Hainan Province, China. Faculty of Environmental Studies. Waterloo, University of Waterloo. Masters in Environmental Studies: 95

Palmer T. and Riera, A. (2003) 'Tourism and environmental taxes. With special reference to the Balearic ecotax', *Tourism Management*, 24(6) 665–74

Parker, S. (2000) Collaboration in tourism policy making: environmental and commercial sustainability on Bonaire, NA. In: B. Bramwell and B. Lane (eds) *Tourism Collaboration and Partnerships: Politics, Practice and Sustainability*. Toronto: Channel View Publications

Pereira, T. (2009) 'Sustainability: an integral engineering design approach', *Renewable and Sustainable Energy Reviews*, 13: 1133–37

Perez-Salom, J.R. (2001) 'Sustainable tourism: Emerging global and regional regulation', *Georgetown Environmental Law Review*, 13(4): 801–37

Phi Phi Releve Toi (3 Feb 2006) Actualite181 les tractations au point mort. Retrieved 6 Nov 2007 from http://www.phiphi-releve-toi.com/en/actualites.php?nid+203&npage=0

Pigram, J.J. and Ding, P. (1999) Tourism – environmental interaction: the greening of Australian beach resorts. In: Singh and Singh (eds), *Tourism Development in Critical Environments*. USA: Cognizard Communications Corporation, pp 35–50

Pine, R. (2002) 'China's hotel industry: serving a mass market', *Cornell Hotel and Restaurant Administration Quarterly*. 43(3): 61–70

Pine, R., Zhang, H.Q. et al (2000) 'The challenges and opportunities of franchising in China's hotel industry', *International Journal of Contemporary Hospitality Management*, 12(5): 300–7

Portney, K.E. (2003) *Taking Sustainable Cities Seriously: Economic Development, the Environment, and Quality of Life in American Cities*. USA: MIT Press

Post, J.E., Lawrence, A.T. et al (1999) The corporation and its stakeholders. In: J.E. Post, A.T. Lawrence and J. Weber (eds), *Business and Society*. Boston: Irwin McGraw-Hill, pp 1–29

PPT (Pro Poor Partnership) and CTO (Caribbean Tourism Organization) (2006) *Making Tourism Count for the Local Economy in the Caribbean: Guidelines for Good Practice*. London: UK Travel Foundation

Priestly, G. and Mundet, L. (1998) 'The post stagnation phase of the resort cycle', *Annals of Tourism Research*, 25(1): 85–111

Pryce, A. (2001) 'Sustainability in the hotel industry', *Travel and Tourism Analyst*, 6: 3–23

Puppim de Oliviera, J.A. (2003) 'Government responses to tourism development: Three Brazilian case studies', *Tourism Management*, 24(1): 97–110

Rebollo J. and Baldal, J. (2003) 'Measuring sustainability in mass tourist destinations. Pressures, perceptions and policy responses in Torrevieja, Spain', *Journal of Sustainable Tourism*, 11(2/3): 181–203

Reddy, M.V. (2008) 'Sustainable tourism rapid indicators for less-developed islands: an economic perspective', *International Journal of Travel Research*, 10: 557–76

Reid, M. and Schwab, A. (2006) 'Barriers to sustainable development', *Journal of Asian and African Studies*, 41(5–6): 439–57

Richter, L.K. (1984) 'A search for missing answers to questions never asked: reply to Kosters', *Annals of Tourism Research*, 11: 613–15

Riedmiller, S. (1991) Environmental Education in Zanzibar : Proposals for Action. Department of Environmental, Finnida, Zanzibar

Riedmiller, S. (1998) 'The Chumbe Island coral park project: management experiences of a private marine conservation project', *ITMEMS Proceedings*, pp 222–35

Riedmiller, S. (2000) Private sector management of marine protected areas: the Chumbe island case. In Herman Cesar Cordio (ed) Collected *Essays on Economics of Coral Reefs*. CORDIDO, SID

Riedmiller, S. (2003) Private sector investment in marine protected areas – experiences of the Chumbe island coral park in Zanzibar/Tanzania. 5th World Parks Congress. Sustainable Finance Stream. Durban, South Africa

Ritchie, B. and Crouch, G. (2005) 'Application of the analytic hierarchy process to tourism choice and decision making: a review and illustration applied to destination competitiveness', *Tourism Analysis*, 10(1): 17–25

Ritchie, J.R. and Crouch, G. (2003) *The Competitive Destination: A Sustainable Tourism Perspective*. Cambridge: CABI

Rivera, J. (2001) Does it pay to be green in the developing world? Participation in a Costa Rican Voluntary Environmental Program and its impact on hotels' competitive advantage. Denver, Colorado: Graduate School of Public Affairs, University of Colorado, pp 1–5

Rivera, J. (2002a) 'Assessing a voluntary environmental initiative in the developing world: the Costa Rican certification for sustainable tourism', *Policy Sciences*, 35: 333–60

Rivera, J. (2002b) Voluntary Green Behaviour in Emerging Markets: The Costa Rican Certification for Sustainable Tourism. Academy of Management Annual Conference, George Mason University

Rivera, J. and DeLeon, P. (2005) 'Chief Executive Officers and voluntary environmental performance', *Policy Sciences*, 38: 107–27

Robertson, S. (1989) *Society: A Brief Introduction*. New York: Worth

Robinson, S. (2000) 'Key survival issues: practical steps toward corporate environmental sustainability', *Corporate Environmental Strategy*, 7(1): 55–69

Royle, S.A. (2001) *A Geography of Islands: Small Island Insularity*. London: Routledge

Ruhahen, L. (2008) 'Stakeholder participation in tourism destination planning', *Tourism Recreation Research*, 34(3): 283–94

Russo, M.V. and Fouts, P.A. (1997) 'A resource based perspective on corporate environmental performance and profitability', *Academy of Management Journal*, 40(3): 534–60

Ryan, C. (2002) 'Equity, management, power sharing and sustainability – issues of the 'new tourism', *Tourism Management*, 23: 17–26

Salima Sulaiman, M. (1996) Islands within islands: exclusive tourism and sustainable utilization of coastal resources in Zanzibar. In: Bruguglio et al (eds), *Sustainable Tourism in Island and Small States: Case Studies*. London: Pinter, pp 32–49

Sautter, E.T. and Leisen, B. (1999) 'Managing stakeholders. A tourism planning model', *Annals of Tourism Research*, 26(2): 312–28

Scott, A., Christie, M. and Tench, H. (2003) 'Visitor payback: panacea or pandora's box for conservation in the UK?', *Journal of Environmental Planning and Management*, 46(4) 583–604

Scheyvens, R. and Momsen, J.H. (2008a) 'Tourism and poverty reduction: Issues for small island states', *Tourism Geographies*, 10(1): 22–41

Scheyvens, R. and Momsen, J.H. (2008b) 'Tourism in small islands states: from vulnerability to strengths', *Journal of Sustainable Tourism*, 16(5): 491–510

Selin, S. (1999) 'Developing a typology of sustainable tourism partnership', *Journal of Sustainable Tourism*, 7(3,4): 260–73

Selwyn, P. (ed) (1975) *Development Policy in Small Countries*. London: Croom Helm

Sharif, R. and Hoti, S. (2005) 'Small island tourism economies and country risk ratings', *Mathematics and Computers in Simulation*, 68: 557–70

Sharpley, R. (2000) 'Tourism and sustainable development: Exploring the theoretical divide', *Journal of Sustainable Tourism*, 8(1): 1–19

Sharpley, R. (2009) *Tourism Development and the Environment: Beyond Sustainability?* London: Earthscan

Sharpley, R. and Knight, M. (2009) 'Tourism and the State of Cuba: from the past to the present', *International Journal of Tourism Research*, 11: 241–59

Sharpley, R. and Telfer, D.J. (eds) (2002) *Tourism and Development: Concepts and Issues*. Buffalo, NY: Channel View

Sheller, M. (2003) *Consuming the Caribbean*. London: Routledge

Silva, M. (2002) Caribbean and Intra-Caribbean Tourism Current Situation and Perspectives. At the 8th Meeting of the Special Committee on Sustainable Tourism of the Association of Caribbean States, CTO, Port of Spain

Sinclair, D. and Jayawardena, C. (2003) 'The development of sustainable tourism in the Guianas', *International Journal of Contemporary Hospitality Management*, 15(7): 402–8

Singh, V. and Singh, S. (1999) Tourism and the Himalayan Tribes: searching for sustainable development options for the Bhotias of the Bhyundar Valley. In: D. Pearce and R.W. Butler (eds), *Contemporary Issues in Tourism Development*. New York: Routledge, pp 192–210

Slinger-Friedman, V. (2009) 'Ecotourism in Dominica: studying the potential for economic development, environmental protection and cultural conservation', *Island Studies Journal*, 4(1)

Sofield, T.H.B. (1996) Anuha Island resort: a case study of failure. In: R. Butler and T. Hinch (eds) *Tourism and Indigenous Peoples*. London: Routledge, pp 176–202

Sommer, B. and Sommer, R. (1991) *A Practical Guide to Behavioural Research. Tools and Techniques*. New York: Oxford University Press

Stabler, M. and Goodall, B. (1996) Environmental auditing in planning for sustainable tourism. In: Briguglio et al (eds), *Sustainable Tourism in Islands and Small States: Issues and Policies*. UK: Pinter, pp 170–96

*The Standard* (Tuesday, 1 Nov 2005) Phi Phi Upgrading hotels to woo well-heeled tourists. China's Business Newspaper. Retrieved 6 Nov 2007 from http://www.the-standard.com.hk/news_detail.asp?pp_cat=17&art_id=4603&sid=5262204&...

Stewart, N. (2006) 'Cree Village Ecolodge: Living Lightly on the Land', *Northern Ontario Business*, 6 August 2006

Stipanuk, D.M. (1996) 'The U.S. Lodging industry and the environment: a historical view', *Cornell Hotel and Restaurant Administration Quarterly*, 37(5): 39–49

Stone, M. and Wall, G. (2003) 'Ecotourism and community development: case studies from Hainan, China', *Environmental Management*, 33(1): 12–24

Svensson, P., Rodwell, L.D. and Attrill, M.J. (2009) 'Privately managed marine reserves as a mechanism for the conservation of coral reef ecosystems: a case study from Vietnam', *Ambio*, 38(2): 72–8

210 | SUSTAINABLE TOURISM IN ISLAND DESTINATIONS

Swanson, K.E., Kuhn, R.G. et al (2001) 'Environmental policy implementation in rural China: a case study of Yuhang, Zhejiang', *Environmental Management*, 27(4): 481–91
Swarbrooke, J. (1999) *Sustainable Tourism Management*. New York: CABI
Taste of Arran. Accessed July 2008 from www.taste-of-arran.co.uk
Telfer, D.J. (2004) Development theories and tourism theory. In: R. Sharpley and
    Telfer, D.J. (ed) *Aspects of Tourism: Tourism and Development Concepts and Issues*. Clevedon: Channel View, pp 35–80
TDI Corporation (2002) St Kitts and Nevis Strategic Plan for Tourism Development
    Prepared for the St Kitts and Nevis Tourism Industry, St Kitts
Theobald, W.F. (1998) Foreword. In: W.F. Theobald (ed), *Global Tourism*, 2nd edn.
    Oxford: Butterworth-Heinemann
Thomas-Hope, E. (ed) (1999) *Solid Waste Management: Critical Issues for Developing
    Countries*. Canoe Press: University of the West Indies
Thompson, D. (1997) Environmental management. In T. Fleming (ed), *The
    Environment and Canadian Society*. Toronto: International Thomson, pp 219–56
Thorne, E.T. (2005) 'Land rights and Garifuna Identity', *NACLA*, 38(2), 21–5
TIAC (Tourism Industry Association of Canada) (2005) Press Release: National
    Awards Recognize Canada's Tourism Excellence. Last Accessed 19 March, 2010,
    http://www.creevillage.com/TIAC_Oct24_2005.pdf
Tinsley, S. (2002) 'EMS models for business strategy development', *Business Strategy
    and the Environment*, 11: 376–90
Tomm (2008) Kangaroo Island at a Glance. Available at http://www.tomm.info
    (accessed December 2009)
Tosun, C. (2001) 'Challenges of sustainable tourism development in the developing
    world: the case of Turkey', *Tourism Management*, 22: 289–303
Tourism Authority of Thailand (2007) Statistical Update of Thai Tourism Situation
    2006. Last accessed on 31 October 2007, retrieved from http://www.tatnews.org/
    tat_release/3301.asp
Tsaur, S.H., Tzeng, G. and Wang, K. (1997) 'Evaluating tourist risks from fuzzy per-
    spectives', *Annals of Tourism Research*, 24(4): 796–812
Twining-Ward, L. and Butler, R. (2002) 'Implementing STD on a small island: devel-
    opment and use of sustainable tourism development indicators in Samoa', *Journal
    of Sustainable Tourism*, 10(5): 363–83
UNCSD (1999) *Tourism and Sustainable Development: Sustainable Tourism: A Non-
    Governmental Organization Perspective*. New York: Commission on Sustainable
    Development
United Nations Commission for Sustainable Development (2000) *Indicators of
    Sustainable Development: Guidelines and Methods*. New York: UNCSD
United Nations (2003) Erosion of the Mediterranean Coastline: Implications for
    Tourism, Parliamentary Assembly Report, United Nations Committee on Economic
    Affairs and Development. Doc 9981
United Nations (2003a) Comparative Review of Coastal Legislation in South Asia,
    GPA Coordination Office, the Netherlands
UNEP (1996) Guidelines for Integrated Planning and Management of Coastal and
    Marine Areas in the Wider Caribbean Region, Caribbean Environmental
    Programme, Kingston, Jamaica
UNEP and ICLEI (2003) *Tourism and Local Agenda 21: The Role of Local Authorities
    in Sustainable Tourism*. France: UNEP
UNEP, WTO and Plan Blue (2000) Final Report: International Seminar on Sustainable
    Tourism and Competitiveness in the Islands of the Mediterranean, Italy, 17–20 May
    2000

United Nations University (2005) Terms of Reference paper for Expert Group meeting on Secure Tenure: New Legal Frameworks and Tools. UN Conference Center, Bangkok, 8–9 December 2005

UNWTO (2005) Definition of Sustainable Tourism. Accessed from www.world-tourism.org, 17 June 2007

UNWTO (2006) Tourism Barometre. Retrieved 15 February 2007 from http://www.world-tourism.org/facts/menu.html

Veitayaki, J. (2006) 'Caring for the environment and the mitigation of natural extreme events in Gau, Fiji islands: a self-help community initiative', *Island Studies Journal*, 1(2): 239–52

Vera, F. and Rippin, R. (1996) Decline of a Mediterranean tourist area and restructuring strategies. In: G.K. Priestley, J.A Edwards and H. Coccossis (eds), *Sustainable Tourism: European Perspectives*. UK: CAB International

Wall, G. (1997) Sustainable tourism – unsustainable development. In: S. Wahaband and J.J. Pilgram (eds), *Tourism, Development and Growth: The Challenge of Sustainability*. London: Routledge, pp 33–49

Warnken, J. and Buckley, R. (1998) 'Scientific quality of tourism environmental impact assessment', *Journal of Applied Ecology*, 35: 1–8

Weaver, D. (2001) Mass tourism and alternative tourism in the Caribbean. In: D. Harrison (ed), *Tourism and the Less Developed World: Issues and Case Studies*. UK: CABI Publishing, pp 161–74

Welford, R. (ed) (1997) *Corporate Environmental Management 2: Culture and Organizations*. New York: Earthscan Publications

Wheeler, B. (1993) 'Sustaining the Ego', *Journal of Sustainable Tourism*, 1: 121–29

Wild, W. and Marshall, R. (1999) 'Participatory practice in the context of Local Agenda 21: a case study evaluation of experience in three English local authorities', *Sustainable Development*, 7(3): 151–62

Wilkinson, P.F. (1989) 'Strategies for tourism in island microstates', *Annals of Tourism Research*, 16(2): 153–77

Wilkinson, P.F. (1997) *Tourism Policy and Planning: Case Studies from the Commonwealth Caribbean*. New York: Cognizant Communications Corporation

Williams, A.M. and Shaw, G. (1998) Tourism policies in a changing economic environment. In: A. N. Williams and G. Shaw (eds), *Tourism and Economic Development*, 3rd edn. Chichester: Wiley, pp 375–91

Williams, P.W. and Ponsford, I.F. (2009) 'Confronting tourism's environmental paradox: transitioning for sustainable tourism', *Futures*, 41(6): 396

Wong, P.P. (1998) 'Coastal tourism development in South East Asia: relevance and lessons for coastal zone management', *Ocean and Coastal Management*, 38: 89–109

World Commission on Environment and Development (WCED) (1987) *Our Common Future*. Oxford: Oxford University Press

The World Factbook (2008) Central Intelligence Agency. Retrieved on 8 May 2008 from https://www.cia.gov/library/publications/the-world-fact-book/geos/ho.html#Econ

World Tourism Organization (1998) *Guide for Local Authorities on Developing Sustainable Tourism*. Spain: WTO

World Tourism Organization (2001) Sustainable Development of Tourism Policy. Report, prepared by WTO for the UN Division of Sustainable Development. Spain: WTO

World Tourism Organization (1994) *National and Regional Tourism Planning: Methodologies and Case Studies*. London: Routledge

World Tourism Organization (2003) *Tourism Highlights*. Spain: WTO

World Tourism Organization (2004) *Indicators of Sustainable Development for Tourism Destinations: A Guidebook*. Madrid, Spain: WTO

World Tourism Organization (2004) *World Tourism Barometer* 2 (3). Spain: WTO

World Tourism Organization (2005) *World Tourism Barometer* 3 (1). Spain: WTO

World Travel and Tourism Council (2009) Tourism news. Retrieved on 7 March 2009 from http://www.wttc.org/eng/Tourism_News/Press_Releases/Press_Releases_2008/2008_Tourism_For_Tomorrow_Winners_Announced/

World Travel and Tourism Council (2002) Tourism Statistics <http://www.wttc.org/ecres/pdfs/WLD.pdf – last accessed August, 2003

World Travel and Tourism Council (2004) Economic Research, Country League Tables. On WWW at www.rea.ru/hotel/TourMaterials/WTO/2004%20League %20Tables.pdf

World Travel and Tourism Council (2006) Tourism Reports. Retrieved 18 September 2008, from http://www.wttc.org/eng/Download_Centre/ Printed_Publications

World Travel and Tourism Council (2007) www.wttc.com. last accessed August 2007

Xie, P. and Wall, G. (1999) Guidelines for the Development of Hainan Eco-Province. Proceedings of the International Symposium on Strengthening Eco-Environmental Planning and Management, Haikou, China

Xie, P. and Wall, G. (2002) 'Visitors' perceptions of authenticity at cultural attractions in Hainan, China', *International Journal of Tourism Research* 4: 353–66

Younis, T. (1990) *Implementation in Public Policy*. UK: Billing

Younis, E. (2000) Tourism sustainability and market competitiveness in the coastal areas and islands of the Mediterranean. In: *Sustainable Travel and Tourism*. UK: ICG, pp 65–7

Yu, L. and Huat, S.G. (1995) 'Perceptions of management difficulty factors by expatriate hotel professionals in China', *International Journal of Hospitality Management*, 14(3/4): 375–88

Zhang, H.Q., Pine, R. et al (2005) *Tourism and Hotel Development in China: From Political to Economic Successes*. New York, Hawthorne

# Appendix: Resources

**Alliance of Small Island States (AOSIS)**
http://www.sidsnet.org/aosis/index.html

The Alliance of Small Island States (AOSIS) is a coalition of small islands and low-lying coastal countries that share similar development challenges and concerns about the environment. Specific focus about island vulnerabilities and climate change are discussed. The website also provides documentation and links to SIDS and the UN system.

**Coral Reef Initiative**
http://www.icriforum.org/

The International Coral Reef Initiative (ICRI) aims to preserve coral reefs and related marine ecosystems. It is a voluntary partnership among governments, international organizations and non-government organizations. The ICRI website offers resolutions, decisions, recommendations and initiatives brought forth by these partners to improve the management and protection of coral reefs.

**Eldis – livelihoods approach**
http://www.eldis.org/go/livelihoods/

This website shares best practices in development policy, practice and research. There is a special section on sustainable livelihoods.

**First International Conference on Island Sustainability**
http://www.wessex.ac.uk/10-conferences/islands-2010.html

**Forum for Island Research and Experience**
http://www.fireonline.org/

The original aim of FIRE was to bring together researchers from the Institute of Archaeology for discussion and comparative debate. However, the forum has gradually expanded in response to the growing interest from other researchers around the United Kingdom and further afield.

### Global Sustainable Energy Islands Initiative
http://www.gseii.org/

The Global Sustainable Energy Islands Initiative was founded in 2000 to support SIDS to the impacts of climate change. The initiative works to increase renewable energy and energy efficiency facilitates the transition away from fossil fuels and benefits the islands' economies and the environment.

### Global Islands Network
http://www.globalislands.net/

The Global Islands Network 'represents a hub that connects and coordinates efforts to help ensure a healthy and productive future for islanders'. Their objectives include:

- facilitating the capacity of islanders to acquire, disseminate and utilize knowledge resources;
- improving access to existing data and generating original information about islands;
- providing technical assistance and supporting initiatives which further integrated development on small islands;
- encouraging collaborative projects and comparative studies between and among islands;
- fostering cooperation by sharing good practices and offering a forum for discussion;
- strengthening the voice of island communities as well as their representatives in intergovernmental and policy making bodies.

### Global Island Partnership (GLISPA)
http://www.cbd.int/island/glispa.shtml

The Global Island Partnership (GLISPA) aims to conserve and sustainably utilize island natural resources by bringing together island nations and nations with islands. Main objectives include mobilizing leadership, increasing resources and sharing skills, knowledge, technologies and innovations in a cost-effective and sustainable way. The website offers examples of strategies, initiatives and commitments of countries and organizations that have utilized GLISPA to advance their collaboration, planning and implementation.

### IFAD – enabling poor rural people to overcome poverty
http://www.ifad.org/sla/index.htm

The International Fund for Agricultural Development (IFAD) is a specialized agency of the United Nations. IFAD is dedicated to eradicating rural poverty in *developing countries*. This website outlines different elements that are encompassed in the sustainable livelihoods approach including a *framework* that helps in understanding the complexities of poverty and a set of *principles* to guide action to address and overcome poverty. There are also links to case studies, toolkits and additional resources.

### Island vulnerabilities
[b]http://www.islandvulnerability.org/

Ilan Kelman's site offers information and resources about island vulnerability as well as a list of publications and island resources.

**Institute of Island Studies**
http://www.upei.ca/iis/

The Institute of Island Studies is a research, policy and education institute which focuses on the culture, environment and economy of small islands.

**Insula**
http://www.insula.org/

INSULA contributes to the 'economic, social, and cultural progress of islands throughout the world as well as to the protection of island environment and the sustainable development for their resources'.

**International Coral Reef Action Network**
http://www.icran.org/

The International Coral Reef Action Network (ICRAN) aims to promote best practices by collecting case studies on sustainable tourism. This case study showcases the initiative to minimize impacts along the Meso-American Reef Alliance by improving environmental business practices.

**Integrated Coastal Zone Management (ICZM)**
http://ec.europa.eu/environment/iczm/home.htm

The European Commission has been working to identify and promote measures to remedy coastal zone deterioration and to improve the overall situation in coastal zones. This is a detailed site which outlines impacts as well as strategies and practical steps for implementing ICZM.

**Islands & Small States Institute**
http://www.um.edu.mt/islands/

Malta's Islands & Small States Institute 'promotes research and training on economic, social, cultural, ecological and geographical aspects of islands and small states. It also offers postgraduate courses on islands and small states studies'.

**Micronesia Conservation Trust**
http://www.mctconservation.org/

The main objective of the Micronesia Conservation Trust (MCT) is to support biodiversity conservation and related sustainable development for the people of Micronesia. The organization offers long-term, sustained funding to community-based organizations and other non-governmental organizations through a grants programme. MCT provides a forum to discuss challenges facing natural resource management for national, state and local governments with private enterprises and organizations.

**North Stradbroke Island Sustainable Tourism Vision (Queensland, Australia)**
http://www.more2redlands.com.au/SiteCollectionDocuments/_Moreto/Moreto%20Do
cuments/Business%20documents/NSI_Visioning_Report_2.pdf

The main objective of the North Stradbroke Island Sustainable Tourism Visioning project has been to propose a framework and a set of values to guide the future development of sustainable tourism on the island. The project's aim is to guide the establishment of strategic priorities for ensuring the long-term sustainability of tourism on North Stradbroke Island.

## Pacific Regional Environmental Programme
http://www.sprep.org/

The governments and administrations of the Pacific region established the Pacific Regional Environment Programme (SPREP) to protect and manage the region's environment and natural resources. SPREP aims to send a clear signal to the global community of the deep commitment of the Pacific island governments and administrations towards sustainable development. The site offers publications concerning nature conservation, pollution prevention, climate change and variability, environmental assessments, national legislation and regional and international conventions, international waters projects, education and awareness and marine species as well as a library and resource centre.

## Palau Conservation Society
http://www.palau-pcs.org/

Palau Conservation Society (PCS) is a local non-profit organization dedicated to the protection of biodiversity, natural resources and local communities that use those resources. PCS also supports the establishment and management of conservation areas, the development of sustainable resource use policies, and an increase of environmental awareness. PCS partners with local communities as well as Palauan government agencies and the international scientific and conservation community to promote sustainable development. The PSC website offers a variety of educational materials such as fact sheets, publications and reports.

## ReefBase: A Global Information System for Coral Reefs
http://www.reefbase.org/pacific/

ReefBase Pacific project's main objective is to improve quality and accessibility of data and information on reef-associated livelihoods, fisheries and biodiversity. It is the regional focus of the global ReefBase project and the website provides a collection of information such as Internet, DVD and printed formats of information to facilitate distribution and accessibility across a wide range of stakeholders and users for the Pacific region.

## SIDS
http://www.sidsnet.org/

Established in 1997 the primary goal of small island development states (SIDS) network is to support the sustainable development of SIDS through enhanced information and communication technology (ICT). The website offers specific reports on sustainable tourism development in SIDS.

## Sustaining Tourism
http://www.sustainabletourism.net/islands.html

This website offers best practices, case studies and examples of sustainable tourism in islands as well as other tourism destinations.

## UNESCO
http://portal.unesco.org

The United Nations Educational, Scientific and Cultural Organization's (UNESCO) Unit for Relations with Small Member States aims to contribute to a 'general policy and a global approach for the specific needs of small Member States, to ensure their full participation in UNESCO's activities and facilitate access to the assistance that UNESCO can provide'.

**UNEP Island Directory**
http://islands.unep.ch/isldir.htm

This United Nations website includes a detailed introduction and explanation about islands of all kinds including criteria for inclusion, island characterization by geological type (atolls, low, coral, volcanic, continental), ecology (conservation, endemic species, protected areas) and economy, society and human impact (density, islands at risk etc.). The site also has detailed listings of all islands and their size, population and more.

# Index